First World War
and Army of Occupation
War Diary
France, Belgium and Germany

5 DIVISION
Divisional Troops
Machine Gun Corps
5 Battalion
1 April 1918 - 31 May 1919

WO95/1539/1

The Naval & Military Press Ltd
www.nmarchive.com
Published in association with The National Archives

Published by

The Naval & Military Press Ltd

Unit 10 Ridgewood Industrial Park,

Uckfield, East Sussex,

TN22 5QE England

Tel: +44 (0) 1825 749494

www.naval-military-press.com

www.nmarchive.com

This diary has been reprinted in facsimile from the original. Any imperfections are inevitably reproduced and the quality may fall short of modern type and cartographic standards.

© **Crown Copyright**
Images reproduced by permission of The National Archives, London, England, 2015.

Contents

Document type	Place/Title	Date From	Date To
Heading	WO95/1539/1		
Heading	5 Division Troops 5 BN Machine Gun Corps 1918 Apr to 1919 May 205 Machine Gun Coy 1916 Oct to 1917 Nov 5 Division Anti Gas School 1917 Oct to 1919 Mar.		
Heading	5th Divisional Troops Formed From The Brigade & Divisional M.Gs 26th April 1918 5th Battalion Machine Gun Company April 1918		
Heading	War Diary of 5/Battn. Machine Gun Corps For The Month Of April 1918		
War Diary	Battn H. Qrs at Thienne	26/04/1918	30/04/1918
War Diary	Fotest De Nieppe L1 & L2 Sub Sector	25/04/1918	26/04/1918
War Diary	L1 & L2 Sub Sector	27/04/1918	30/04/1918
War Diary	Fired (Italy)	01/04/1918	04/04/1918
War Diary	Field (France)	04/04/1918	17/04/1918
War Diary	Field	19/04/1918	30/04/1918
War Diary	Haverskerque	25/04/1918	30/04/1918
Miscellaneous	Organisation of The Machine Gun Battalion	25/03/1918	25/03/1918
Miscellaneous	Organisation of Machine Gun Battn	29/03/1918	29/03/1918
Miscellaneous	O.C. 5/M.G. Battn	25/04/1918	25/04/1918
Miscellaneous	P.O.M. O.O No.49	29/04/1918	29/04/1918
Miscellaneous	A Form Messages And Signals	27/04/1918	27/04/1918
Miscellaneous	Disposition Of M.Guns 5/Battn MGC	26/04/1918	26/04/1918
Miscellaneous	Disposition Of M.Guns 5/Battn MGC	30/04/1918	30/04/1918
Map	Map		
Heading	5th Divisional Troops 205th Machine Gun Company April 1918		
Heading	D. Coy 5th M.G Battn (205th M.G. Coy) War Diary April 1st-30th 1918		
War Diary	C. Basso Pojana	01/04/1918	11/04/1918
War Diary	Haverskerque	12/04/1918	30/04/1918
Heading	War Diary of 5th Battalion Machine Gun Corps For The Month Of May 1918		
War Diary	In Trenches Approx Frontage Bois De Nieppe La Bassee Canal Left Flank 29th Division Right Flank 61st Division	01/05/1918	02/05/1918
War Diary	In Trenches	02/05/1918	31/05/1918
Heading	5/Battn M Gun Corps War Diary Appendix "A"		
Miscellaneous	5th Battalion Machine Gun Corps	05/05/1918	05/05/1918
Map	Map		
Miscellaneous	XI Corps	10/05/1918	10/05/1918
Miscellaneous	O.C. " " Company.	11/05/1918	11/05/1918
Miscellaneous	5th Division S/60	18/05/1918	18/05/1918
Miscellaneous	Report Of A Minor Operation On The 20th Of May 1918	21/05/1918	21/05/1918
Miscellaneous	5th Divisional Intelligence Summary	21/05/1918	21/05/1918
Miscellaneous	Preliminary Examination Of Prisoners Of 48th Reserve Division Captured On 20th May 1918	21/05/1918	21/05/1918
Operation(al) Order(s)	5th Division Operation Order No.224	17/05/1918	17/05/1918
Operation(al) Order(s)	61 Division Order No.162	21/05/1918	21/05/1918

Type	Description	Date From	Date To
Operation(al) Order(s)	5th Battalion Machine Gun Corps Operation Order No.2	22/05/1918	22/05/1918
Operation(al) Order(s)	5th Battalion Machine Gun Corps Operation Order No.3	23/05/1918	23/05/1918
Miscellaneous	20 H.Q 13/Inf Bde & 5/Battn M.G.C from O.C "A" Company 5/Battn M.G.C	29/05/1918	29/05/1918
Operation(al) Order(s)	5th Battalion Machine Gun Corps Operation Order No.4	27/05/1918	27/05/1918
Miscellaneous	C.M & Coy O.O No. 55 Ref No 26A N.E 1/20000	29/05/1918	29/05/1918
Map	Map		
Heading	War Diary of 5th Battalion Machine Gun Corps For The Month Of June 1918		
War Diary	In Trenches Approx Frontage Foret De Nieppe to La Bassee Canal Battn H Qrs Thiennes Left Flank 29/Division Right Flank 61/Division	01/06/1918	02/06/1918
War Diary	Trenches	03/06/1918	30/06/1918
Heading	5th Battalion Machine Gun Corps War Diary For June Appendices "A" & "B"		
Operation(al) Order(s)	C Machine Gun Company O.O No. 56	02/06/1918	02/06/1918
Operation(al) Order(s)	5th Battalion Machine Gun Corps Operation Order No.5	03/06/1918	03/06/1918
Miscellaneous	XI Corps No. I.G. 82	09/06/1918	09/06/1918
Miscellaneous	Gas Projection Operation Carried Out by No.1 Special Company R.E in The Right Brigade Sector in The Morning of 7/6/18	07/06/1918	07/06/1918
Operation(al) Order(s)	5th Battalion Machine Gun Corps Operation Order No. 6	11/06/1918	11/06/1918
Operation(al) Order(s)	5th Battalion Machine Gun Corps Operation Order No. 7		
Operation(al) Order(s)	5th Battalion Machine Gun Corps Operation Order No. 9	19/06/1918	19/06/1918
Operation(al) Order(s)	5th Battalion Machine Gun Corps Operation Order No. 10	26/06/1918	26/06/1918
Operation(al) Order(s)	No.5 Machine Gun Battalion Operation Order No. 8	16/06/1918	16/06/1918
Miscellaneous	Appendix "A" to Accompany No.5 Battn M.G.C O.O No.8		
Miscellaneous	Appendix "B" to Accompany No.5 M. Gun Battn O.O No.8 Administrative Arrangements		
Miscellaneous	To O.C Detachment 39th Bn M.G.C.	27/06/1918	27/06/1918
Miscellaneous	W.23/8	27/06/1918	27/06/1918
Miscellaneous	Reference No 5 Machine Gun Battalion No.8	26/06/1918	26/06/1918
Operation(al) Order(s)	5th Battalion Machine Gun Corps Warning Order No. 6	14/06/1918	14/06/1918
Miscellaneous	Reference No. 5 Machine Gun Battn O.O No.8	26/06/1918	26/06/1918
Miscellaneous	W.23/4/1	18/06/1918	18/06/1918
Miscellaneous	Reference 5th Machine Gun Battalion Operation Order No.8	17/06/1918	17/06/1918
Map	Map		
Operation(al) Order(s)	No.5 Machine Gun Battalion Operation Order No.11	30/06/1918	30/06/1918
Map	Map		
Miscellaneous	Syllubus of Training carried out by Companies when in Divisional Reserve at I.16.a near Thiennes	05/06/1918	05/06/1918
Heading	5th Division 5th M.G.C July To December 1918		
Heading	War Diary For Month Of July 1918 Vol 4		
War Diary	Trenches	01/07/1918	31/07/1918
Operation(al) Order(s)	No.5 Machine Gun Battalion Operation Order No. 12	01/07/1918	01/07/1918
Operation(al) Order(s)	No.5 Machine Gun Battalion Operation Order No. 13		

Type	Description	Date From	Date To
Operation(al) Order(s)	No.5 Machine Gun Battalion Operation Order No. 14	09/07/1918	09/07/1918
Miscellaneous	O.C. "C" Company	16/07/1918	16/07/1918
Miscellaneous	Reference No.5 Machine Gun Battalion Operation Order No.14	11/07/1918	11/07/1918
Operation(al) Order(s)	No.5. Battalion Machine Gun Corps Operation Order No 15	16/07/1918	16/07/1918
Operation(al) Order(s)	No.5. Battalion Machine Gun Corps Operation Order No 18	23/07/1918	23/07/1918
Operation(al) Order(s)	No.5. Battalion Machine Gun Corps Operation Order No 19	28/07/1918	28/07/1918
Miscellaneous	Annexe to 5th Divisional Intelligence Summary	26/07/1918	26/07/1918
Miscellaneous	Annexe to 5th Divisional Intelligence Summary		
Map	Map		
Miscellaneous	Training Programme For Week Ending 21st July 1918	21/07/1918	21/07/1918
Miscellaneous	Training Programme For Week Ending 28th July 1918	28/07/1918	28/07/1918
Miscellaneous	Increases And Decreases In Battalion Strength During Period 1st To 31st July 1918	31/07/1918	31/07/1918
Heading	No.5 Battalion Machine Gun Corps War Diary For The Month of August 1918 Vol 5		
War Diary	In Line Division Front Approximately Foret De Nieppe to Canal De La Lys	01/08/1918	02/08/1918
War Diary	In Line	03/08/1918	04/08/1918
War Diary	Trenches	04/08/1918	06/08/1918
War Diary	Wardrecques Area 36 A/40000	06/08/1918	14/08/1918
War Diary	Frevent Sheet 57d 1/40000	15/08/1918	15/08/1918
War Diary	Frevent	16/08/1918	18/08/1918
War Diary	Doullens	19/08/1918	19/08/1918
War Diary	Fonquevillers Sector	20/08/1918	31/08/1918
Heading	Appendix "A" War Diary 5/battn Machine Gun Corps August 1918		
Miscellaneous	Battalion Strength On 1.8.18		
Miscellaneous	No.5 Battalion Machine Gun Corps Officer Reinforcements from Base Depot during the Month of Aug 18		
Miscellaneous	No.5 Battalion Machine Gun Corps List of Awards to N.C.O.'s and Men of the above Battalion during the month of Aug 1916	28/06/1918	28/06/1918
Operation(al) Order(s)	5th Division Operation Order No. 243	04/08/1918	04/08/1918
Miscellaneous	Administration Instructions To Accompany 5th Division Order No.243 Ref Sheet / 36 A NE And N.W. I/20000		
Operation(al) Order(s)	No.5 Battalion Machine Gun Corps Operation Order No.21	04/08/1918	04/08/1918
Miscellaneous			
Operation(al) Order(s)	5th Battalion Machine Gun Corps Operation Order No.20	03/08/1918	03/08/1918
Operation(al) Order(s)	5th Battalion Machine Gun Corps Operation Order No. 21/I	06/08/1918	06/08/1918
Map	Map		
Map	Lines of Defence		
Operation(al) Order(s)	5th Division Operation Order No.244	12/08/1918	12/08/1918
Miscellaneous	O.C. "A" Company	12/08/1918	12/08/1918
Miscellaneous	Administrative Instructions For The Entrainment Of The Division	12/08/1918	12/08/1918
Miscellaneous	Administrative Instructions Etc	12/08/1918	12/08/1918
Miscellaneous	5th Division C.C./639/2 Administrative Instructions	13/08/1918	13/08/1918
Miscellaneous	Orders For Entrainment		

Type	Description	Date From	Date To
Miscellaneous	O.C. "A" Company	16/08/1918	16/08/1918
Operation(al) Order(s)	No. 5 Battalion Machine Gun Corps Operation Order No. 23	18/08/1918	18/08/1918
Operation(al) Order(s)	No. 5 Battalion Machine Gun Corps Operation Order No. 25	19/08/1918	19/08/1918
Operation(al) Order(s)	5th Division Operation Order No.247	19/08/1918	19/08/1918
Operation(al) Order(s)	5th Division Operation Order No.246	19/08/1918	19/08/1918
Miscellaneous	Supports and Reserves		
Miscellaneous	Intelligence Notes to Accompany 5th Division O.O No. 246		
Operation(al) Order(s)	No. 5 Battalion Machine Gun Corps Operation Order No. 26	23/08/1918	23/08/1918
Operation(al) Order(s)	5th Division Operation Order No. 248	22/08/1918	22/08/1918
Operation(al) Order(s)	5th Division Warning Order No. 2.	22/08/1918	22/08/1918
Miscellaneous	Action Of Machine Guns During The Operations Of The 5th Division From 21st August To 31st August	31/08/1918	31/08/1918
Heading	War Diary of No.5 Battalion Machine Gun Corps For The Month Of September 1918		
War Diary	In Line Divisional Frontage Approx From 1.8.c 0/5 To 1.20.c.95/60	01/09/1918	02/09/1918
War Diary	In Line	02/09/1918	04/09/1918
War Diary	G.23.d Near Bihucourt	05/09/1918	11/09/1918
War Diary	G.23.d	12/09/1918	13/09/1918
War Diary	In Line	14/09/1918	21/09/1918
War Diary	Trenches	21/09/1918	30/09/1918
Heading	War Diary Appendix "A" For Month Sept 1918		
Operation(al) Order(s)	5th Division Operation Order No.254	01/09/1918	01/09/1918
Miscellaneous	Operation 1st To 3rd Sept 1918	07/09/1918	07/09/1918
Miscellaneous	5th Divn S.70/55	13/09/1918	13/09/1918
Operation(al) Order(s)	No.5 Battalion Machine Gun Corps Operation Order No. 27	13/09/1918	13/09/1918
Miscellaneous	Relief Table To Accompany Operation Order No.27	13/09/1918	13/09/1918
Miscellaneous	No 5 Battalion Machine Gun Corps Administrative Instructions	13/09/1916	13/09/1916
Operation(al) Order(s)	5th Division Operation Order No.257	13/09/1918	13/09/1918
Miscellaneous	Relief Table To Accompany 5th Division Operation Order No.257		
Operation(al) Order(s)	No. 5 Battalion Machine Gun Corps Operation Order No. 28	17/09/1918	17/09/1918
Operation(al) Order(s)	5th Division Operation Order No. 258	17/09/1918	17/09/1918
Miscellaneous	Programme of Training for Reserve Company No 5 Battn Machine Gun Corps 19th Sept to 21st Sept	19/09/1918	19/09/1918
Miscellaneous	Programme of Training for Reserve Company For 5 Days	22/09/1918	22/09/1918
Map	Disposition Of M.G		
Map	Map		
Operation(al) Order(s)	No. 5 Battalion Machine Gun Corps Operation Order No. 30	22/09/1918	22/09/1918
Miscellaneous	Table Of Moves To Accompany No.5 Bn M.G Corps O.O. 30		
Operation(al) Order(s)	No. 5 Battalion Machine Gun Corps Operation Order No. 29	20/09/1918	20/09/1918
Miscellaneous	Table Of Moves To Accompany 5/Bn M.G Corps O.O No.29		
Operation(al) Order(s)	No. 5 Battalion Machine Gun Corps Warning Order No. 31	24/09/1918	24/09/1918

Miscellaneous	Account of Operation From 12th September 1918 To 30th September 1918	08/10/1918	08/10/1918
Operation(al) Order(s)	No. 5 Battalion Machine Gun Corps Operation Order No. 30	22/09/1918	22/09/1918
Miscellaneous	Table Of Moves To Accompany No.5 Battalion M.G.C Operation Order No.30		
Operation(al) Order(s)	No. 5 Battalion Machine Gun Corps Operation Order No. 32	25/09/1918	25/09/1918
Miscellaneous			
Map	Map		
Heading	War Diary No.5 Battalion Machine Gun Corps October 31st 1918 Vol 7		
War Diary	Bertincourt	01/10/1918	08/10/1918
War Diary	Bantouzelle	09/10/1918	10/10/1918
War Diary	In Line	11/10/1918	23/10/1918
War Diary	Caudry	23/10/1918	31/10/1918
Miscellaneous	No.5 Battalion Machine Gun Corps-Programme of Training	03/10/1918	03/10/1918
Miscellaneous	To O.C "A" Company W.23/68	09/10/1918	09/10/1918
Operation(al) Order(s)	No. 5 Battalion Machine Gun Corps Operation Order No. 33	09/10/1918	09/10/1918
Operation(al) Order(s)	No. 5 Battalion Machine Gun Corps Operation Order No. 35	10/10/1918	10/10/1918
Miscellaneous	No.5 Battalion Machine Gun Corps Defence Scheme	13/10/1918	13/10/1918
Operation(al) Order(s)	No.5 Battalion Machine Gun Corps Operation Order No.36	15/10/1918	15/10/1918
Operation(al) Order(s)	No.5 Battalion Machine Gun Corps Operation Order No.6	16/10/1918	16/10/1918
Operation(al) Order(s)	No.5 Battalion Machine Gun Corps Operation Order No.37	18/10/1918	18/10/1918
Map	Map		
Operation(al) Order(s)	No.5 Battalion Machine Gun Corps Operation Order No. 38	21/10/1918	21/10/1918
Miscellaneous	No.5 Battalion Machine Gun Corps Account of Operations For Period 19th October 1918-23rd October 1918	23/10/1918	23/10/1918
Miscellaneous	A/10	27/10/1918	27/10/1918
Map	Map		
Heading	4th Division 11th Infy Bde 1st Bn Hampshire Regt March April May 1919 Missing		
Miscellaneous	H.Q. 5th Division	30/11/1918	30/11/1918
Heading	War Diary for the month of November 1918 No.5 Battalion Machine Gun Corps		
War Diary	Battn: H.Q Caudry	01/11/1918	02/11/1918
War Diary	Beaurain	03/11/1918	04/11/1918
War Diary	Neuville	05/11/1918	05/11/1918
War Diary	Louvignies	06/10/1918	06/10/1918
War Diary	Jolimetz	07/10/1918	08/10/1918
War Diary	Pont Sur Sambre	09/10/1918	10/10/1918
War Diary	Le Quesnoy	11/10/1918	12/10/1918
War Diary	Jolimetz	13/10/1918	30/10/1918
Heading	No.5 Battalion Machine Gun Corps War Diary "Appendix "A"		
Operation(al) Order(s)	No. 5 Battalion Machine Gun Corps Operation Order No. 39	02/11/1918	02/11/1918

Type	Description	Date From	Date To
Operation(al) Order(s)	No.5 Battalion Machine Gun Corps Warning Order No. 10	02/11/1918	02/11/1918
Operation(al) Order(s)	5th Division Operation Order No.273	10/11/1918	10/11/1918
Operation(al) Order(s)	5th Division Operation Order No.274	10/11/1918	10/11/1918
Operation(al) Order(s)	No. 5 Battn M. Gun Corps Operation Order No. 40	10/11/1918	10/11/1918
Miscellaneous	No.5 Battalion Machine Gun Corps Supply Arrangements		
Operation(al) Order(s)	No. 5 Battalion Machine Gun Corps Operation Order No. 41	12/11/1918	12/11/1918
Miscellaneous	Account of The Operations From 2nd-12th Novr 1918	12/11/1918	12/11/1918
Map	Map		
Operation(al) Order(s)	5th Division Operation Order No.275	14/11/1918	14/11/1918
Miscellaneous	5th Division IV Corps No. 17/1/10	24/11/1918	24/11/1918
Miscellaneous	No.5 Battn M.G. Corps Programme of Training	30/11/1918	30/11/1918
Heading	No.5 Battn Machine Gun Corps War Diary For The Month of December 1918		
War Diary	Jolimetz	01/12/1918	22/12/1918
War Diary	Temploux & Suarlee	22/12/1918	31/12/1918
Heading	No.5 Battalion Machine Gun Corps War Diary For The Month of December 1918		
Miscellaneous	Notes on Conference of Corps And Divisional Commanders Held At Army Headquarters 30th Novr 1918	30/11/1918	30/11/1918
Operation(al) Order(s)	5th Division Operation Order No.276	04/12/1918	04/12/1918
Miscellaneous	Programme of Training	06/12/1918	06/12/1918
Miscellaneous	O.C. "A" Company W.5/23/3	10/12/1918	10/12/1918
Miscellaneous	Programme of Training From 9th To 11th Decr 1918	09/12/1918	09/12/1918
Operation(al) Order(s)	No. 5 Battalion Machine Gun Corps Warning Order No.20	13/12/1918	13/12/1918
Operation(al) Order(s)	No. 5 Battalion Machine Gun Corps Operation Order No. 43	12/12/1918	12/12/1918
Miscellaneous	No. 5 Battalion Machine Gun Corps Programme of March	12/12/1918	12/12/1918
Heading	War Diary for the month of January 1919 No.5 Battalion Machine Gun Corps Vol 10		
War Diary	Temploux & Suarlee	01/01/1919	31/01/1919
Heading	War Diary for the month of January-1919 No.5 Battalion Machine Gun Corps Appendix "A"		
Diagram etc	Plan Of 5th Div Wing Infantry Barracks Charleoi		
Miscellaneous	Programme of Training fro the Week Ending 18th Jany 1919	12/01/1919	12/01/1919
Heading	War Diary No.5 Battalion Machine Gun Corps For The Month Of February 1919		
War Diary	Temploux And Suarlee	01/02/1919	28/02/1919
Heading	War Diary of No.5 Battalion Machine Gun Corps For Month Of March 1919		
War Diary	Temploux and Suarlee	01/03/1919	16/03/1919
War Diary	Sombreffe	17/03/1919	31/03/1919
Heading	Appendix "A" War Diary of No.5 Machine Gun Corps March 1919		
Miscellaneous	O.C. "A" Company	04/03/1919	04/03/1919
Miscellaneous	O.C. "A" Company D. 1/156	06/03/1919	06/03/1919
Diagram etc	Infantry Barracks Charleroi		
Miscellaneous	No.5 Battn M.G. Corps 5th Division S. 55/17/1	06/03/1919	06/03/1919
Miscellaneous	5th Divn A.M/3900/436	13/03/1919	13/03/1919
Miscellaneous	W.23/100/2	16/03/1919	16/03/1919

Operation(al) Order(s)	No. 5 Battalion Machine Gun Corps Operation Order No. 44	13/03/1919	13/03/1919
Miscellaneous	Special Order Of The Day	17/03/1919	17/03/1919
Operation(al) Order(s)	No. 5 Battn Machine Gun Corps Warning Order No. 10	31/03/1919	31/03/1919
Heading	War Diary of No.5 Battalion Machine Gun Corps For The Month Of April 1919		
War Diary	Sombreffe	01/04/1919	01/04/1919
War Diary	Charleroi (Ref. Map Namur 8 1/100,000)	02/04/1919	02/04/1919
War Diary	Charleroi	03/04/1919	03/04/1919
War Diary	Sieglar	04/04/1919	26/04/1919
War Diary	Kreigsdorf	10/04/1919	26/04/1919
War Diary	Oberlar	10/04/1919	26/04/1919
War Diary	Eschmar	10/04/1919	30/04/1919
Heading	Appendix "A" War Diary of No.5 Battn Machine Gun Corps April 1919		
Miscellaneous	5th Division Cadre 5th M. Gun Battalion		
Miscellaneous	5th Division AM./3900/533	01/04/1919	01/04/1919
Miscellaneous	5th Battn M.G Corps		
Operation(al) Order(s)	No.5 Battn Machine Gun Corps Operation Order No.91		
Heading	War Diary of No.5 Battalion Machine Gun Corps For The Month Of May 1919		
War Diary	Sieglar	01/05/1919	02/05/1919
War Diary	Kreigsdorf	03/05/1919	04/05/1919
War Diary	Eschmar	04/05/1919	05/05/1919
War Diary	Oberlar	06/05/1919	14/05/1919
War Diary	Godesberg	15/05/1919	31/05/1919
Heading	Appendix "A" War Diary of No.5 Battalion Machine Gun Corps Month Of May 1919		
Operation(al) Order(s)	No. 5 Battn Machine Gun Corps Operation Order No. 91	14/05/1919	14/05/1919
Miscellaneous	5th Bn Machine Gun Corps Xth Corps No. 9/507/Q	19/05/1919	19/05/1919
Miscellaneous	Xth Corps No. G.43/2/115	16/05/1919	16/05/1919
Miscellaneous	Tenth Corps Rhine Army No A 602/1 (0)	16/05/1919	16/05/1919

No 95/1539/1

5 DIVISION. TROOPS.

5 BN MACHINE GUN CORPS
1918 APR TO 1919 MAY.

205 MACHINE GUN COY.
1916 OCT TO 1917 NOV.

5 DIVISION ANTI GAS SCHOOL
1917 OCT TO 1919 MAR.

1539

5th Divisional Troops.

Formed from the Brigade & Divisional M.Gs
26th APRIL 1918.

5th BATTALION

MACHINE GUN COMPANY

APRIL 1918.

A: B: C & D Companies attached.

Confidential

Register No: A.5/8.
Part No: 1.
Volume No: 1.

War Diary
of
5 Battn: Machine Gun Corps.

for the month of
April, 1918.

30.4.1918.

L. Watling Lieut: Col:,
Commanding 5 Battn: M. G. Corps.

Original. April 1918. Page 1.

5/Battalion Machine Gun Corps.

Map Reference Sheet 36A 1/40,000.

Army Form C. 2118.

WAR DIARY

~~INTELLIGENCE SUMMARY~~

(Erase heading not required.)

Instructions regarding War Diaries and Intelligence Summaries are contained in F.S. Regs., Part II. and the Staff Manual respectively. Title pages will be prepared in manuscript.

Place	Date	Hour	Summary of Events and Information	Remarks and references to Appendices
Battn: H.Qrs. at THIENNE			The formation of the 5/Battn: M.Gun Corps comprising the following Machine Gun Companies was carried out in accordance with instructions received from the War Office:	For details regarding formation see Appendix "A"
			Officers O.R's	
			13th Machine Gun Company 7 169	
			95th Machine Gun Company 6 171	
			15th Machine Gun Company 9 179	For Company details see Appendix "B"
	26th.		205th Machine Gun Company 10 185	
			32 704
			Strength of Battn. on formation.	
	27th.		Weather dull, situation quiet.	
	28th.		Weather fine but dull. Internal relief commenced, "B" Coy: being relieved by "A" Company in Left Sector of Divisional front.	For details of relief see Appendix "A/2"
	29th.		Weather dull. Internal relief completed.	
	30th.		Weather wet. Major Stuart reports for duty with Battn: & is posted to "A" Company, 2nd in Command.	For disposition of Officers see Appendix "A/3"

H. Welling Lieut: Colonel
Commanding 5/Battn: Machine Gun Corps

Army Form C. 2118.

"B" Company
5/Batt: MGC Corps

April 26th 1918.

WAR DIARY
or
INTELLIGENCE SUMMARY.
(Erase heading not required.)

Place	Date	Hour	Summary of Events and Information	Remarks and references to Appendices
	26th		[illegible handwritten entries]	

Army Form C. 2118.

WAR DIARY
or
INTELLIGENCE SUMMARY.
(Erase heading not required.)

Instructions regarding War Diaries and Intelligence Summaries are contained in F. S. Regs., Part II. and the Staff Manual respectively. Title pages will be prepared in manuscript.

Place	Date	Hour	Summary of Events and Information	Remarks and references to Appendices
[illegible]	27		The enemy have put down a very heavy barrage and are attacking. [illegible] heavy shelling & machine gun fire during the night. [illegible] quiet. The enemy kept up intermittent shelling during the day. [illegible] attack was made against our line at 6.15 p.m. but was broken up by our artillery & machine gun fire. Our casualties were [illegible] No 4 decker. [illegible]	
-do-	28		The enemy again shelled our line heavily. A very heavy [illegible] (Brigade) test was put down at 10.30 p.m. by the enemy but no attack developed. [illegible] 2nd Lieut [illegible] wounded. Other casualties amongst O.R. 5 killed 17 wounded.	
-do-	29		[illegible] casualties during the day wounded 1 O.R. The enemy shelled our lines during afternoon. Our casualties have been considerable. [illegible] 1 & 2 decker [illegible] companies to the Regt [illegible] 2 R.S. 8 O.R. wounded, [illegible] killed. [illegible] held reception [illegible] quiet.	
-do-	30		Intermittent shelling the day. No [illegible] attack. Night was quiet but in the hours [illegible] 2 O.R. during the night. The work of relieving of heavy positions all day.	

(Sgd) [illegible] Lieut
Cmdg 16 Company [illegible]

Army Form C. 2118.

WAR DIARY
or
INTELLIGENCE SUMMARY.
(Erase heading not required.)

Claston Batt. M.G.C.   **June 1918.**

Place	Date	Hour	Summary of Events and Information	Remarks and references to Appendices
Field (ITALY)			No Return Worth note &c	
			Raining VILLA CORNARA VALMARZENA. Weather settled was foggy.	
			Arrived SVICENZA	
Field (FRANCE)			Long Journey via Mt Cenis tunnel. 11:00 Residence WB.N.F.	
			Detrained at PREVENT. Front to ROCHIN AUX.	
			Moved to LILLERS & HINDICOURT	
			At rest	
			Came into line. 2nd CANADIAN DIVISION cancelled. Entrained on tactical train at BAILEUL	
			Detrained at AIRE. The enemy having broken through at MERVILLE, the Bren was (?) to action, 15th Brigade in advanced Posn. Marched to MOLINGHAM thence via St VENANT to CROIX MARMISSE (F 27-80) Shelled in BIVOUACS.	
			Casualties. 35592 Pt Gordon killed. 35345 Cpl Dutton M.C. (r.M.) 16299 L/Cpl Davies J 48965 L/Cpl Adams E, 2-R. 108763 Pt Gabrielson E, 4 Sergts 7 Pt Pinson, J 10581, Pt Blunt F, 16809, Pt Moore W, wounded received. an66 Pt Moore An (?), Pt Bedford Mitchell 35255, Pt Noblett F W. (?) Pt Shires attached transfused wounded in action. 4957 Pt Wilson in Jones Coy, from Reposalia.	
			Remained in Diamond Reposn. Cant 4 Yds + 8 Guns in DR Line &	
			Bois des Vaches.	
			Relieved 9th M.G. Coys 11 ft Sector in front of Forêt de Nieppe 8 Guns in Br le Bigottere 8 subsections in line.	

C Company 6th Bn MGC
April 1918

Army Form C. 2118.

WAR DIARY
or
INTELLIGENCE SUMMARY.

(Erase heading not required.)

Instructions regarding War Diaries and Intelligence Summaries are contained in F. S. Regs., Part II. and the Staff Manual respectively. Title pages will be prepared in manuscript.

Place	Date	Hour	Summary of Events and Information	Remarks and references to Appendices
Field	April 17 1918		2 Platoons in position as said in orders last by German O.C. on march	
			102 Platoon in action with 2nd Bn Devons, O	
	20		Mnrs Operation in conjunction with 92nd Brigade a night reconnaissance and re-construction of line from K.15.c. to K.20.d was carried out about midnight. 3 Guns assisted in this operation & by the barrage were across the line K.15.a. & K.20.a.5 and 1 gun by subsidiary fire with M.G.s running through to line K.21.c.	
			The operation was successful and 3 Guns were placed on the new line at K.21.a.35 and K.21.a.6.6	
		2 night	A counter attack & turn on the new position was repulsed with the assistance of the 2 guns. Further pressure during night the enemy succeeded in working round one flank of the 3 guns into action along after the others were taken out, but out of action.	
			Casualties 4236 Sgt Stotch I. 258/27th Coy L.C. Sooth 7th Division G.C. 116032. Pte SMITH N. wounded. 19314. Pte CAPPER R.J. 16050 Pte CARTER S. Killed. Relieved by 132 M.G. Coy), 5 Guns withdrew to BOIS DES VACHES 7.8 to Divisional Reserve at T.20.d.0.6. 1 O.R. reinforcement 45177 Pte LOCKHART J.	
		20th April	70-1 Pte ASHBY W. (1 Norfolk Regt attchd) reported MISSING from 17/4/18 & returned 26/4/18 to Company under escort	

M. Tuffill.
Comd C Coy 6th Bn MGC

Army Form C. 2118.

D Comp[any]
WAR DIARY
or
INTELLIGENCE SUMMARY.
(Erase heading not required.)

Place	Date	Hour	Summary of Events and Information	Remarks and references to Appendices
HAVERSKERQUE			COY. HQRS:- HAVERSKERQUE J.27.d.9.7	
	25/4/18		No 1 Sec No 2 No 3 In reserve in HAVERSKERQUE	Sheet 36A NE
			Lewis J.23.c.cent. J.17.cent. 2 along the road	
			2 " J.29.a.0.5. 2 " J.23.a.5.8. 20 + J.28.a & J.34.B	
			2 " Nyis J.28.17.5 Nyis Longue Rue J.28a along the road	
			J.11.C.17.	
			Situation normal. Heavy artly fire as enemy raiding right	
			24/25. Between 10.30pm & 12 enemy sent over 450 shells. S.A.A expended	
			10 rounds (No.1 P.). 1 O.R. to hosp. acct.	
	26/4/18		Situation normal. Firing of locations continued & strengthening	
			of trenches & emplacements. Heavy H.V. shelling to the interior towards	
			No 4 position.	
	27/4/18		Situation normal. S.A.A. expended nil. Casualties nil. Some	
			600 shells in vicinity of positions. Two enemy artillery pieces seen.	
	28/4/18		Situation normal. 160 rounds S.A.A expended at enemy aircraft.	
			Work of strengthening positions carried on. Intermittent artillery shells	
			during night 27/28.	
	29/4/18		Situation normal. 300 rounds S.A.A expended against enemy	
			aircraft during positions. Intermittent shells during night 28/29.	

Army Form C. 2118.

WAR DIARY
or
INTELLIGENCE SUMMARY.
(Erase heading not required.)

Instructions regarding War Diaries and Intelligence Summaries are contained in F. S. Regs., Part II. and the Staff Manual respectively. Title pages will be prepared in manuscript.

Place	Date	Hour	Summary of Events and Information	Remarks and references to Appendices
HAVRINCOURT	30/11/18		Situation quiet. Fought enemy shelling during day, bursts of enemy M. Gun firing of positions carried on.	

G. Shank
Capt for Major
Cmdg B. Coy
5th Bn

5th DIVISION.

ORGANISATION OF THE MACHINE GUN BATTALION.

1. In accordance with instructions issued by the War Office the Machine Gun Companies of the Division will be organised into a Machine Gun Battalion.

2. The Battalion will consist of a H.Q. and 4 Companies of 4 Sections each ; total 64 guns.

The 13th M.G. Company will become "A" Company.
    95th   do.   "B" "
    15th   do.   "C" "
    205th   do.   "D" "

Under this organisation the Battalion will become the accounting Unit, thereby relieving the Companies of the majority of the administrative details for which they are now responsible.

3. The organisation is based on the principle that it is preferable to detach guns from the Division to the Brigades for specific operations rather than to withdraw guns from the Brigade to meet the requirements of the Division. The Battalion formation renders this feasible and permits of the detachment to Brigades of such numbers of guns as may be considered necessary for any specific operation and the organisation is designed to ensure that the Brigade can at all times have a proportion of guns directly under the Brigade Commander, the actual number being dependent on the tactical requirements.

Where the tactical situation permits Machine Gun Companies will operate with the Brigades to which they were previously affiliated.

The O.C. Machine Gun Battalion will be responsible for the discipline, administration and training of the battalion.

4. The establishment of a Section allows for 8 Privates per gun, exclusive of range takers and scouts, thereby providing sufficient men for the actual manning of the gun and for its ammunition supply. The attachment of Infantry to Machine Gun Companies as carrying parties is consequently no longer necessary and will be discontinued.

The attached Infantry at present with the Machine Gun Companies who are not employed as No.1 or 2 on gun teams will be returned to their units when the battalion is raised to its new establishment. Those men who are employed as No.1 or 2 on gun teams will be transferred to the Machine Gun Corps.

5. The details of the organisation will be arranged by Div. "Q".

6. The date on which the battalion formation will be adopted will be notified later.

G. W. Gordon Hall
Lieutenant-Colonel,
General Staff, 5th Division.

25th March 1918.

Copies to :- 13th, 15th & 95th Inf. Bdes. 13th, 15th, 95th & 205th M.G. Companies. 5th Division "Q". D.M.G.O.

SECRET   S/Dwn: No. C.C.508

ORGANISATION OF MACHINE GUN BATTN:

1. The following W.O's, N.C.O's and men will be required for employment on Battn: A.Q.H. as stated.

13th M.G Company
- S.M. Boston to be employed as Q.M. Sergt.
- L/Cpl. Lipter " " " Fitter (Wheelwright)
- One Private " " " Policeman.

15th M.G. Company
- Lieut. A.G.W.W. STANLEY to be employed as Adjutant.
- Sergt. Wilson " " " Provost Sergt.
- Pte. Woodward " " " Butcher

95th M.G. Company
- S.M. McAra to be employed as R.S.M.
- Sergt. Hannel " " " Signalling Sergt.
- One Private " " " Policeman.

205/M Gun Company
- Lieut. C.E.J. McDonald (M.C.) to be employed as Transport Officer
- Transport Corpl. " " " Transport Cpl.
- Pte. Keighley " " " Fitter (Wheelwright)
- One Private " " " Policeman.
- Pte. India " " " { M.O's Orderly / rank of Cpl.
- One Private " " " { M.O's Orderly / Driver

2. The above mentioned personnel will be attached for rations and discipline to the 205/M.G Coy. until the formation of the Battalion. They will report to 205/M.G Coy. by 12 noon, 30th inst. & will bring with them their rations for 31st and their blankets.

O.C. 205/M.G.Coy. will report to D.M.G.O. the completion of assembly of this personnel.

3. This attachment is at present provisional & no pay of appointment, or permission to wear badges of higher rank in case of promotion is granted until the M.Gun Battn is actually formed.

29/March 1918

(sd) O.W. WHITE Lieut.Col,
A.A. & Q.M.G. S/Dwn

SECRET   5/Div CC/508/1

O.C. 5/M.G. Battn.

        Further to this office No. CC/508 of 29/3/18

1. The M. Gun personnel of the Division will be formed into No 5/Machine Gun Battalion, with effect from 26/April, 1918.

2. The following appointments in the Battn. are made:

Commanding Officer	Lieut. Col. P.H. Cutting (MC) /Devon R. M. Gun Corps
2nd. in Command	A/Major D.G. KYDD (7/R.Scots) M. Gun Corps
Adjutant	A/Captain A.C.W.U. STANLEY (R INNIS FUS) M. Gun Corps
Signal Officer Medical Officer Quartermaster	To be notified later
Transport Officer	Lieut. C.B.J. MacDONNELL, M.G. Corps

"A" Company (13/M.G. Coy)
  O.C.
  2nd. Command   } to be notified later

"B" Company (95/M.G. Coy)
  O.C.   A/Major. A.S. NICHOLL M.C. (7/R. Scots) M.G.C.
  2nd. in command   A/Capt. R.M. DADD (KOSLI) M.G. Corps.

"C" (15/M. Gun Company)
  O.C.   A/Major. H. TUFFILL M.G. Corps
  2nd. in C.   to be notified later.

"D" Company (205/M. Gun Coy)
  O.C.   A/Major. O. COOPE, M.G. Corps.
  2nd. in C.   A/Capt. A.J. SHANKS M.G. Corps.

    Claims have been submitted for the above named officers & the G.O.C. authorises their wearing the badge of their acting ranks.

3. The necessary adjustments of transport will be carried out in accordance with the establishment of M. Gun Battalion. Indents for new tournaments will be submitted forthwith.

4. The O.C. M.G. Battn. will demand personnel required to make up to establishment on the A.F.B.213 for the current week.

5. The signal section for the Battalion has been demanded by O.C. 5/Signal Section.

25/4/18
                                            (sd). Major
                                            D.a.a.G. 5/Divn.

SECRET   REF. MAP. FRANCE 36A. N.E. 1/20,000

P.O.M. O.O. N° 49

1. POM will be relieved by PORPOISE on the night 28/29 April.

2. Guides as under will be at Ration Dump at 8.30 p.m.

	Opposite number
C Section 2 guides (1 for each pair of guns)	N° 1 Sectⁿ
D Section (K14d) 1 guide	} N° 3 "
A " (K9a) 1 "	
B " 2 guides	N° 2 "
A " (Right) 1 guide	} N° 4 "
D " (Right) 1 "	

Care must be taken that guides pick up their correct opposite numbers.

3. Belt boxes & all trench stores will be handed over & receipts obtained.

4. On relief A & D Sections will man the positions in the Divisional Line around BOIS DES VACHES. B & C. Sections will withdraw to reserve at J20d 0.5. After relief 2/Lt WILSON will assume command of A Section. 2/Lt FAIRGRIEVE will return to POM REAR.

"A" Form
MESSAGES AND SIGNALS.

Army Form C. 2121 (in pads of 100).

TRANSPORT. The T.O. will arrange for two limbers to be at the Ration Dump from 9.30 p.m. onwards. One limber will take A & D Sections' Guns etc to BOIS DES VACHES. One limber will take B & C. Sections' equipment to Reserve at J 20 d. 0.5.
On completion of Relief Coy HQ. will close at J 6 d 0.9 + reopen at J 20 d 0.5.
Completion of relief to be reported by Code Word "BING"

Issued at 3.0 p.m.
27-4-18

H. Tuffill, Major
Comdg P.M.

Disposition of M. Guns 1/Battn. M.G.C. on 26/4/18

Ref Map. 36A. N.E.

B Company

~~Left~~ Right sector guns at:
- K.21 a. 60/80
- K.21 a. 45/80
- K.21 a. 30/80 (2)
- K.30 b. 10/10
- K.30 b. 25/30
- K.30 d. 25/40
- K.30 d. 60/50
- K.34 b. 05/10
- K.36 b. 20/62
- K.36 b. 05/60
- K.28 d. 05/50
- K.21 a. 60/70
- K.21 a. 70/80
- J.36 a. 45/60
- J.31 a. 80/10

C Company

~~Right~~ Left sector guns at:
- K.red 85/60 (2)
- K.9 a. 85/10
- K.9 c. 90/10
- K.15 d. 60/80
- K.15 d. 50/60
- K.9 d. 65/75
- K.21 a. 20/50
- K.9 c. 05/20 (2)
- K.8 a. 50/20
- K.8 a. 50/0
- K.15 b. 10/20
- K.9 d. 65/40
- K.9 d. 40/28
- K.9 d. 95/90

D Company

Durable line guns at:
- J.34 b. 4/2
- J.34 b. 26/6
- J.34 b. 6/4
- J.34 b. 8/6
- J.29 a. 4/4
- J.29 a. 05/05
- J.23 b. 25/05
- J.23 b. 35/40
- J.23 a. 65/5
- J.23 a. 8/9
- J.17 b. 6/4
- J.17 b. 00/05
- J.27 b. 80/28
- J.27 b. 89/20
- J.27 d. 0/3
- J.27 d. 85/67

A Company

Reserve guns at:
- J.6 c. 50/25
- J.12 c. 0/4
- J.6 d. 45/20
- J.6 d. 50/40

} Dual Line

also 8 guns about
J.20 a. 2/4

26/4/18

Disposition of M. Guns, 5 Batt: M.G.C. on 30/4/18

"B" Company

~~Left~~ Right Sector guns at

K 21a	60/80		J 36a	45/60
K 21d	45/50		J 36a	80/40
K 21a	20/20 (2)		K 31a	60/70
K 20b	10/10		K 31a	70/80
K 20b	25/25		K 25d	95/50
K 20d	45/40		K 26b	05/60
K 20d	60/50			
K 26b	05/60			

"A" Company

~~Right~~ Left Sector guns at

K 9a	05/10		K 9c	05/20 (2)
K 9c	90/90		K 8a	50/20
K 9b	60/60		K 8a	55/10
K 9b	68/52		K 9c	82/20
K 15d	60/50		K 9d	68/40
K 15d	20/60		K 9d	45/48
K 14d	85/60 (2)		K 9d	95/70

"D" Company

Dwnl. Line guns at

J 34b	4/2		J 23a	65/45
J 34b	45/15		J 23a	5/9
J 34b	6/9		J 17a	9/1
J 34b	6/8		J 17b	00/15
J 29a	1/44		J 27b	80/28
J 29a	05/35		J 27b	87/20
J 23b	30/35		J 27d	9/3
J 23b	35/40		J 27d	85/39

"C" Company

Reserve guns at

J 6c	30/25 (2)	⎫
J 12c	0/4 (2)	⎬ Dwnl. Line
J 6d	40/25 (2)	⎪
J 6d	80/40 (2)	⎭

8 guns about J 20d 2/4

MACHINE GUN POSITIONS ON 5/1st Suffolk (5)Battn:MGC) FRONT on 30.4.1918.

5th Divisional Troops.

205th MACHINE GUN COMPANY

APRIL 1918.

D. Coy
5th M.G. Batt'n
(205th M.G. Coy)

WAR DIARY

APRIL 1st - 30th 1918

Army Form C. 2118.

WAR DIARY
or
INTELLIGENCE SUMMARY.
(Erase heading not required.)

Instructions regarding War Diaries and Intelligence Summaries are contained in F. S. Regs., Part II. and the Staff Manual respectively. Title pages will be prepared in manuscript.

Place	Date	Hour	Summary of Events and Information	Remarks and references to Appendices
C. BASSO	1/4/18		Coy in training 2 OR to Locualrick.	
POIANA	2/4/18		Coy march to POIANA & entrain at 23-57 for France	
	3/4/18		In train en route to France	
	6/4/18			
	7/4/18		Coy detrain 8-30 pm at FREVENT & proceed by march route to LUCHEUX & billet there	LENS 11.
	8/4/18		Coy in training at Lucheux.	
	10/4/18		Coy stage to MONDICOURT & entrain for THIENNES.	
	11/4/18		Coy detrain at THIENNES 10am & all 4 sections proceed to the line to cover reserve line in advance of coro frontier by 1/6 A.J.H from HAVERSKERQUE TO LE PARC - Coy H/O established at J.27.d.8.7. 4 guns in K.E. outs of LETOUQUET T.25.d.	Officer Comdg.
HAVERSKERQUE	12/4/18		4 guns in H.E. outs of LETOUQUET T.25.d. Vic. Aguns H.guns) R.O.1. Appy LA RUE DES MORTS. No.2. In reserve in HAVERSQUE No.3. 4 guns along the Haversque road T.28.b T.34.L	Lieut. BENE 36 BN

(A7092). Wt. W12839/M1293. 750,000. 1/17. D. D. & L., Ltd. Forms/C.2118.14.

WAR DIARY
or
INTELLIGENCE SUMMARY.

Army Form C. 2118.

Place	Date	Hour	Summary of Events and Information	Remarks and references to Appendices
HAVERSKERQUE	13/4/18		Situation quiet during the early hours but been very restless during the daytime. Sections well dug in by night. 3 O.R. slightly wounded.	
	14/4/18		Situation normal. Periodic bursts of enemy shelling. 1 O.R. killed & 1 O.R. wounded to Sheaho (3rd R.) in command proceed to 13 Filipoep 20 Lorry. C.O.	
	15/4/18		Situation quiet. Casualties nil. Sections moved to positions as follows:- No 1. 2 guns J.17 central J 23 a 5 8 2. Rey Hqrs Forestier House J 11. C. 17. Nos 3 & 4 Sections remain as before.	No 1 2 guns J 23. C central 2 guns J 99. a. 05. 36 A N E Hqrs J 15 & 75.
	16/4/18		Situation normal. 1 OR killed & 2 to Hosp. sick	

WAR DIARY
or
INTELLIGENCE SUMMARY.

Army Form C. 2118.

Place	Date	Hour	Summary of Events and Information	Remarks and references to Appendices
HAVERKER SQUE.	17/4/18 - 19/4/18		Situation quiet. Nothing special to report. Casualties nil.	
	20/4/18		Situation normal. Casualties nil. 2 guns moved from J.34.d.77 to J.34.d.50 in the trenches J.34.d.8 & J.27.d.50 in the trenches.	
	21/4/18		Situation quiet. Our artillery very active during night. Enemy sent over 300 shells. The gun crews all who indexed up to seize violently part of making forward & strengthening positions carries on.	
	22/4/18		Situation normal. 1 O.R. slightly wounded. Ranges registered & recoveries made for ammunition. Target No. 1 gun shells thrown into FORÊT DE NIEPPE positions vicinity shells during the afternoon.	
	23/4/18		Situation normal. Anti-aircraft movement continued, parties & forwards made. Harassing fire & green lights on night front of No 2 position. Rain fell heavily during night. Bombarded enemy sent H.E. & H.E. shells into buildings J.77.C.2.4 for a few mins. 2 O.R. to hosp. sick.	

WAR DIARY
or
INTELLIGENCE SUMMARY.

Army Form C. 2118.

Place	Date	Hour	Summary of Events and Information	Remarks and references to Appendices
HAZEBROUCK	24/4/18		Situation normal. Reliefs carried out to schedule & emplacements deluged by shell fire & artillery overnight during night. Our artillery extremely hampering. Several SOS went up owing to enemy of River LYS at night & our own. SOS went up owing to enemy of River LYS at night. Several aerial activity just before dawn, heavy day experienced.	
	25/4/18		Situation normal. Heavy artillery fire at intervals during the night 24/25. Between 10-30 p.m. midnight enemy sent over gas shells (LPM) expended 10 rounds (AP) 1 SB shell, air.	
	26/4/18		Situation normal. During hours of darkness continued strengthening of trenches & emplacements. Heavy H.V shelling to the westward of 70 & howrs.	
	27/4/18		Situation normal. S.A.A expended nil. Casualties nil. Some gas shells in vicinity of trenches but enemy activity quiet than usual	
	28/4/18		Situation normal. 160 rounds S.A.A expended at present. Enemy bent of strengthening positions carried on interm- ittenly fuels during night 27/28	

Army Form C. 2118.

WAR DIARY
or
INTELLIGENCE SUMMARY.
(Erase heading not required.)

Instructions regarding War Diaries and Intelligence Summaries are contained in F. S. Regs., Part II. and the Staff Manual respectively. Title pages will be prepared in manuscript.

Place	Date	Hour	Summary of Events and Information	Remarks and references to Appendices
HAMERSKER QUE	29/4/18		Situation normal. 300 rounds N.A.A expended on enemy aircraft. Enemy positions lightly shelled during day	
	30/4/18		Situation quiet. Light enemy shelling during day on rear of enemy. Strengthening of positions carried on	

A. Thank
Capt. for Major.
Comdg. D Coy
5th K.R.R.C.

Vol 2

Registered No: W.20/4.
Volume No: 2
Part No: 1

C O N F I D E N T A L.

O R I G I N A L.

W A R D I A R Y.

O F

5 TH:BATTALION MACHINE GUN CORPS.

FOR THE MONTH OF M A Y 1918.

31/5/18.

R H Cutting Lieut-Colonel,

Commanding 5th:Battalion Machine Gun Corps.

Page 1.

Map Reference - Sheet. 36 A. 1/40000.

Original. – May 1918.

5/Battn: M. Gun Corps. –

Army Form C. 2118.
5/Bn: M.G.C/2.

WAR DIARY
INTELLIGENCE SUMMARY.

(Erase heading not required.)

Place	Date May	Hour	Summary of Events and Information	Remarks and references to Appendices
In Trenches	1st.		Weather fine but dull. Disposition of Battn: as follows:-	
approx: frontage			"A" Company in Left Brigade Sector. (Vickers system) — 16 guns.	For exact
Bois de NIEPPE			"C" Company in Left Brigade Sector. (Support) – 8 guns, also 8 gun Dual: location see
— LA BASSEE —			"B" Company in Right Brigade Sector. (Vickers system). — 16 guns.	Appendix A/1
CANAL.			"D" Company in Right Brigade Sector (Support) — 16 guns.	
Left Flank 29th Division			Strength of Battalion. Officers 32. O.R. 703.	
Right Flank 61st Division			attached. 1. 93.	
			Situation: normal. Our arty. very active, houses in enemy line at K.21.b & K.21.b.2/3 set	
			on fire causing ammunition to explode. Hostile M. Guns were active during night	
			especially on cross roads at K.8.c. 65/20. Hostile arty: active all day. No.1 Section H.Q.	
			& road in vicinity of No:4 Section were shelled with 5.9's. and also trench	
			Mortared. Mortar located at K.16.c. 60/30. Work. Companies were employed	
			improving positions generally. 2nd positions constructed by "B" Coy. at K.21.a.3/5	
			& K.25.b.9/3. went C.T. to forward position. Lieut: ANDERSON joined from Base Reported.	
			to "C" Company assuming duties of 2nd i.c. Casualties. 2. O.R. Wounded.	
— do: —	2nd.		Weather dull. Situation normal Arty: on both sides active, "A" Company's Section	

Original.
Page 2.

Army Form C. 2118.

WAR DIARY / INTELLIGENCE SUMMARY

Place	Date	Hour	Summary of Events and Information	Remarks and references to Appendices
In trenches	2nd:	—	H.Qrs. and horses about K.9.a.8.6. heavily shelled by the enemy. Our support lines were shelled during the night. Hostile aircraft flew low over our lines at 7pm: dropping a few bombs in FOREST de NIEPPE. Enemy M.G's & T.M's. very active. Work: "D" Company wiring and improving their positions in support line. Lieut: B.E.BISHOP & Lieut: J.E.D. PACKER join from Base & one posted to "B" Company. 5. O.R. rejoin from C.C.S. — 3 to "A" Coy: — 1 to "B" Coy: — and 1 to "D" Coy: No: casualties.	
— do: —	3rd:	—	Weather fine. Situation normal. Our artillery active especially at 10:30pm: when there was a great deal of activity S. of our line. Hostile Arty: bombarded our front line in Left Sector with light shells at 10:30 a.m... At 3pm: shells of 8" calibre fell in our front line in same sector. a few of these shells also fell in: "No Man' Land" & the enemy's front line system. Work: "A" Coy: took up extra bombs & S.A.A. & belt boxes to positions in left sector, parapets of positions strengthened & fields of fire altered where necessary. Position about K.14.d. 70/55. Camouflaged & improved. "B" Company carried out deepening of existing trenches & sheepherd parapets in Right Sector. Infantry relief commences K.15/h/y: Bde: relieving 25/h/y: Bde.	
— do: —	4th:	—	Weather fine. Infantry relief completed. Situation Quiet. Our field guns & heavies	

Original

Page 3
Army Form C. 2118.

WAR DIARY
INTELLIGENCE SUMMARY
(Erase heading not required.)

Instructions regarding War Diaries and Intelligence Summaries are contained in F. S. Regs., Part II. and the Staff Manual respectively. Title pages will be prepared in manuscript.

Place	Date	Hour	Summary of Events and Information	Remarks and references to Appendices
In Trenches	4th.	Contd.	fired on LE SART in afternoon setting fire to houses at K.27.d.1/2 & K.33.a.2/6. Field guns and Leaches harassed Cross roads & punished hostile M.Guns which were very active. Our aircraft active all day. Hostile artillery was active and advanced H.Q: of "D" Company were moved to J.2.d.5/3; enemy shelled LA MOTTE BAUDET at 11.30 am. and LA RUE des MORTS with H.E. for 20 minutes. 5 oh. "A" Company built new position at K.a.3 and 2 at K.14.b 60/70. 2 60/65. respectively; reserve of 40,000. S.A.A. distributed along hedges at K.15.c.95/80. 4 guns of "A" Company commence indirect fire on tracks & road at K.10.b.20/10. & K.16.a.60/10. during evening.	
In Trenches	5th.		Weather fine. 4 Guns of "A" Company expended 3500 rounds in indirect fire on 4th. At 3-50am: till 3-45am: 8 guns ("A" Coy:) in Left Sector fired on K.11.a; 24,000 rounds were expended and assistance given to 29th division who executed a raid. Situation normal. Our artillery active on LE SART & HERVILLE. Our aircraft active mostly on Wissening, bombing & firing Rear H.Guns. Whilst our Leaches were firing at HAVERSKERQUE a premature occurred wounding 1 man of "D" Company. Hostile Arty: active, back in K.20.c. got much attention and 1.H. Gun position of "D" Company at K.26.a. received a few shells — no damage. "A" Company reported light shelling on K.9.b.	

A6945 Wt. W14422/M1160 350,000 12/16 D.D. & L. Forms/C./2118/14

Original.   Page 4.
Army Form C. 2118.

WAR DIARY
INTELLIGENCE SUMMARY.

Place	Date	Hour	Summary of Events and Information	Remarks and references to Appendices
In Trenches	5th:	cont:	also on road near HQrs at K.9.c. Hostile M.Guns were not so active. Both "A" Company continuing alternate positions for front line guns, screens were erected and S.A.A. brought up for night firing. "B" Company employed on changing of trenches and gun positions in Support line. Casualties nil. Lieut: G.D.M. ABBOTTS joined & posted to "A" Company.	
-do-	6th:		Weather fine but dull, slight rain. Situation quiet. Enemy artillery shelled Section HQrs of "B" Company at K.9.C. and also M. Gun positions at K.9.b. 50/40. one of these positions being destroyed as a result. Aircraft very active on both sides. Hostile airmen dropping bombs at CROIX MARRAISE and HAVERSKERQUE during afternoon. One enemy machine was brought down by our machines near ST VENANT. Work. General improvement to positions Trenches. "A" Company rebuilt M.Gun positions which was destroyed by enemy shell fire. Lieut: A.G. SMYTH (to "A" Coy). Lieut: V.F. WALKLETT (to "A" Coy). & Lieut: R.J. WALTER (B. Coy) joined from Base Depot and posted to Companies as above.	
-do-	7th:		Weather fine dull and little rain early morning. Situation quiet. Ourarty: active. M. Guns in Right Sector (B. Coy) carried out harassing fire throughout night & early morning on tracks from LE SART in K.27.c.8. on Canal from K.33. a 0/1; 5000 rds being expended.	

Page 5.

Original.

Army Form C. 2118.

WAR DIARY
INTELLIGENCE SUMMARY

(Erase heading not required.)

Instructions regarding War Diaries and Intelligence Summaries are contained in F. S. Regs., Part II. and the Staff Manual respectively. Title pages will be prepared in manuscript.

Place	Date	Hour	Summary of Events and Information	Remarks and references to Appendices
In trenches	7th	contd.	Hostile arty was active. At 12.45am and again at 2.45am a light barrage was put down on left sector front & support lines. At 3.30am enemy arty shelled K.9.b. During the farm there to the ground. At 4pm a very heavy barrage was put down on the CROIX MARAISE — CORBIE Road. Work S.A.A. taken up to left sector, parapets and positions improved by "A" B.& D. Coys. Casualties 1. O.R. Wounded (remained at duty).	
— do —	8th:		Weather fine. Situation Quiet. Our arty shelled LE SART & carried out harassing fire throughout the night. H.Gs. also carried out harassing fire, firing on tracks radiating from LE SART. Hostile arty was very active shortly after midnight, firing over a wide area, particular attention being given to edge of WOOD at K.2.a. At midday LES LAURIERS heavily shelled, at 10.30pm Heavy barrage put down about GLOSTER FARM and LE VERT BOIS. Both Minor alterations to positions in left sector. Change of dispositions takes place.	
— do: —	9th:		Weather fine. Situation normal. Arty active throughout day and night. Our H.Gs. active in neighbourhood of LE SART & in region of CANAL; it was noted that our fire on the village drew almost instant retaliation whilst fire about CANAL was ignored by the enemy. Enemy guns quiet during day but especially active	

Original.

Page 6.

Army Form C. 2118.

WAR DIARY
INTELLIGENCE SUMMARY.
(Erase heading not required.)

Place	Date	Hour	Summary of Events and Information	Remarks and references to Appendices
Trenches		9pm:	Contalmaison in Left Sector very heavily bombarded with gas shells, all Calibres, special attention also given by the enemy to reserve area Left Sector at 6pm: RUE DES MORTS & Company H.Q's: "A" Company shelled heavily with 5.9's & between 11.30 & 12.30pm same places received number of gas shells. Indirect harassing fire carried out during early morning of 9th: by "A" & "B" Companies on following targets K.U.b. 50.50 (Occupied house) K.22.a. 35.95. (Trench Mortar position in orchard), K.33.a. 80/99. (Occupied house) rounds fired 5750.	
do:		10am:	Weather fine. Situation quiet. In conjunction with Right Flank Divn. the 15/R.I.Ble. carried for details of out a raid at 2am: on the house at K.21.b.61. Operation quite successful, very little opposition raid by 15/R.I.B. was encountered — Six prisoners taken. Hostile arty: quiet in Right Sector, in the Left Sector light shelling of front line & back areas. After dusk hostile snipers & M.Guns were particularly active. "A" Company withdrew to reserve after relief by "C" Company & Tk. Trench round Gun positions of "B" Company taken over etc.	see App: of/42
do:		11pm:	Fine but dull, very misty after dusk. Our arty: very active especially at 4.30pm, 7pm, 8.15pm for new Our M.Guns carried out harassing fire during early morning on the following targets Dispositions M.G. at K.10 a. 55/55. Bn.G. at K.10 a 05/50, 4,000 rounds were fired, silencing the hostile M.Gun. see App: of/43

Original

Page 1.

Army Form C. 2118.

WAR DIARY
INTELLIGENCE SUMMARY.
(Erase heading not required.)

Instructions regarding War Diaries and Intelligence Summaries are contained in F.S. Regs, Part II. and the Staff Manual respectively. Title pages will be prepared in manuscript.

Place	Date	Hour	Summary of Events and Information	Remarks and references to Appendices
Neulos	12th.		Duel, slight showers. Situation normal. Arty: active all day concentrating at times on LE SART & the left of that village. Our M.Gs carried out usual harassing fire the following targets being engaged, Hostile M.Gs at K.21.b.4/6, K.10.d.2/1 & K.10.d.10/35. "C" Company expended 5,000 rounds on bridge across marsh at K.32.d.8/4 & tracks from direction of MERVILLE. Hostile Arty: only slightly active, vicinity of LES LAURIERS shelled with 5.9s but enemy batteries silenced by our Counter batteries. Several Balloons were up but 7-1.50cm. One enemy balloon shelled & brought down by our guns occupants descending in parachute. Work "A" Company working on reserve positions erecting temporary shelters etc. about J.20.d. "B" Company strengthened & deepened position & built 2nd emplacement at K.14.b.5/5. Jealous M.Gs. strengthened & sandbagged. 2 O.R. to hospital sick.	
-do:-	13th.		Fine, heavy rain after dusk. Our M.Gs. carried out harassing fire on hostile H.Q. at K.21.b.4/5. Bridge over canal at K.29.A. & on exits from HERVILLE. "C" Coy guns fired 10,000 rounds on tracks in K.32 & 24.b in conjunction with artillery. Hostile arty: exceptionally quiet, slight shelling of CHAPLE BOOM with 5.9s & the CANAL bank with 4.2s. Enemy M.Gs. active all night in spite of our counter-measures.	

A6945 Wt. W11422/M1160 350,000 12/16 D.D.&L. Forms/C/2118/14.

Original.

Page 8.
Army Form C. 2118.

WAR DIARY
INTELLIGENCE SUMMARY

Place	Date	Hour	Summary of Events and Information	Remarks and references to Appendices
Trenches	14th		Fine but windy. Situation Quiet. Our arty. very active on enemy communications and opened out at 11.30 pm. Hostile guns fairly active, our front & support lines being lightly shelled. CHAPLE BOOM also received attention. On the whole field guns were more than usually active. LES LAURIERS was shelled with shells of large calibre and at 9.30 pm the BOIS des VACHES received some gas shells. There was a great deal of aerial activity on both sides. Our M.Gs active during night firing up 800 rounds harassing fire. Work "A" Company constructed 4 A.A. positions. "B" Company commenced 6 embrasures for Batty work. Trenches cleared and parapets thickened. 1. O.R. wounded.	
-do-	15th		Situation normal. Our arty. active day & night on positions behind enemy lines. Several large fires being observed in consequence. At midnight a house at K.21.b.95.98 containing S.A.A. & very lights was burnt down. Large volumes of smoke from HERVILLE at midnight. Hostile arty. was quieter than usual at 1.30 pm the canal at K.31.a. was shelled for half an hour & at 10.30 pm. the road in K.25.c. and K.20.c. shelled considerably at midnight. A raid was made at 1 am by the Brigade heavily shelled. CHAPLE BOOM received the usual attention. Our support line in	

Page 9.
Original
Army Form C. 2118.

WAR DIARY
INTELLIGENCE SUMMARY
(Erase heading not required.)

Place	Date	Hour	Summary of Events and Information	Remarks and references to Appendices
Dreches	15th.	cont.	on our left to which the enemy replied feebly although the reply to his S.O.S came down quickly. Our M. Guns harassed enemy M. Gun positions at K.10.d. 25/30, K.16.a. 40/50.	
— do —	16th.		Weather fine till 8am. Our arty: active; concentration on K.21.b and K.15.d at 4-30pm. Hostile guns were quiet; a few 5.9s: on LES LAURIERS and some large calibre shells on COBRE at 11am: our support line was shelled at 6·30pm: Hostile bombing machines were active during early hours of morning on our back areas. Machine Guns on both sides were active. Our firing 5,000 rounds. Reinforcements 3 O.R.	
— do: —	17th.		Weather fine; situation normal. Our 18 pdrs & 4·5's fired on the enemy front and support lines & carried out harassing fire straight MERVILLE Sad shelled by our Howitzers at 4-4-30pm. At 4-4-5pm: a ten minutes concentration was put down on hostile positions from K.21.b 4/4 to K.24.b 7/8, at 4·45pm: a good concentration was put down on wire & huts in K.15.b. Hostile Artillery was active on WICTES at 2pm: CAUDESCURE & CHAPLE BOOM shelled by 11am. all day. HAVERSQERQUE recorded as shelled at 11pm. Our M. Gun positions in J.29.a 2/5 were gas shelled & the artillery billet near by was hit on fire.	

Original
Page 10.
Army Form C. 2118.

WAR DIARY or INTELLIGENCE SUMMARY.

(Erase heading not required.)

Place	Date	Hour	Summary of Events and Information	Remarks and references to Appendices
Trenches	18th:		Weather fine. Our arty: carried out shoot on house at K.10.c. 80/90 at 4:30 p.m. also small quantity of T.A.A. exploded there. Heavies shelled MERVILLE & LES AIRES BECQUES. at 5:30 p.m. our field arty: concentrated on hostile positions at K.26.d.2/5 & K.26.c. 6/5. Hostile arty: active day & night, from 2:30 a.m. to 3:45 a.m.; roads & our support line in right sector were shelled. Hostile M.G. active during early morning impeding the work of our patrols in left sector; tracks behind right sector were harassed by enemy M.G. firing from K.26.b.7/4 & K.26.b. during night. Our guns carried out a little night firing, 1900 rounds being fired. Work: "C" Company engaged in filling in grenade shell holes at J.29.a.2/5. Small improvements to positions. "B" Coy: completed position for battery; also 2 new positions in K.9.d. Completed. 2 O.R.s adm: to Hospital Sick. 2 O.R. Wounded.	
- do:-	19th:		Weather fine. Hostile aircraft very active bombing our back areas in early morning. Situation normal. Our field guns shelled ARREWAGE & P. TOURNANT - from 2 to 4 p.m. Our heavies shelled PONT RONDIN, LE CORNET PERDUE & enemy line in K.15 & 16. Also MERVILLE. Hostile guns active during day; at night edge of the BOIS MOYEN intermittently shelled. Rt: Bde: Hdqt: shelled from 4 p.m. onwards with gas shells.	

Page 11.
Army Form C. 2118.

WAR DIARY
INTELLIGENCE SUMMARY

Original

Place	Date	Hour	Summary of Events and Information	Remarks and references to Appendices
Trenches	20th		Weather fine. Gas alarm at 5 am: for practice in manning battle positions in Divl: lines. At 4.30 pm: An operation was carried out by 1st E. Surrey Regt: (95th Inf. Bde.) assisted by "B" Company 16th Bn. M.G.C. which was quiet successful and resulted in the closing up of re-entrant between PONT TOURNANT (K.15) and ARLEUX (K.10). 22 Prisoners and 2 M. Guns were taken. Our new line was held in spite of heavy bombardment & a counter attack. Casualties were 3 O.R. killed & 7 O.R. wounded. Our M.Gs. active all day & night on tasks he Hostile Arty: very active during & after our operations.	For particulars of Gas Alarm see Appendix A/4. For report on operations See appendix A/5.
do:	21st		Weather fine. Situation normal. Our Arty: active 2P. day fright & especially at 11-15 pm: on left. Our M.Gs: fired on enemy bridges over the River K.16.b. & 6.10.d. also on K.33.a. 80/05. J. Mortars quiet. Enemy arty: were active day and night against our support & Reserve line but pretty quiet on front line. Gas shells were sent over from 4-30 am: to 5-7 am: on to our M. Gun Battery in: J.36.b. Work: "B" Company engaged in consolidating new positions in our new line. Both ours and the enemy's aircraft were very active day and night. 39th Bn: M.G.C. substituted to Army Reserve.	For withdrawal 39 Bn: M.G.C. see App. A/6.

WAR DIARY
INTELLIGENCE SUMMARY

Place	Date	Hour	Summary of Events and Information	Remarks and references to Appendices
Trenches	22nd		Weather fine. Situation normal. Our artillery quieter than usual. H. Guns fired on enemy bridges over the river at K.16.b, K.10.d, K.11.c & K.26.d. 80/30. Hostile Arty. rather more active than usual. Houses at K.9.c. 29/23. received several direct hits. Our support lines shelled at intervals during the day. A few shells dropped in the vicinity of Café Brigade H.Q. during night. Hostile M. Guns and Trench Mortars were inactive. Relief of the 95/Inf. Bde. by the 15/Inf. Bde. commenced. Our adjustment made to dispositions of Machine Guns in the HAVERSKERQUE – LA MOTTE Line.	For change in dispositions see Appendix 94
Trenches	23rd		Weather very dull & windy. Inter-Brigade relief (95th & 815th) completed. Our artillery fairly active. Hostile guns were active and a number of enemy shells dropped in his own lines where a number of rockets were sent up by the enemy. During a ten minute barrage put down by us at 10 p.m. on K.2.b.d. & K.2.9.c. the enemy put up GREEN lights but nothing noteworthy followed. The road & houses at 7.36.b. were shelled at 6.40 p.m. Gas shells freely at R.E. AMN HALTE and in certain parts of the WOOD. Hostile M. Guns were not active. Our M. Gs fired at K.32.b. 50/60. & tracks & bridges over the Stream.	

Original.

Page 13.
Army Form C. 2118.

WAR DIARY
or
INTELLIGENCE SUMMARY.
(Erase heading not required.)

Place	Date	Hour	Summary of Events and Information	Remarks and references to Appendices
Trenches	23rd.		Captain & Qr.Mr. DEVOTO joined Battn. for duty. Relief of B Company by "C" Company completed. Work 2 new gun positions constructed by "A" Company at K.35.b. & 18/33, telephone wires repaired. 1. O.R. wounded.	C Company relieved B in left sector see Appendix No 8
–do:–	24th.		Weather wet. Situation normal. Arty: fairly active on both sides. Between 8 and	
		2pm.	Hostile guns were active on the HALTE also on the HAVERSKERQUE – ST. VENANT Road. A house at T.34.b.5/0. & a cordite dump near by were set on fire. A.M. Gun position of "A" Company at K.25.b was shelled at intervals throughout the day. Track at T.22.d also received considerable attention. Hostile M. Guns were very active during evening, two firing from about K.10.d & 6.b. Draft arrived from Base Depot. 1 officer (2/Lieut: BLAIR) & 140 o.Ranks. Casualties 3. O.R. wounded.	
–do–	25th.		Weather fine. Situation Normal. Hostile Arty. shelled K.25 a & b. all morning, from 8 to 10pm. J.17 central – BOIS des VACHES – RUE des MORTS & J.5a & b. were shelled. Our support line in left sector was heavily shelled for half an hour at 9.30pm with large calibre shells. The wood was again shelled throughout the night over a large area. Our M. Guns fired 9,000 rounds at various targets. Casualties 7.O.R. wounded. 1. O.R. missing.	

Original.

Page 14.
Army Form C. 2118.

WAR DIARY
INTELLIGENCE SUMMARY.

(Erase heading not required.)

Place	Date	Hour	Summary of Events and Information	Remarks and references to Appendices
Brerles	26/5/18		Gen. Situation Normal. Hostile arty: active THIENNES shelled at intervals from 4-30 a.m. to 12 noon causing a few casualties. Our support line in the left sector were regularly shelled. "A" Company M.G. Batty: in orchard at K.9.c.9.5 (positions at J.26d & K.31a. were shelled, shortly two crates & appeared to be searching. K.9.c & J.51.b. & the CHATEAU at D.30.c. were shelled at various times a large proportion of Gas Shells being used with H.E. The road CROIX MARRAISE — LE SART was harassed day & night. Our arty. was active especially during early morning in view of abnormal movement reported around ESTAIRES. Our M.Gs. fired 4,000 rds at various targets. Casualties — 2 O.Rs wounded.	
–do–	27/5/18		Weather fine. Hostile Arty: active on our suppt. lines. Areas in the left sector were shelled heavily at 3 a.m. At 3 p.m. the road HAVERSKERQUE – ST. VENANT was shelled with 8" shells & m.au. LA MOTTE – CORBIE – LE SART road reported. Our arty: very active day & night. Our M.Gs. fired 5,000 rounds Hostile M.G. very active especially one firing from direction of the orchard in K.9.d. Casualties nil. Lt: C.B.J. Mc. DONNELL rejoins from Veterinary Course.	For disposition of M. Guns see app: a/11.

Page 15.
Army Form C. 2118.

WAR DIARY
INTELLIGENCE SUMMARY.
(Erase heading not required.)

Place	Date	Hour	Summary of Events and Information	Remarks and references to Appendices
Inchebat	28/5/18		The situation normal. Enemy artillery shelled VIA-ROMA and HALT dump at 8pm and road about J.30.c.40/00. Gas shelled with gas shells heavily at 10pm. A heavy barrage was put down at K.25.d.20/10 from 12.40am to 1.30am. But very little damage was done to our trenches. Our guns were active day and night causing a Bigfire in MERVILLE at 6.15pm. One M gun assisted in raids carried out by the infantry. 10 guns assisting the 15/R. War: R. & 3guns assisting the 1/R. W. Kent R:- 40,000 rounds being expended. THIENNES was shelled by A/V guns from 4.30pm: to 10.30pm: at irregular times. The following officers arrived for duty from Base Depot:-	To detail of minor operation see App: A-9
			2/Lt: P.M. BREEN. to "A" Company	
			2/Lt: A. THOMAS. to "B" — do —	
			2/Lt: W.H. WARNER. to "B" — do —	
			2/Lt: R.M. BROADFOOT to "C" — do —	
			2/Lt: F.W. ROBSON to "D" — do —	
			2/Lt: P.W.G. RUSSELL. to "D" — do —	

Original

Page. 16.

Army Form C. 2118.

WAR DIARY
INTELLIGENCE SUMMARY.

Instructions regarding War Diaries and Intelligence Summaries are contained in F. S. Regs., Part II and the Staff Manual respectively. Title pages will be prepared in manuscript.

(Erase heading not required.)

Place	Date	Hour	Summary of Events and Information	Remarks and references to Appendices
Trenches	29/5/18		Gen: situation normal. Enemy artillery shelled FORET de NIEPPE between 1am. and 2am. the BOIS des VACHES received numerous gas shells and the CROIX MARAISE – LE SART Road received attention a large number of gas shells being included. Our aircraft were active. An enemy machine attacked and brought down in flames one of our Observation Balloons at 8.45pm: at J.17.central. Our M.Gs: fired 1,700 rounds in harassing fire – 1 O.R. Killed – 2 O.Rs wounded	
– do: –	30/5/18.		Gen: situation normal. Enemy shelled J.30.c.40 & J.29.a.20 at intervals – gas shells being included. DOLL'S HOUSE was shelled at 5-30pm. and enemy was active in LES LAURIERS & ROUSSEL FARM. THIENNES was shelled spasmodically day & night. M Guns active day & night on both sides. 6 enemy aircraft flew low around our lines and were engaged by M.Guns – 2 of these machines came down out of control S.W. side of ST. VENANT – Arty. A.A. fire was active at the time and our guns were the only one firing. Several indecisive combats took place during the day. 2 Lt: J.E.F. PACKER wounded but remained at duty. Casualties – 1 O.R. killed	

Original
Page 17.
Army Form C. 2118.

WAR DIARY
INTELLIGENCE SUMMARY
(Erase heading not required.)

Place	Date	Hour	Summary of Events and Information	Remarks and references to Appendices
Trenches.	31/5/18		Situation normal. Hostile Arty. was slightly livelier - the enemy carried out several 5 minutes bombardments of our trenches at irregular intervals. - K.15.c. 75/60 road in K.4.a.d and orchard at K.9.b. were intermittently shelled. Our guns were fairly active. Our M. Guns were active carrying out harassing fire on bridges and tracks in K.16.a.& selected areas. The relief of "A" Company in the Right Sector by "B" Company is completed. TRENNES was shelled by hostile H.V. gun day & night at irregular intervals. — Casualties — 2. O.R. wounded. Strength of Battalion. Officers — 48 O.R. 875 attached pending transfer to M.G. Corps 24.	For details please see Appendix 9/10

A.M. Cutting Lieut. Colonel
Comdg: No. 5 Battn. M. Gun Corps

Original
May 1918

5/Battn. M Gun Corps

— War Diary —

Appendix "A"

1/6/1918.

SECRET.  Copy No: a/1

5th. BATTALION MACHINE GUN CORPS.

LOCATION OF MACHINE GUNS. to 12 noon 5/5/18.

Battalion Headquarters at TRIENNES.

Left Brigade Front.   "A" Company.

Guns at K.15.c. 7/2.   K.14.d.85/60.   K.9.a.90/65.
         K.15.c.85/35.   K.14.d.90/65.   K.9.b.65/45.
         K.15.b. 1/7.   K.9.c.05/15.   K.9.d.60/45.
         K.9.d. 5/2.   K.9.c.05/25.   K.8.a.55/10.
         K.9.d. 6/6.   K.9.c. 9/9.   K.8.a. 5/3.
         K.9.d. 9/8.

Company Hd:Qrs: at J.16.c.70/10.

Right Brigade Front.   "C" Company.

Guns at K.26.c.05/60.   K.20.d.65/35.   K.20.b. 2 /20.
         K.31.a. 9/8.   K.20.d.75/55.   J.36.a. 7/4.
         K.31.a. 7/7.   K.21.a. 1/5.   J.36.a. 70/55.
         K.26.c. 1/7.   K.21.a.15/35.   J.30.c.55/70.
         K.26.a.05/40.   K.20.b. 0/1.   J.30.c.55/80.
         K.26.a.25/60.

Company Hd:Qrs: at J.16.c.70/10.

In Support   Divisional Line.   "D" Company.

Guns at J.34.b. 4/2.   J.28.a.65/75.
         J.34.b.45/15.   J.23.a. 5/9.
         J.34.b. 6/9.   J.17.   .00/5.
         J.34.b. 6/6.   J.17. b 0/ 1.
         J.29.a. 1/4.   J.27.b.80/25.
         J.29.a.05/35.   J.27.b.87/20.
         J.23. c 30/35.   J.27.b. 9/3.
         J.23. c 35/40.   J.27.d. 85/30.

Company Hd:Qrs: at J.27.d. 5/3.

In Support   Divisional Line   "B" Company.

Guns at J.8.c.50/25.   2 Guns.
         J.12.c. 0/4.   2 "
         J.8.d.40/25.   2 "
         J.8.d.80/40.   2 "

8 Guns in reserve at about J.20.d. 2/4.

5/5/18.   Lieut-Colonel,
                            Commanding; 5th.Battn.Machine Gun Corps.

SECRET.

XI Corps.

1. 183rd Infantry Brigade are carrying out an operation on the South bank of the CANAL on the night 10th/11th May, the left of its objective being K.31.b. 9/0.

2. 15th Infantry Brigade will take advantage of this operation to raid the two houses in K.31.b. 6/1 which are suspected of containing machine guns.

3. The operation of the 61st Division will be carried out under a creeping artillery barrage. This barrage is to extend as far North as the northern bank of the CANAL.

4. ZERO hour will be notified later.

5th Division.   Major-General,
10/5/18.   Commanding 5th Division.

Copies to :- 61st Division.
                15th Inf. Bde.
                5th Div. "Q".
                5th Sig. Coy.
                5th M.G. Battalion.

SECRET.   G.M.8.

O.C." " Company.

In order to equalise the work of the Machine Gun Companies of the Battalion, the following dispositions have been taken up.

Forward System.

Each Brigade in the Line has 3 Section of their affiliated Machine Gun Company and 1 Section of "D" Company in action. The Section of "D" Company will be under the orders of the O.C. Brigade Company.

HAVERSKERQUE - LA MOTTE LINE.   This Line is garrisoned by:

1 Section of "D" Company.
1 Section of the Right Brigade Company.
1 Section of the Left Brigade Company.
2 Sections of the Reserve Brigade Company.

DIVISIONAL RESERVE.

The Divisional Reserve consists of 2 Sections of the Reserve Brigade Company and 1 Section of "D" Company.

O.C. Brigade Companies in the Line will notify O.C. "D" Company of any proposed relief between their Section in the HAVERSKERQUE LA MOTTE Line and the Forward System. Completio of such reliefs will be reported to O.C. "D" Company.

O.C. "D" Company will be responsible for the continuity of the work on the emplacements in this line South of J.11.d.4/5. and also for the discipline of the Section in this portion of the Line.

11/5/18,   Lieut-Colonel,

Commanding 5th: Battalion Machine Gun Corps.

CONFIDENTIAL.   5th:Division. S/60.

1.   Test alarm for practice in manning Battle Stations will take place on the early morning of the 20th:May.
        B.G.Cs:13th & 95th Infantry Brigades will satisfy themselves that Battalions in Brigade Reserve have all necessary preparations made for moving to assembly positions. A small party of Officers should move forward to their positions and test the time likely to take the Battalions to reach these points; otherwise the troops in the Front Line will not eb affected.

2.   The Brigade in Divisional Reserve will rendezvous in J.16.b. & d,

        The Battalion at STEENBECQUE will move by route march and the time and route taken to reach their position will be noted.
        The Battalions at THIENNES and TANNAY will move by Light Railway, 2 Companies from THIENNES and 2 Companies from HARSTONE.
        Detraining Stations for 4 Companies - EDITH STATION, West end of VIA ROMA.
        Detachments, Transport and Wagon Lines etc: will occupy alarm Positions. 1/6th: A & S Highlanders and Field Coys: R.E. will occupy the HAVERSKERQUE - LA MOTTE line.
        1st:King Edwards Horse, Corps Cyclists and "D" Coy: 39th:Battn:M.G.C. will occupy the MORBECQUE Line.
        As soon as C.Os: are satisfied that their men are in position they can be dismissed and sent home.
        The following times will noted and reported to this office:-

        (1) Time order received.
        (2) Time Troops ready to move.
        (3) Time Troops in position.

18th:May 1918.   Lieut-Colonel,
                                            General Staff, 5th:Division.

Copy to XI Corps.

REPORT OF A MINOR OPERATION ON THE 20th. OF MAY 1918.

Map:- 36.A. N.E. 1/20,000.

"B" Company, 24th. Battalion Machine Gun Corps, took part in a small operation undertaken by the 95th. Infantry Brigade.

The idea was to capture the enemy trench as indicated in Brigade Operation Orders.

Zero hour was 4.30 p.m.

The attack was carried out by the 1st. Battalion East Surreys, and was supported by Artillery, T.M. and M.G. barrages.

Two guns of "B" Coy. were instructed to go forward with the Infantry. 2/Lt. RYALS was in charge of these guns.

The disposition of the guns previous to the attack, were as follows:-
Guns doing barrage:6 of these were at K.16.d.1/5 (left gun); 2 at K.14.d. 85/90; 4 guns in support, 3 at K.9.c.1.95/45, and 1 in orchard K.9.b.95/40, one in orchard K.9.b.60/10.

4 Guns in front doing direct fire as follows:-

2 at K.16.a.25/15. enfilading of fugitives.
2 at K.15.c.95/85. head of Circus road K.15.b.
2 guns in front of orchard at K.15.b.45/95. to go over.

A belt of smoke was ordered to be put down across the left flank but this was not carried out as the wind was unfavourable. At 4.30 p.m. the Artillery barrage was opened and was immediately followed by Machine Guns and Trench Mortars.

The preliminary barrage lasted 3 minutes and at 4.33 p.m. the East Surreys went forward and got their objective fairly easily. Their advance was covered by Artillery and Machine Gun barrage. The 2 Machine Guns went forward ten minutes after the Infantry and got into position as follows:-

1 Gun at K.15.b.87/80.
1 Gun at K.15.b.8/5.

These guns went forward under cover of the orchard and only suffered one casualty on the way.

Guns, tripods, spare parts, and 16 belt boxes per position were got forward with the first party. When the barrage opened the enemy left their trenches and ran back and the guns in front on the left got some nice targets. It is estimated that about 50 Germans were killed or wounded at this time by Machine Gun fire.

These Gun teams suffered no casualties. The teams on the right front had 2 men killed and 2 wounded by one shell which struck a tree in front of their positions.

The enemy made a feeble reply at first except by Machine Guns, these were firing from about K.21.a. and b.

About 9.p.m. the enemy sent a large number of shells and large number of heavy Trench Mortars on to our new line, inflicting several casualties to gun teams. This was continued right through the night.

Immediately after dusk ~~~~~~~~~~~~~ 2/Lt. RYALS and myself proceeded to reconnoitre the new positions for the forward guns in vicinity of K.15.d.3/5, but found it impossible to get the guns across owing to the shell fire. I then decided to put them back in their original positions at K.15.c.95/85.

They were got there safely by midnight.

The Barrage Guns remained in their positions all night and carried out harassing fire on the enemy trenches K.16.a.& K.10.d., Orchard K.16.d. Road K.16.c.& d. and Orchard K.16.b.

Their S.O.S. Line was their original Barrage Line for the night.

At 3.5.a.m. the enemy attacked our new positions on both sides of the Canal and on the Left Front a party got into our trenches on Right of the Canal but were immediately thrust out and all killed. On the Left some Germans got into our line and bombed along the trench but were soon checked and another platoon of the East Surreys came in again on the Left and so there they are still being gradually killed off.

The S.O.S. was sent up by the Infantry and it was at once complied with by our Machine Guns which fired rapid for five minutes when the situation was cleared up.

Previous to this attack the enemy put down a heavy barrage. Several shells hit the advanced Company H:Qrs: setting the farm on fire and the place was burned down. The Infantry here had several casualties but our people got away. Some signalling equipment has been lost but some of this may be salved to-night.

One of our S.A.A. Dumps was blown up.

One Gun was completely destroyed in the front Line. It was a Trench Mortar that hit this gun. This was replaced from the Support Section and again from Barrage Guns and it is hoped that the new gun will be up in position to night.

The Infantry were very well satisfied with the work of the Mahine Guns and thought that the Barrage was splendid. The C.O.12th:Gloster's said that the reply to S.O.S.was the quickest and best that he had ever seen. In addition to barrage the enemy put down gas in K.15.b.

Our Battery Line held right through the operations but the line to the front Battalions was badly cut. We were not asked to take on any special targets by the Infantry.

My last Report from the front Section was at 2 a.m.

30000 rounds were fired during the operations.

(sd). A.S.NICOLL,Major,
Commanding "B"Company,
5th:Battalion Machine Gun Corps.

21/5/18.

5th DIVISIONAL INTELLIGENCE SUMMARY.

For 24 hours ending 6 a.m. 21/5/18.

Not to be taken into the Front line trenches.

OPERATIONS.   An attack was carried out by the left Brigade at 4.30 p.m. 20th instant on enemy front line from K.15.b. 6/0 to K.9.d. 9/2 including houses at K.15.b. 5/0 - K.15.b. 6/2, K.15.b. 7/8.   Artillery, trench mortars and machine guns co-operated.   All objectives were gained.

During the early morning of the 20th instant an observed shoot by 4.5" Hows., and 18-pdrs destroyed the wire in front of enemy positions, the attack barrage was excellent and enormously facilitated the Infantry advance.   During the attack the enemy showed little resistance, the greater number abandoning arms and equipment and fled.   The houses at K.15.b. 6/2 were strongly held but the garrison endeavoured to escape across country.   On the right the enemy endeavoured to make a stand but was killed or taken prisoner.   Snipers who went over with the attack scored 20 hits after the situation had quietened down.   All objectives were gained at 4.38 p.m.   24 prisoners (including 8 wounded, one of whom has since died) and 8 M.G's were captured.   At 3 a.m. a party of the enemy gained a footing under cover of a heavy mist in our recently captured trench at K.15.b. 9/9, they immediately commenced bombing down the trench towards the ORCHARD and were held up by a block formed at K.15.b. 8/8, our bombing sections attacked killing 12 of the enemy and completely restored the situation.   The line gained was consolidated during the night, and the right battalion of the left Brigade also advanced their line from K.15.d. 6/8 to K.15.c. 9/0 to keep touch with the attacking battalion.

Artillery.   Enemy.   Left Brigade.   Retaliation to the attack consisted of a light shrapnel and 4.2" barrage on our front line. At 4.45 p.m. a fairly heavy 5.9" and 4.2" barrage was put down for a short time on the left battalion front by ARREWAGE and some scattered shelling of Support and reserve areas continued till dusk.   At 3 a.m. a very heavy barrage was opened on our new front, on Orchards at K.15.b. 7/7 and K.15.c. 9/8 and road running S.E. from ROUSSEL FARM.   Fires were caused in houses in K.8.d. and K.14.b.   M.G. and T.M. forward H.Qrs at K.15.a. 05/40 was destroyed after several direct hits.   Mustard and Blue Cross gas shells were fired along the whole front. Fire was kept until 4.30 a.m. when it was confined to slow rate on our support line in K.8, 9, 14 & 15.

Right Brigade.   At 10 a.m. a 77 mm battery shelled cottages at K.25.a. 5/5 employing H.E. and one mustard gas shell.   At dusk and at intervals during the night K.25.a. 5/5 was shelled with 77 mm. and 4.2"   At about 3.30 a.m. a few gas shells fell near WICTES and on the edge of BOIS MOYEN in K.25.a.   4.2" shells were fired at T.M. position at K.25.a. 5/5.

Trench Mortars.   Ours.   6" NEWTONS fired in retaliation to ELSIE (K.32.a. 8/7) L.T.M's fired occasional shells at ORCHARDS in K.26.c. and K.32.a. during the night.

Hostile.   At 2.15 a.m. a few L.T.M. shells fell in K.15.b. From 8 p.m. onwards Heavy and M.T.M's were very active firing from about K.16.a. 1/0 and K.10.d. 20/05.

Machine Guns.   Ours.   Our M.G's fired on the front of L.3 sub-sector.

Hostile.   Were active during the night.   Very little activity during the attack.   2 M.G's. were seen firing against our low-flying aeroplanes from T. shaped trenches near hedge at K.10.c.5/1 and K.10.c.6/2.

Aircraft.   Ours.   Contact planes flew over our front and obtained exact location of line by flares.   5 CAMELS flew low at 5.45 p.m. and fired M.G's into the enemy lines. Many other machines - scouts and artillery - were flying throughout the day - 2 balloons being brought down in flames.

Hostile.   At 6.5 and 8.40 p.m. an E.A. flew about 500 ft over the captured ground, firing a signal at latter time over house K.15.b.8/9 which was later registered with shrapnel.   5.25 a.m. An E.A. flew low

over our front. All low-flying E.A. were engaged by M.G. and L.G. fire
DEFENCES. The strong point at K.16.c.15/90 was the scene of much
movement during the attack. Enemy line appears to be approx.
K.9.d.9/0 - K.16.a.0/9 - K.15.b.7/5 - K.15.d.55/90.
The enemy is reported to be erecting much wire on the right Bn.
of the right Bde. A small trench at K.31.b.7/1 is now occupied
and lights are fired from here at night. An enemy working party
was observed at K.26.c.8/5. and dispersed by L.G. fire.
OUR PATROLS. Patrols from the right Bde. report wiring and
digging observed on the line K.21.c.3/7 to K.21.b.0/2., large
enemy party observed sandbagging and wiring from K.21.c.6/9 to
K.21.c.35/55 and a post strongly held at about K.21.c.3/7.
GENERAL. The house at K.31.b.6/1 is probably used as an O.P.
as the window has been boarded up. Men wearing steel-helmets
entered house ar K.16.b.12/90. Men wounded were seen making
towards NEUF BERQUIN in the evening.
S.O.S. Double Green and Double Red were used on left of front
attacked.

                                                                            Captain
                                            Lieutenant.
21st May 1918.   Intelligence Officer. 5th Division.

PRELIMINARY EXAMINATION OF PRISONERS OF 48th RESERVE DIVISION CAPTURED ON 20th May 1918.

IDENTIFICATIONS. - 2nd, 7th, 8th & 11th Coys. of 223 R.I.R.

DISPOSITIONS. 1st Battalion in rest, 2nd Battn. in line, 3rd Bn. in support.

RELIEFS. Prisoner's statement and a captured Regimental Order show that last night the 1st Bn. was to relieve the 2nd, and 2nd Bn. was to go into support and the 3rd into rest.

TOUR OF DUTY. 6 or 7 days.

1st BATTALION. Men of 2nd Coy who were captured were members of the advance party of the 1st Bn. and had come up to reconnoitre trenches and take over stores.
STRENGTH. 2nd Coy. about 75. 7th Coy. about 80. 8th Coy. about 80-90.
ORDER OF BATTLE. N. to S. 222 R.I.R. (48th Res.Div.) 223 R.I.R. (48th Res.Div.), 49 I.R. (4th Div.)
BATTALION DISPOSITIONS. N. to S. 8th Coy., 6th Coy. and 7th Coy. in line. 5th Coy. - close support at K.15.b.7/2.
SECTORS. 7th Coy., Southern boundary at PONT TOURNANT, extended about 260 - 280 metres.
WORK. Work is proceeding steadily at night. Wire is being put out in front of front line, support and reserve positions. Trenches are being improved as far as possible and are being joined up, short communication trenches have been started. Trenches are not good as in most places it is impossible to dig down more than ¾ metre without finding water.
HOSTILE INTENTIONS. As far as the 48th Res. Div. was concerned it was no longer fit to hold the line, still less to make an attack on a large scale. All prisoners expected to be relieved shortly and to go out to rest and refit. N.C.O's. of experience considered that after rest the Division would again be capable of offensive operations, though they did not anticipate any such operations in the immediate future.
CONDITIONS AND MORALE. Considering the heavy losses suffered when the 48th Res. Div. attacked on April 14th and the fact that they have not been relieved since that date, morale is very fair. Prisoners were in good health and appeared satisfied with their rations which were adequate. After a period of rest the 48th Res. Div. is likely to prove a good Div.
LIGHT M.G's. The average number appears to be 5 per Infantry Coy., of which four are usually in the line and one in reserve.
TRENCH MORTARS. Battalions of 223 I.R. normally have 2 L.T.M's. each, but at present 4 T.M's. are always left in the line in the front line battalion sector. Reliefs of personnel do not correspond with those of the Infantry. At present Light T.M's. had orders to fire only in answer to S.O.S.
OUR ATTACK. About 2 hours before our attack word had been sent down from the right Coy. of the Battalion that BRITISH trenches were being manned more strongly than usual. The Coy. at PONT TOURNANT had been warned to expect an attack at sunset.
SUPPORT POSITIONS. Small sections of trench in K.17.d.
REST BILLETS. In scattered houses South of NEUF BERQUIN - ESTAIRES road in and about L.21.c.
ROUTES TO TRENCHES. Cross-country tracks are exclusively used. Units are allowed great latitude in choosing their own units, the only stipulation being that they reach their destination and avoid shell-fire as much as possible.
COMMUNICATIONS. Between Coys and Battalion H.Q. the only communication is by runner. S.O.S. - GREEN.
PONT TOURNANT. 4 days ago the Germans tried to blow up PONT TOURNANT. The project was abandoned as it was found impossible to work quietly.
OUR FIRE. One N.C.O. said he would rather be in the front line than in support or in rest. They were constantly harassed when out of the line. Some prisoners confirmed previous statements as to the trying effect on the nerves of our T.M. fire.
23rd FIELD ARTILLERY REGT. A prisoner from the 23rd Field Artillery Regt. was taken in K.4.c. early this morning (May 21st). This Artillery

Regt. belongs to the 16th Division which was in line opposite the Southern sector of our front until May 3rd. Prisoner does not know to which his Regt. is attached, but it seems possible that the 16th Div. Arty. is covering part of the front of the 48th Res.Div. "x Div. This prisoner states that last night in the enemy's lines opposite our left sector he met troops of the 223 R.I.R. and of the 23 R.I.R. The 223 R.I.R. is normal, but the 23 R.I.R. belongs to the 12th Res. Div. which is believed to have attacked on this front on or before April 14th. As the 48th Division is expecting immediate relief it is possible that its relief by the 12th Res. Div. began last night. Prisoner said that there was considerable confusion behind the enemy's lines last night and probably this relief was not completed.

Prisoner's battery was in action East of MERVILLE and he stated that there were many troops and much material of all kinds in the road-triangle of MERVILLE - NEUF BERQUIN - ESTAIRES. Prisoner's battery consists of 4 77 mm guns of which one is an anti-tank gun. His description of the location of this gun was vague but it appears to tally with the gun marked on a captured on aviators map at K.22.b. 8/8.

[signature]
Lieutenant.
Intelligence Officer, 5th Division.

21st May 1918.

S E C R E T.   Copy No:

5th:Division Operation Order No:224.

17th:May, 1

1.   At a time and a date to be notified later the 95t
Infantry Brigade will capture the enemy front line from K.15.b.
to K.9.d.9/2. as soon as the operation has been successfully
carried out our present front line will be advanced to conform
with the flanks of the objective.
2.   The operation will be covered by a creeping barrag
shrapnell and H.E. and supported by 3" and 6" Trench Mortars.
Heavy Artillery will bombard selected points and be employed on
counter-battery work.
3.   O.C.Machine Gun Battalion will arrange Machine Gun
Barrage and Supporting Fire.
4.   The Left flank of the Operation will be covered by
a Smoke Cloud which will be formed by 3" and 4" STOKES Mortars
from K.10a. and c. if the wind conditions are favourable.
5.   The necessary wire cutting will be carried out by
short Bombardments on the 18th:,19th: & 20th:May.
            Between the 16th: &20th:May similar Bombardments wi
be carried out on other points of the enemy's front opposite the
5th:, 20th: & 31st:Divisions.
6.   If the wind conditions are favourable No:1 Special
Company R.E. will project Gas into the houses and orchards about
K.9f.c.9/1. on the night 19/20thMay.
7.   At Zero Hour 13th:Infantry Brigade will carry out a
demonstration against the enemy's trenches in K.9f.c.
8.   15th:Infantry Brigade will place the 15th:Trench
Mortar Battery at the disposal of 95th:Brigade for this operation
9.   A Contact Plane will call for Flare at Zero plus 30
minutes.
            Scouting Machines will co-operate with the harassing
fire after Zero plus 5 minutes.

10.   ACKNOWLEDGE.

Issued at 8a.m.   (sd).   Major,
                                                 General Staff.

SECRET.   Copy. No. 24

61 DIVISION ORDER No. 162.

21st May, 1918.

1. 39th Bn. M.G.C. is being withdrawn into Army Reserve at ROMBLY.

2. The 22 guns of 39th Bn. M.G.C. now in position in the AMUS-OIRES - HAVERSKERQUE System will be relieved by 16 guns of 61st Bn. M.G.C. after dark on the night of May 21st/22nd under arrangements to be made by Battalion Commanders concerned.

3. The Company of 61st Bn. M.G.C. in Divisional Reserve in O.16.b. will remain intact.

4. Completion of relief will be reported to this office.

5. ACKNOWLEDGE. ✓

A. Anderson
Lieut. Col.,
G.S., 61st Division.

Issued at 7 a.m.

DISTRIBUTION :-

Copy No. 1.	A.D.C. for G.O.C.	13 - 14.	61 Div. Train.
2.	61 Signal Coy.	15.	" "
3.	16 Div. Art.	16.	"G"
4.	C.R.E.	17 - 18.	War Diary.
5.	61 Bn. M.G.C.	19 - 21.	Spare.
6.	1/5 D.C.L.I.	22.	XIth Corps.
7.	182 Inf. Bde.	23.	4th Division.
8.	183 Inf. Bde.	24.	5th Division.
9.	184 Inf. Bde.	25.	3rd Can. Div.
10.	A.D.M.S.	26	8th Can. Inf. Bde.
11.	D.A.D.O.S.		(through 3rd Can. Div.).
12.	A.P.M.	27.	39th Bn. M.G.C.

SECRET.

5th: Battalion Machine Gun Corps,
Operation Order No: 2.

22/5/18.

Reference Map 36.A. 1/40000.

1. An adjustment in the disposition of the Machine Guns along the HAVERSKERQUE - LA MOTTE Line will take place forthwith.

2. The two positions in J.23.a. will be vacated and the gun teams thus relieved will relieve the two teams of "A" Company in J.23.a.

3. After relief the two teams from J.23.a. will relieve the two teams of "C" Company in J.12.C.

4. On completion of the above reliefs "C" Company will withdraw the right Section from the BOIS DES VACHES area into Divisional Reserve at J.20. central.

5. On completion of this adjustment all Sections in the HAVERSKERQUE - LA MOTTE Line will come under the orders of O.C. "D" Company.

6. No alteration will be made in the disposition of A.A. Machine Guns along this Line.

7.. Completion of this adjustnebt will be reported to Battalion H.Qrs: in B.A.B. Code.

8. ACKNOWLEDGE.

Issued at 12.30.p.m.

(sd) R.H. CUTTING, Lieut-Colonel,

Commanding 5th: Battn: Machine Gun Corps.

Copies to:-
(1) O.C. "A" Company.
(2) O.C. "B" Company.
(3) O.C. "C" Company.
(4) O.C. "D" Company.
(5) 13/Infy:Bde:
(6) 15/Infy:Bde:
(7) 95/Infy:Bde:
(8) 5/Division.
9 & 10 War Diary.

S E C R E T.
8th: Battalion Machine Gun Corps
Operation Order No: 3.

Copy No: 9.
22/5/18.

Reference Map 58.A. 1/40000.

1. "C" Company will relieve "B" Company in the line on the night of 23/24th: inst: Details to be arranged between Company Commanders concerned.

2. On completion of relief "B" Company will withdraw three sections into Divisional Reserve. The fourth section will take up the positions vacated by "C" Company in the morn bye-vaches.

3. The three sections of "B" Company in Divisional Reserve will be accommodated in billets in I.15.a. and b.

4. The Battalion Signalling Officer will arrange to connect the H.Q. of "B" Company in I.15.a. with Divisional Exchange.

5. Completion of relief will be reported to Battalion H.Qrs: in B.A.B. Code.

6. ACKNOWLEDGE.

Issued at 2.p.m.

Lieut - Colonel,

Commanding 8th: Battalion Machine G.C.

Copies to:-
No: 1. A. Company.
No: 2. B. Company.   No:
No: 3. C. Company.   No: 9. File.
No: 4. D. Company.   No: 10 & 11. War Diary.
No: 5. 5/Division.
No: 6. 15/Infy:Bde:
No: 7. 16/Infy:Bde: No: 12. Signalling Officer.
No: 8. 95/Infy:Bde:

To H.Q. 13/Inf. Bde & 5/Battn: M.G.C.
From O.C. "A" Company, 5/Battn: M.G.C.

Intelligence Report

Enemy Artillery

Very active during day & night. At 10pm road at J.30.c.40/00 was shelled with Gas shells. Enemy barrage was heavy at K.25.a.1/8 from 12.40am. — 1-30am. but little damage done to the trenches. A fire was observed in MERVILLE at 6-15pm.

Enemy aircraft were more active than usual.
Enemy M.G's less active than usual.

In co-operation with the Infantry the guns of "A" Company were employed as follows:—

15/Warwicks raid ———— 10 guns co-operated

No. of Guns	Position	Target	No. of rds. expended
2 guns	J.36.a.76/80	K.32.a.95/80	6000
2 guns	J.36.a.85/40	K.32.a.15/25	6400
2 guns	J.36.a.30/40	K.26.c.40/35	5,000
2 guns	J.30.c.58/45	K.26.b.85/30	5,500

The following 2 guns at K.26.c.05/30. did direct fire on X roads & orchards in K.26.c.80/05. These 2 guns had excellent targets and fields of fire and no retaliation from BOSCH, M.G's or rifles, but at time hostile arty. as reported above was heavy. Rounds fired 4,000 rounds. During the operation BOSCH put up RED, GREEN & GOLDEN Rain flares from his first line.

'R.W.Kents' raid ———— 3 guns co-operated.

1 gun at K.21.a.25/35 took on K.21.c.50/70 with direct fire.
1 gun at K.21.a.40/40 ———— do ————
1 gun at K.20.d.65/00 on K.21.c.35/45.

These 3 guns fired 3,250 rds direct fire into the enemy line.

Other work done, new Section H.Q. work continued, Guns Emp's & S.A.A. cleaned, new positions at K.25.b.65/29 made.

May 29th
8.15 am.

(sd) G.S. THARBY Lieut
for O.C. "A" Company.

SECRET.   8th:Battalion Machine Gun Corps.   Copy No: 10.

Operation Order No: 4.   27/5/18.

Reference Map W.A. 1/40000.

1.   "B" Company will relieve "A" Company in the line on the night of 30th:May – 31st:May. Details to be arranged between Company Commanders concerned.

2.   On completion of relief "A" Company will withdraw three Sections to the Divisional Reserve. The fourth Section will take up the position vacated by "B" Company in the BOIS DES VACHES.

3.   "A" Company will arrange for a small party under an officer to take over the present billets of "B" Company on the afternoon of the 30th: inst:.

4.   Completion of relief will be reported to Battn: H.Qrs: in B.A.B. Code.

5.   ACKNOWLEDGE.

                                              Major,
                                      for Lieut-Colonel,
Issued at 12 Noon.
                              Commanding 8th:Battalion Machine Gun Corps.

Copies to:-
    1.   5th:Division.
    2.   13/Infy:Bde:
    3.   15/   "   "
    4.   95/   "   "
    5.   O.C. A.Company.
    6.   O.C. B.Company.
    7.   O.C. C.Company.
    8.   O.C. D.Company.
    9.   File.
    10 & 11. War Diary.

SECRET

C. M.G. Coy. O.O. Nº 55

Ref Map. 36A NE 1/20000

On the night 30/31 May the following relief will take place. Nº 4 Section will relieve Nº 3 Section. Guides to be at the HALT at 10.0 p.m.

On relief Nº 3 Section will relieve Nº 1 Section in the Battery Position. Nº 1 Section will then occupy the positions in the Divisional Line formerly occupied by Nº 6 Section. For this purpose Nº 1 Section will send a man to Coy. H.Q. This man will reconnoitre the position & will meet Nº 1 Section on VIA ROMA (K.1.d.5.0.) & conduct them to their positions.

No limbers will be supplied for this relief. All trench stores including tripods will be handed over.

Rations. Nº 4 Section's rations will be dumped at the HALT. Nº 3 Section as usual. The rations for Nº 1 Section will be handed over to D Coy who will deliver them as usual.

After relief Nº 1 Section will come under the command of O.C. D Company.

Completion of relief to be reported to C Coy H.Q. by Nº 1 Section.

A. Tuffill.
Major.
Comdg C Coy 5th R.F. Battⁿ

29-5-18

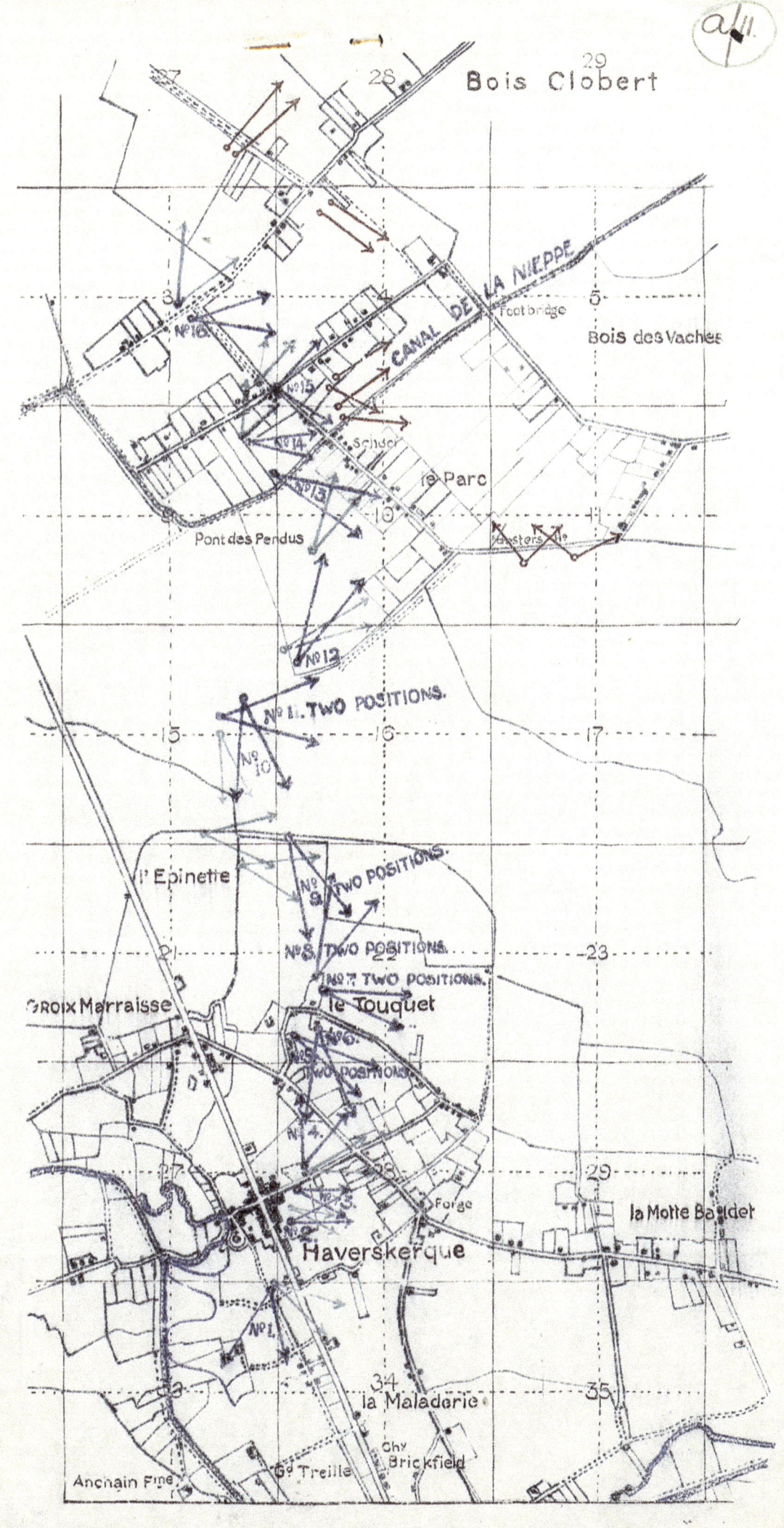

C O N F I D E N T I A L.

Register No: W.20/5.
Volume No: 3
Part No: 1

Vol 3

W A R D I A R Y

of

5th:Battalion Machine Gun Corps.

for the Month of JUNE 1918.

R H Cutting

Lieut-Colonel,

Commanding 5th:Battalion Machine Gun Corps.

30th:June,1918.

No. 5 BATTALION.
M.G. CORPS.

Map. Reference Map. 36A. 1/40,000.

Original. June 1918.

1. 5 Battn: M. Gun Corps.

Army Form C. 2118.
Page. 1.

WAR DIARY
INTELLIGENCE SUMMARY
(Erase heading not required.)

Place	Date	Hour	Summary of Events and Information	Remarks and references to Appendices
In Trenches	1st.		Weather fine. Situation normal. Hostile Arty: much quieter than usual. From 12 midnight to 2am: enemy shelled our A.A. M.Gun positions in the wood with gas & H.E.	For disposition
Approx: frontage FORET de NIEPPE to LA BASSÉE CANAL.			THIENNES was shelled intermittently day & night by H.V. guns. LES LAURIERS was shelled & destroyed during the day by fire. Our arty very active during day shelling the enemy's lines about ARLEWAGE also the vicinity of MERVILLE. Hostile M.Guns were silenced by our Lewis gun & rifle fire in the Left Sector.	off M.Guns of Battn: see Appendix B/1.
Battn: HQrs. THIENNES.			3 hostile guns reported firing from K.26.c.5/4 on to our night Bn: Front.	
Left Flank 29 Division			Major A.S. NICOLL (B. Company) and Lt. J.M. Mc.KINNEL (Battn: HQs:) Sounded but remained at duty.	
Right Flank 61 Division			Battn: Strength. Officers. O.Rs. 48 - 872.	
	2nd:		Weather fine. Situation normal. Enemy artillery shelled our M. Gun batteries during day & night and what appeared to be an ammunition dump in MORBECQUE direction was set on fire. Hostile M. Guns were very active in both sectors but our shooting high. Ours carried out harassing fire on the following K.26.B 60/80 K.26.b 90/85 tracks and bridges in K.16. Battn: HQ, moves from THIENNES to 120.c. 4/3.	

No. 5 BATTALION MACHINE GUN CORPS.

Page 2.
Army Form C. 2118.

WAR DIARY
INTELLIGENCE SUMMARY

(Erase heading not required.)

Place	Date	Hour	Summary of Events and Information	Remarks and references to Appendices
Trenches	3rd		Line. Situation Normal. Enemy artillery quiet during day – at 10.30a.m: a 77m.m: Batty: shelled K.21.a.10.10. for 10mins: LES LAURIERS was shelled at 10.30a.m: also. 5.9 shrapnel R.H.E. was put over our forward area during the morning. At "Stand to" in evening gas shells were put over in light scale over I.29.c. at 1.15a.m: & 2a.m: the vicinity of Company H.Q. at DOLL'S HOUSE was shelled with Fieldartl. 5.9. H.E. & gas. The Desinfector was shelled with Yellow + gas shells during night. Raid see Our arty: was very active during night. At 11.45p.m: a raid was successfully Appendix carried out by 16/R: War: R: assisted by guns of "C" Company 10,500 rds: were expended. A/2. 3 prisoners of 103 I. Regt: 32 Saxon Divn: were taken. 1 OR. wounded. Reinforcements 1 OR.	
– do: –	4th:		Line. Situation Normal. Hostile arty: shelled K.14.b at 12-15 with 5.9 and the transport track from I.23.d.04. to I.30.a.25.30 was shelled intermittently from 9.30p.m: to 3.30a.m: the RUE des MORTS was shelled all day. Our Machine Guns engaged tracks and bridges in the enemy lines at K.16.b & K.10.d. firing 8,000 rounds. Hostile arty: was very active bringing down one of our arty: machines and an observation balloon in flames. Casualties 2 O.R. wounded. Inter-Brigade relief commences the 13/H/f/Bde: relieving 15/H/f/Bde:	

WAR DIARY
INTELLIGENCE SUMMARY

No. 5 BATTALION MACHINE GUN CORPS

Page 3 / Army Form C. 2118.

Place	Date	Hour	Summary of Events and Information	Remarks and references to Appendices
Trenches	5th:		Situation Normal. Enemy was Quiet except for lively barrage put down on our Support line and Right Edge of WOOD in K.20-25 and 26. At 1-30am. LE TOUQUET was fairly heavily shelled. Gas shelling of MALADERIE — LE TOUQUET — BOIS des VACHES. Our arty: was slightly less active than usual. Our MGs fired 2000 rounds Harassing fire on usual targets. A'escaped probes apprehended by a Machine Gunner of "B" Company in Dist. Lis. Relief of "C" Company by "A" Company in Left Sector commenced.	See Appendix a/3 for internal Coys. Relief. For details of Capture of probes see appendix a/4
do:	6th:		This Situation normal. Our arty: active at intervals during day but Quieter than usual during night. Hostile arty: Quiet up to 3pm: when LE TOUQUET was shelled. ST VENANT — MALADERIE — CROIX MARAISSE and Road junction at J.28.d.f.f. received attention (5.90 & 4.25). Gas and H.E. shells were fired on road at J.23.a.8.8. from 10 to 11pm: Our M. Guns fired 3,000 rounds at K.32.b.30/45 & y.4. Hostile aircraft were active flying low over our lines at 8am, 6pm: and 8pm: they dropped 3 bombs near ROUSSELL FARM at 3pm.	
do:	7th:		Weather fine. Our arty: active at intervals and Co-operated in conjunction with gas projection on Right Brigade sector front. Hostile arty: put down	For gas projection operation see Appendix a/5.

Page H.
Army Form C. 2118.

No. 5 BATTALION,
MACHINE GUN
CORPS.

WAR DIARY
INTELLIGENCE SUMMARY.
(Erase heading not required.)

Place	Date	Hour	Summary of Events and Information	Remarks and references to Appendices
Inchea	7th.	contd.	a gas shell barrage on our support line & edge of the WOOD in K.20, 25 & 26. During the night, the enemy also shelled our batteries behind LE TOUQUET and HAVERSKERQUE. Roads around ST VENANT — MALADERIE & LE TOUQUET received attention. The house at STATION INN was set on fire by arty. fire. Enemy M.Gs less active than usual, one gun very active at house K.15.b 80/45 until silenced by our Lewis gun & rifle grenades. Our M.Guns fired 13,500 rounds harassing fire and in support of projector of gas in right sector. Weather fine. Situation Normal. Hostile Arty. was active and intermittently	
do: —	8th.		shelled K.8.d. and K.14.a & b. CHINESE Compound was shelled from 10-11am. The Wood around road at J.9.c. heavily shelled with gas shells mixed with H.E. HAVERSKERQUE and ST VENANT were also shelled. Our arty. was active and at 12.15am: a concentration from Arty. T.Ms and small arms was carried out on enemy M.Gun positions about BOTAR FARM. Hostile M.Guns were much less active after this shoot. Our Machine guns fired upwards of 6000 rounds harassing fire on no usual targets. Aircraft were active on both sides. Casualties — 1 O.R. Wounded.	

A6945 Wt. W1442/M1160 350,000 12/16 D.D.&L. Forms/C./2118/14.

Page 5.

Army Form C. 2118.

WAR DIARY
INTELLIGENCE SUMMARY.
(Erase heading not required.)

Instructions regarding War Diaries and Intelligence Summaries are contained in F.S. Regs., Part II. and the Staff Manual respectively. Title pages will be prepared in manuscript.

No. 8 BATTALION
MACHINE GUN
CORPS.

Place	Date	Hour	Summary of Events and Information	Remarks and references to Appendices
Trenches	9th.		Weather fine. Situation Normal. Enemy arty: less active than usual, a few gas shells around HAVERSKERQUE at 4am and at intervals during the day. At 4am large number of gas shells fell in WOOD 8 LE TOUQUET. "A" Company's M. Gun Battery shelled for 15 minutes at midnight - H.E. & Gas - no damage done. Our arty: less active during day, but fired a number of Gas shells on enemy back areas during night. 4,000 rounds were expended by our M. Guns on enemy tracks & bridges. Hostile M. Guns replied vigorously to fire of our Guns in the Right Sector. - Casualties nil. - Reinforcements 1 O.R.	For Nuneaton gunners carried out see app B/2 period 1 - 12/9/18
do:	10th.		Weather fine. Situation Normal. Hostile Arty: showed her usual activity. TAXI FARM was shelled at 5:00am. and the Orchard at K.1.w.b.4/7 at 12 midnight. HAVERSKERQUE & CROIX MARRAISE received usual attention. Gas shells fell in the areas around J.34.b. and road in J.28.d. WOOD and LE TOUQUET were shelled with H.E. and shrapnel at 4 am. Enemy aircraft very active especially do from 6pm to 8pm. flying low over our positions, they were engaged & driven off by our L.T. M.S. and Lewis Guns. Reinforcements 21 O.R. from Base Depot.	

Page 6.

Army Form C. 2118.

WAR DIARY
INTELLIGENCE SUMMARY.
(Erase heading not required.)

No. 5 BATTALION MACHINE GUN CORPS

Place	Date	Hour	Summary of Events and Information	Remarks and references to Appendices
Treslea	11th		Weather fine. Situation normal. Our artillery were active 4.5" Hows: cutting wire from 6p.m. to 7p.m. in K.10a.2.c. and K.16.b. and also shelled enemy trenches opposite Right Brigade Sector LE SART and MERVILLE Station during the day. Enemy arty. shewed normal activity. Enemy machine guns engaged our aircraft during the day and fired on our tracks and trenches at night. One hostile M. Gun was located at K.10c.65/20 and engaged by one of our Vickers guns.	
do	12th		Weather dull. Arty: fairly quiet during day becoming more active during the night at 12 midnight the enemy heavily shelled the road at J.28a and again at 12.30 a.m. At 12.45 a.m. gas shells fell at J.22.c. He cross roads at J.30d 3/1 and the CORBIE road were heavily shelled with 4.2s including gas shells. The enemy also active on our back areas and on HAVERSKERQUE main road at same time. Our arty: active 4.5" how: firing on enemy wire around BONAR FARM on S.A.A. dump in the vicinity was set on fire explosions continuing for 20 minutes. Reassed field guns fired on MERVILLE and LE SART and cross roads at K.22 a 10/25. Enemy aircraft shewed some activity. Our aircraft activity frequent on the enemy trenches & carrying out reconnaissances at low altitudes.	For relief of "B" Company by "C" Company in LE SART Sector see appendix A/6.

Page 1.

Army Form C. 2118.

No. 5 BATTALION
MACHINE GUN
CORPS

Instructions regarding War Diaries and Intelligence Summaries are contained in F. S. Regs., Part II. and the Staff Manual respectively. Title pages will be prepared in manuscript.

WAR DIARY
INTELLIGENCE SUMMARY
(Erase heading not required.)

Place	Date	Hour	Summary of Events and Information	Remarks and references to Appendices
Trenches	13th.		Weather fine. Our heavy arty. shelled VIEHOUCK GARS BRUSCHE (F.56) LE CORNET PERDU & L'EPINETTE, in latter farm was set on fire. Enemy explosion of S.A.A. very bright. Field Guns fired on enemy wire in K.16a. Sparticular attention was given to enemy support line. A fire was caused in Regal Lodge (L.9b) where some S.A.A. was destroyed. Hostile arty. furly quiet. TANKARD FARM shelled at 10am, and area around. CHAPLE BOOM received number of 5.9s & 4.2s. The edge at K.20B.2/6 & K.20.C.5/b. was shelled intermittently during the day. Casualties. Nil. Lt G.S.TUTT, "A" Company reported "Missing".	
do.	14th.		Weather fine. Our arty: actise shelling ITCHEN FARM which was set on fire, the houses were destroyed at K10d.45/45 & 50/75. MERVILLE LE SART BRICKFIELDS the ORCHARDS in K.2b.c. and the wire in K.10a & opposite the Right Brigade front were all engaged by our guns. Hostile arty: was fairly actve & shelled CHINESE CAMP CAUDESCURE VIA ROMA and the WOOD in K.25a&b. during the day. The enemy' Machine Guns were quieter than usual but showed some activity between midnight and 2am. Casualties 1 O.R. ("A" Company) Wounded	

Page 1.

No. 15 BATTALION
MACHINE GUN
CORPS

WAR DIARY

INTELLIGENCE SUMMARY

Place	Date	Hour	Summary of Events and Information	Remarks and references to Appendices
Trenches	15th		Weather fine. Situation Normal. Enemy arty; Quiet during the day. HAVERSKERQUE and surroundings were shelled from 1-2pm: also at 5pm: The forge at J.28.a received attention. Our trenches in K.25.b & the neighborhood of K.19.d were intermittently shelled. Our arty; active shelling PONT RONDIN LE CORNET PERDUE GARS BRIGADE & L'EPINETTE. Field guns were active Cattle guide. Enemy M.G's were active during night. Aircraft active on both sides, at 1.30pm an enemy Balloon was brought down in flames 8.30-11-45pm. Another was observed to break away Schrft: 1 section "C" Company relieved 1 Section "D" Company in the LE SART Sector. Casualties nil.	For details LE CORNET relief in the LE SART Sector see app: aff.
do	16th		Weather fine. Situation Normal. Enemy Arty; active firing 9.00 H.E shells on CORBIE Road J.30.d. K.25.c at 2pm: LES LAURIERS K.HOOD & HAVERSKERQUE K.19.d received attention. Our heavies shelled LE CORNET PERDUE K.18.d PONT RONDIN and LA GORGUE, Field guns shelling enemy wire, the trenches in K.10.a and harassing tracks etc. during the night. Enemy M.Guns family active. Our Machine Guns carried out harassing fire on LE SART & tracks in that neighborhood. Casualties 1 O.R. Wounded.	

Page 8
Army Form C. 2118.

WAR DIARY
or
INTELLIGENCE SUMMARY.

Place	Date	Hour	Summary of Events and Information	Remarks and references to Appendices
Neuve Lea.	17th.		Weather fine. Our howitzers shelled L'EPINETTE GARBRIGGHE LE CORNET PERDU & RENNET FARM. At 5.15pm: house at K.16.d.4.5/80 was set on fire by A.i.S"Mort. & 2"mp, thought to be Trench Mortar Ammunition, exploded. A quantity of S.A.A was also destroyed. MERVILLE and LE SART also received attention. Hostile artillery were active carrying out Counter battery work. Our support line in K.14.b. was heavily shelled at 6.20am. Road in K.15.a & BOIS MOYEN were harassed regularly with H.E. & gas shells. Casualties: Lt: SGTHARBY wounded at duty.	
do:	18th.		Weather fine. Situation Normal. Hostile Arty: much quieter than usual, during the night about 1000 gas shells were put over between our support line and the S.E. Corner of the WOOD the wind carrying the gas into the WOOD, between 11pm: and midnight a few 5.9a were scattered about LE CORBIE. Our arty: shelled L'EPINETTE and vicinity and RENNET FARM, harassing fire at night which was heavier than usual. Hostile M.Gs active shooting on K.25.a & the Railway & Road in K.14. Our aeroplanes very active, especially during the evening, at 7pm: an enemy machine was brought down & fell in K.16.b. Casualties. Nil.	

Page 9.
Army Form C. 2118.

WAR DIARY
INTELLIGENCE SUMMARY.
(Erase heading not required.)

Place	Date	Hour	Summary of Events and Information	Remarks and references to Appendices
Trescies	19th.		Situation Normal. Hostile Artillery quiet until 2.30am: when the LE COLBIE Road was shelled. The Communication trench and area around K.25.b 8.h.e HOOD behind were heavily shelled. Causing a violent explosion in the HOOD. Our leaves shelled LE SART – ANCHOVY FARM and hostile M.Guns in the BRICKFIELDS. Our aircraft very active during the evening, an hostile scout attempting to destroy one of our Balloons was forced down near CROIX MARRAISE – one of the enemy O.Bs was brought down in flames by our aircraft at 7-10pm.	
do:	20th.		Weather unsettled. Situation Normal. Hostile arty: Quieter than usual. J.9.c. was shelled from 10pm tonight and at 2.30pm, LA MALADERIE was shelled with shrapnel and again at 9.30pm with HE. The BOIS des VACHES received attention at 10-30 &3pm: Our trenches were shelled (I.M.) lightly from 3am to 4am: Our arty: active on L'EPINETTE & LES PURESBECQUE — BONAR FARM and targets in K.16.c. The enemy's M.Guns were active and one which was located in ITCHIN FARM was particularly so. Aerial activity slight only 3 E.A. seen during the day. "B" "E" Companies of the 39th n: n: n: Corps report their own unit on completion of period of attachment. "B" Company relieves "A" Company in ARKENWRITE sector.	See appendix 9/8 for relief of "A" Company by "B" Company

Page 10.
Army Form C. 2118.

No. 5 BATTALION
MACHINE GUN

WAR DIARY
of
INTELLIGENCE SUMMARY.
(Erase heading not required.)

Instructions regarding War Diaries and Intelligence Summaries are contained in F. S. Regs., Part II. and the Staff Manual respectively. Title pages will be prepared in manuscript.

Place	Date	Hour	Summary of Events and Information	Remarks and references to Appendices
Trenches	21st.		Weather fine. Situation quiet. Our heavy arty. fired on K.22.a. and field guns on LEPINETTE — LES PURESBECQUES and trenches and farms in K.10.d. & K.16.a. Enemy was active on our M.Gun positions in J.11.d. during the day and BOIS des VACHES was shelled at 5pm & 8pm. and 12 midnight. Our Machine Guns were active firing 35/90 rounds at enemy tracks and bridges in K.11.c.& d. and enemy guns retaliated on our tracks etc. Sqk. "B" Company commenced work on 4 positions in K.3.c. 78/32. and 80/35. K.3.c. 88/58 and 90/65 (approximately) The positions at TAXI FARM were improved. Work commenced on open emplacements at PILLBOXES at K.14.b. 83/33 & K.4.b. 90/40.	
do.	22nd.		Weather dull & showery. Our arty. was active on BONAR FARM, the enemy posts situated about K.5.c. & K.17.b. and hostile M.Gun positions at K.10.d. 15/15. MERVILLE and MERVILLE STATION. The enemy shelled BOIS MOYEN — BOIS D'AVAL — BOIS D'AVAL during the day and at night there was the usual shelling of our tracks &c. Hostile Machine Guns fired occasional bursts during the night principly from BONAR FARM and RENNET FARM. Our M.Guns were slightly active. Casualties — nil —	

Page 10.
Army Form C. 2118.

WAR DIARY
INTELLIGENCE SUMMARY.
(Erase heading not required.)

No. 5 BATTALION MACHINE GUN CORPS

Instructions regarding War Diaries and Intelligence Summaries are contained in F. S. Regs., Part II. and the Staff Manual respectively. Title pages will be prepared in manuscript.

Place	Date	Hour	Summary of Events and Information	Remarks and references to Appendices
Trenches	23rd		Weather fine. Enemy active shelling CAUDESCURE & TAXI FARM at intervals. LE CORBIE Road received the usual attention. At 12.30 a.m. artillery activity developed to extent of almost a bombardment in J.30.d. Our field guns very active shelling the enemy's trenches in K.15.a at 3pm. and setting fire to house at K.17.a.4/5. The usual attention was paid by henies to BORIAR FARM & L'EPINETTE & NEUF BERQUIN. M. Guns were active on both sides. Our guns fired 6000 rounds on enemy tracks in LE SART area and on hostile M. Guns situated at K.21b.9/45 & K.16.a. 2/90. Work on PILLBOXES in Kruids. Continued. Section p.Mgs at TAXI FARM strengthened. Section HQrs: (D Coy) made in Jb.a. & shelters for teams in Jbd. Casualties Nil.	
do:	24th		Weather dull - showers. Situation Normal. The enemy's guns were slightly active during the day and very active during the night when a considerable amount of gas shelling of our batteries and back areas occurred. Ours shelled L'EPINETTE — RENNET FARM — BORIAR FARM. Harassing fire was maintained during the night and a large fire caused in MERVILLE. Our M.G's carried out usual harassing of L.E. SART and neighbouring tracks and also silenced a hostile M.G. firing from K.16.c.5/1. Casualties — Nil.	

Page 11.
Army Form C. 2118.

WAR DIARY
INTELLIGENCE SUMMARY.
(Erase heading not required.)

Place	Date	Hour	Summary of Events and Information	Remarks and references to Appendices
Trenches	25th.		Weather fine. Enemy active shelling of our line, K.8.6 and K.9.a and trenches in vicinity of Dene Farm; Annerarge, & Chapelle Roon. House 14.6. 50/42 burnt down by incendiary shell. Our field guns worried the enemy front line. Henriesfried on its backages and K. 17.c all afternoon; LE SART, MERVILLE, and line of communication. During British raid on right M. Guns fired 13,000 rounds. Lynn 45,000 rounds. Work positions generally improved. Section H.Q. (C Company) strengthened. Casualties - 1 O.R. wounded (gas)	
do.	26th.		Weather dull. Enemy artillery showed very little activity during period. Our artillery active day and night. Henries fired on PONT RONDIN, RIVIERE CORNET PERDU, L'EPINETTE, MERVILLE, VIEUX BERGUIN, and exploded dumps near BECKET CORNER. Bombs dropped in several parts of W.O.D. and hostile aircraft active in ARREWAGE sector. Work positions H.Q. (C Coy) strengthened. Henges in front of Pill Boxes thinned. Clearing of Forest continued. Casualties nil.	Territorial Battery relief 300 Coy. M.G.C.

Page 12.
Army Form C. 2118.

No. 5 BATTALION
MACHINE GUN
CORPS.

WAR DIARY

INTELLIGENCE SUMMARY.
(Erase heading not required.)

Place	Date	Hour	Summary of Events and Information	Remarks and references to Appendices
Trenches	27th.		Weather fine. Artillery fairly quiet but was active on our Suppt. lines in the afternoon. Between 2 & 2.30pm. K.25.b. was shelled with 4.2 & 77mm. HE. Ours were active day & night. Our M.Guns carried out usual harassing fire by night. Hostile M.Guns showed some activity especially gun firing across flooded land. Casualties Nil.	
– do: –	28th.		Weather fine. Operation known as "BORDERLAND" was very successfully carried out. The enemy's line being attacked from PONT TOURNANT to LE CORNET PERDU (attack was continued Northwards by our left flank Bn.) Heavy casualties were inflicted on the enemy and following prisoners & material captured 30 officers – 181 O.Rs. 4 H.Machine Guns. Hostile Artillery was very active replying to our barrage at 6.30am: and heavy fire was directed on to our old positions during the day which was not marked between 3 & 5pm: and later at 12.20pm: Our M.Guns were very active nearly in reply to S.O.S. Signals which were sent up at following times:- 4.30pm: 10.30pm: 4.36pm: 11.0pm: S.A.A. expended 24,9,650 rounds.	For details see Appendix A/10.

No. 5 BATTALION,
MACHINE GUN
CORPS.

Page 13.
Army Form C. 2118.

WAR DIARY
INTELLIGENCE SUMMARY.
(Erase heading not required.)

Place	Date	Hour	Summary of Events and Information	Remarks and references to Appendices
Trenches	28th	Cont'd	Total Casualties of Battn: were 1, Officer wounded, 4. O.R. killed, & 36. O.R. wounded & 1 39 Bn: M.G.C. (attached for operations) 1 Officer wounded, 5. O.R. killed, 1. O.R. wounded	
	29th		Weather fine. Our arty: very active. Enemy guns were active on CORPSE Road, VIEITES ARREVAGE CAUDESCURE were subjected to bursts of fire at various periods during the day. Machine Guns were most active on both sides every sweeping our front line continuously. Ours successfully engaged small parties of the enemy during the day. Casualties 10. O.R. Wd.	
	30th		Weather fine. Mobile Artillery fairly quiet except for intermittent shelling between 1.30am: and 3am: The road and area in the WOOD around K.14 was shelled with heavy gas shells from 1.30 to 2.15am: K.25b. was shelled at 9am: with 4.2s. and again at 11am: Activity increased towards midnight when the WOOD, our Batteries, VIA ROMA and the HAVERSKERQUE Road were all heavily shelled. Hostile Machine Guns were active and Our Carried out harassing fire. 31/Bn: M.G.C. relieve some guns of this Battn: on detaching their Divisional Front. Casualties 2. ORs. reported missing of "B" Company	For relief see app: A/H.

No. 5 BATTALION
MACHINE GUN
CORPS

Page. 14.
Army Form C. 2118.

WAR DIARY
or
INTELLIGENCE SUMMARY.
(Erase heading not required.)

Place	Date	Hour	Summary of Events and Information	Remarks and references to Appendices
			Battalion Strength Officers O.R.	
			"A" Company 6 192	
			"B" do 8 193	
			"C" do 9 209	
			"D" do 9 200	
			H.Qrs. 8 68	
			Total 40 862	

B.W. Wilkins, Lieut: Colonel
Comdg: 5 Bn: M.G. Corps.

O R I G I N A L.

5th:Battalion Machine Gun Corps.

W A R D I A R Y

for JUNE

A P P E N D I C E S "A" & "B".

30th:June,1918.

Lt Col.
Comm^d. No 5 Battn MGC.

S E C R E T.   "C" Machine Gun Company O.O. No: 56.

Reference Map 36 A.N.E. 1/20000.

On the night 3rd/4th:June,1918., a small Operation will be carried out by the 16/R.Warwick R.

OBJECTIVE. To raid enclosure and Houses from K.10.C.6/8. to K.10.c.85/95. along the ARREWAGE - LES PURESBECQUE Road.
"C" Machine Gun Company will assist as follows:-
2 Machine Guns of No: 4 Section from Orchard at K.9.b. will take up position at K.10.a.8/4. in the hedge in front of our front line, and there will traverse the enemy front line from K.10.b.9/2. to K.10.b.3/3. taking care not to traverse further Right than K.10.b.0/2.
The 2 Guns of No: 4 Section in the front line will move to positions about the corner of the hedge K.10.a.4/3. and will fire as follows;-
Z to Z plus 3 - Traverse hedge and trench from K.10.c.8/9 to K.10.c.60/75.
Z plus 3 onwards - Switch right and traverse enemy front line from K.10.c.6/4. to K.10.c.4/2/.
Great care must be taken after Z plus 3 not to converge towards the Road.
2 Guns of No: 2 Section from K.9.d.3/4. will move forward to the front line at K.10.c.0/5. and will fire as follows:
Z to Z plus 3 - Enfilading Trench K.10c.6/7/ to K.10.c.8/9.
Z plus 3 onwards - Switch 20 deg: RIGHT and continue firing.

RATE OF FIRE. Z to Z plus 3 - One Belt per minute.
Z plus 3 on wards - One Belt per 4 minutes.
During the raid the 4 Guns in the Battery Positions in K.14.b. will do active harassing Fire on the Bridges and tracks in K.10.d. and K.16.b.
Zero Hour will be issued to all concerned, but the opening of the Artillery Barrage will be the signal for Machine Guns to open fire. Firing will cease with the Artillery.
After the Operation is completed the Guns will return to their Battle Positions.

ACKNOWLEDGE.

(sd), H.TUFFIL, Major,
Issued at 6pm, 2/6/18.   Commanding "C" Company, 5th Battn: M.G.Corps

S E C R E T.   5th Battalion Machine Gun Corps.   Copy No:

Operation Order No: 5.   3/8/18.

Reference Map N.A. 1/40000.

1.   "A" Company will relieve "D" Company in the
Left Sub-Sector on the night of 5th/6th:inst:. Details to be
arranged between C.Os: concerned.

2.   On relief "D" Company will withdraw three
Sections into Divisional Reserve. These Sections will be
accommodated in the billets vacated by "A" Company. The fourth
Section will take up the positions vacated by "A" Company in the
BOIS DES VACHES.

3.   Completion of relief to be reported to Battn:
H.Q. in B.A.B. Code.

4.   ACKNOWLEDGE.

Issued at 11 am.   (Sd) R.H CUTTING.   Lieut-Colonel,

                               Commanding No: 5 Battalion Machine Gun Corps.

Copies to:-
        1. 5th Division.
        2. 13/Infy:Bde:
        3. 15/   "   "
        4. 95/   "   "
        5. O.C. A.Company.
        6. O.C. B.Company.
        7. O.C. C.Company.
        8. O.C. D.Company.
        9. File.
       10. & 11. War Diary.

XI Corps No. I.G.82.

Statement of Albert MALETSKI, escaped German
prisoner from the 117th P.O.W. Coy., CALAIS,
captured near HAVERSKERQUE on 6th June, 1918.

The prisoner was captured on 20/4/17 between MESSINES and
WYTCHAETE: he was in the 4th Grenadier Regt.
Prisoner had been with three P.O.W. Coys., viz:- 45th, 18th and 117th.

Cause of attempt to escape.
Owing to unpunctuality at meals the prisoner was given two days imprisonment.

Method of escape.
He heard that he was to receive punishment, and while on work the previous day brought back a pair of wire cutters from some factory near by, where he stated there were numerous tools, etc. lying about. The wire cutters he wrapped up in a rag and concealed.
The prisoner was locked up in a room on the night of 29th or 30th of April. By means of a small coin he managed to take out the screws of the lock and escaped.

The prisoner appears to have spent a considerable time in CALAIS, nearly three weeks, hiding in barns, old houses and fields in the neighbourhood. He obtained his food from a Chinese Compound, where he was liberally supplied with biscuits and a few scraps of meat.
He visited this camp at night and found no difficulty in entering.
On deciding to leave CALAIS, MALETSKI entered a Sergeant's quarters and stole his uniform, haversack, etc., and afterwards a small scale map of FRANCE and BELGIUM from a French lorry.

Route to the Front.
On leaving CALAIS he proceeded along side roads and across fields in a S.E. direction towards ST.OMER, striking the canal north of ST.OMER after about six days.
From ST.OMER towards the line he followed the north bank of the canal with the exception of two places, where he had to cross to the south bank to avoid posts. He states he was not challenged throughout the journey. Movement was carried out at night.
The canal bank was followed until the ground got swampy, and he was looking for another way through when captured.

Method of capture.
One of our machine gunners noticing that the prisoner was not provided with a steel helmet or gas mask questioned him, and noticing his foreign accent arrested him.

NOTE. This smart capture of a prisoner emphasises the necessity for all ranks to be continually on the alert, in order to prevent the enemy receiving valuable information from this source.

XI Corps (I).
9 - 6 - 18.
FR.

W. M. BECKWITH, Major,
General Staff, XI Corps.

Gas Projection Operation carried out by No:1 Special Company R.E.
in the Right Brigade Sector in the morning of 7/6/18.

This operation was originnally arranged to take place on
May 19th:,1918, but was not carried out owing to unfavourable
weather conditions until 7/6/18.

" At 1.30 am. this morning 680 Gas Projectors were fired on the
following points:-

    Cross Roads.   K.26.c.7/1.
    Area around the Chimney. K.32.a.10/15.
    Cross Roads.   K.21.b.7/5.

        In conjunction 300 C.G. and N.C.T. Mortars
were fired on the enemy Posts:-
        K.26.d. 5/0.
        K.26.d.7/7.
No enemy action resulted, exceptfor slight Machine Gun
fire from the flanks. Operation appeared satisfactory.

At 1.32 - 35am. 2 Batteries Barraged K.26.c.4/3. -
K.26.c.7/7/ K.26.d.1/4.   1 Battery K.31.b.8/2.
At 2.15 - 17 am. K.26.a.6/0. - K.27.c.5/0.
1 Battery Canal Bank K.32.b.6/1. - K.32.a.5/2.
Rate of fire intense for both periods.

No retaliation by the enemy after the Gas Projection. "

(Extract from 5th:Divisional Intelligence Summary 7/6/18.)

SECRET.　　　　　5th. Battalion Machine Gun Corps.　　　Copy No:

　　　　　　　　　　Operation Order No:6.　　　　　　　　11/6/18.

Reference Map 36.A.1/40000.

1.　　　"C" Company will relieve "B" Company in the LE SART Sector on the night of 12th:/13th:inst:. Details will be arranged between C.O's: concerned.

2.　　　On relief "B" Company will withdraw 3 Sections into Divisional Reserve at J.16.a. and take over the billets vacated by "C" Company. The fourth Section will take over the positions vacated by "C" Company in the BOIS DES VACHES, and come under the orders of O.C."D" Company.

3.　　　Relief complete to be reported to Battalion H.Q. by the Code Word "WATER".

4.　　　ACKNOWLEDGE.

Issued at 10.30am.　　　(sd) R.H. CUTTING　　Lieut-COLonel,

　　　　　　　　Commanding 5th: Battalion Machine Gun Corps.

Copies to:-
1. 5/Division.
2. 13/Infy:Bde.
3. 15/ "   "
4. 95/ "   "
5. O.C.A.Company.
6. O.C.B.Company.
7. O.C.C.Company.
8. O.C.D.Company.
9. File.
10 & 11. War Diary.

S E C R E T.   Copy No:

5th: Battalion Machine Gun Corps

Operation Order No: 7.

Reference Map 36.A. 1/40000.

1.   The Section of "C" Company in the Divisional Line will relieve the Section of "D" Company in the LE SART Sector on the night of the 14/15th:inst:,

2.   On relief the Section of "D" Company will occupy the Positions vacated by "C" Company in the Divisional Line.

3.   **ACKNOWLEDGE.**

Issued at 7.pm.   (sd) R.H.CUTTING,   Lieut-Colonel,

Commanding 5th: Battalion Machine Gun Corps.

Copies to:-
1. 5/Division.
2. 15/Infantry Brigade.
3. O.C. "C" Company.
4. O.C. "D" Company.
5. File.

S E C R E T.   5th: Battalion MachineGun Corps.   Copy No: 11
                Operation Order No: 9.

Reference Map 36.A.1/40000.

1.   "B" Company will relieve "A" Company in the ARREWAGE Sector on the night of the 20th:/21st:inst:. Details to be arranged between Company Commanders concerned.

2.   On completion of relief "A" Company will withdraw 3 Sections into Divisional Reserve. The fourth Section will take up the Positions vacated by "B" Company in the BOIS DES VACHES.

3.   The 3 Sections of "A" Company in Divisional Reserve will be accomodated in the Billets vacated by "B" Company in I.16.a.

4.   Completion of relief to be reported to Battalion H.Q. in B.A.B. Code.

5.   ACKNOWLEDGE.

Issued at 12.45.pm.

(sd) D.G.Kydd.   Major,
                  for Lieut-Colonel,
19/6/18.   Commanding 5th:Battalion M.Gun Corps.

Copies to :-
1. 5/Division.
2. 13/Infantry Brigade.
3. 15/Infantry Brigade.
4. 95/Infantry Brigade.
5. O.C. "A" Company.
6. OC. "B" Company.
7. O.C. "C" Company.
8. O.C. "D" Company.
9. File.
10. & 11. War Diary.

SECRET.

Copy No:

5th: Battalion Machine Gun Corps.

Operation Order No. 10.

Reference Map 36.A.1/40000.

1. The following relief will take place to night as soon as possible:-

    2 Guns and Teams of "A" Company from "C" Battery will relieve 2 Guns of "C" Company in PILLBOXES at K.14.d.40/60. and K.20.b.45/85.

2. The Guns and teams of "A" Company thus freed will be available for use in connection with "BORDERLAND".

3. On conclusion of their task the Guns and teams of "C" Company will return to PILLBOXES in relief of "A" Company's Guns, the latter returning to "C" Battery.

4. ACKNOWLEDGE.

Issued at 7.pm.   (sd) D.G.KYDD,   Major,
                                            for Lieut-Colonel,
26/6/18;   Commanding 5:Battalion Machine Gun Corps.

Copies to - 1. O.C. "A" Company.   5. War Diary.
             2. O.C. "C" Company.   6. 13/Inf:Bde:
             3. O.C. 31st:Bn:M.G.Corps. 7. 15/Inf:Bde:
             4. File,

SECRET.   Copy No:

No: 5 Machine Gun Battalion Operation Order No: 8.

Reference Map - Sheet 36.A.1/20000, Edition 7.

1.   On a date and at an hour to be notified later the 5th:
Division will capture the enemy position lying N.W. of the PLATE
BECQUE between the SWING BRIDGE and LE CORNET PERDUE, both
inclusive.
        The attack will be carried out in co-operation with the
Division on our Left.

2.   The attack by the 5th: Division will be carried out by
the 13/Inf:Bde: on the Right and the 95/Inf:Bde: on the Left.
The Attack will be covered by an Artillery and Machine Gun
Barrage.

3. OBJECTIVE.   The Objective of the 5th: Division will be:-
K.15.d.55/88. - K.16.c.35/95. - K.10.d.4/0. - K.10.d.80/45. -
Road Junction.- K.11.b.5/8. - K.6.a.25/00.

4. BOUNDARIES.-- SOUTHERN BOUNDARY.   Road at K.14.a.6/7. to
Bridge at K.15.a.20/55., and thence along the BOURRE River.

        NORTHERN BOUNDARY.   Grid Line running
through the centre of Squares K.3., K.4. and K.5.

        Between Brigades TANKARD FARM inclusive to
the 13/Infantry Brigade - K.10.a.60/45. - K.10.b.20/35. -
K.11.a.3/2. - K.11.b.05/15.

3. ACTION OF MACHINE GUNS.

    (a).   "A" Company, No:5 Bn:M.G.C., less 1 Section, will be
            employed in the local Defence of the captured area
            under the orders of B.G.C., 13/Inf:Bde:.

    (b).   "B" Company, No:5 Bn:M.G.C., less 1 Section, will
            be employed in the Local Defence of the captured area
            under the orders of the B.G.C., 95/Inf:Bde:.

    (c).   "C" Company, No: 5 Bn:M.G.C. will co-operate in the
            protection of the Right Flank of the Objective under
            the orders of B.G.C., 15/Inf:Bde:.

    (d).   The following will be employed on Barrage Work:-

            1 Section of "A" Company, No:5 Bn:M.G.Corps.
            1 Section of "B" Company,   do:
            "D" Company, No: 5 Bn:M.G.Corps.
            2 Companies of the 39/Bn:M.G.Corps.

        Commencing at Zero plus 1 these Companies will
apply protective M.G. Barrage throughout the Attack.
        On reaching the final Protective Barrafe Line,
(SOS) each Battery will apply a Barrage along it for 10 minutes
and will then creep forward to the limit of its range at the rate
of 100 yards per 8 Minutes. The rate of fire during this creep
forward will be half the normal Barrage Rate.

"At Zero plus 80 the Barrage will be applied for 10 Minutes along the whole of the S.O.S. Line and at Zero plus 90 it will creep forward at the rate of 100 yards per 4 minutes to allow patrols to get out to the PLATE BECQUE. The Barrage will cease at Zero plus 100 until it is called for by an S.O.S. Signal when it will open on its S.O.S. Lines.

Barrage Lines are shown on the attached Map.

In case of an S.O.S. Call all Guns will apply an Barrage along their S.O.S. Lines for 10 Minutes. If after this period the S.O.S. Signal is agian sent up the Barrage will be re-applied for 10 Minutes.

The rate of fire throughout the Operation will be:-

Normal Barrage   60 rounds per Minute.
S.O.S. Barrage.   1st: Five Minutes. - Rapid.
                      2nd: Five Minutes. - 100 rounds
                                              per Minute.

6. ORGANISATION OF MACHINE GUN COMPANIES EMPLOYED ON BARRAGE WORK.

RIGHT GROUP. — Covering the 13/Infantry Brigade.

Battery	Position	No: of Guns	Battery Commander to be appointed by.		Group Commander.
"D"	K.14.b.7/0.	8.	"C" Coy: 39/M.G.C.	O.C."C" Coy: 39/Bn:M.G.C.	
"E"	K.14.b.50/65.	8.	do:	do:	
"F"	K.9.c.9/8.	8.	"B" Coy: 39/M.G.C.	O.C."B" Company. 39/Bn:M.G.C.	O.C."C" Company, 39/M.G.C.
"G"	K.9.a.70/65.	8.	do:	do:	

LEFT GROUP. — Covering the 95/Infantry Brigade.

Battery	Position	No: of Guns	Battery Commander		Group Commander.
"H"	K.9.b.65/75.	8.	"D" Coy; 5/M.G.C.	O.C."D" Company. 5/Bn:M.G.C.	
"I"	K.3.d.45/75.	4.	"A" Coy:, 5/Bn:M.G.C.	O.C."B" Coy: 5/Bn:M.G.C.	
		4.	"B" Coy:, 5/Bn:M.G.C.		
"K"	K.4.c.5/5.	8.	"D" Coy:, 5/Bn:M.G.C.	O.C."D" Coy: 5/Bn:M.G.C.	O.C."D" Company, 5/M.G.C.

7. **ASSEMBLY.** Sections employed on Barrage Work will assemble in the Forward Area on Z/Y night.
With the exception of the Sections for "K" Battery Sections will assemble in their Battery Positions.
The Sections for "K" Battery will assemble in Trench at K.8.a.7/5. - K.8.a.6/9. and will move forward to their Battery Positions at Zero.

8. **HEADQUARTERS.**

Advanced M.G.Battn:H.Q. (At Adv:Divn:H.Q.)	J.9.d.7/0.
13/Infantry Brigade. H.Q.	K.8.c.20/18.
95/Infantry Brigade. H.Q.	K.8.c.3/7.
Right Group.	K.14.b.65/95.
Left Group.	K.8.b.60/85.

9. **COMMUNICATIONS.** Batteries will be connected up to their Group H.Q. and Group H.Q. to their the H.Q. of the Infantry Brigade it is covering. For detailed arrangements see Appendix "A".

10. **LIGHT SIGNALS.** The S.O.S. Signal will be a Rifle Grenade Rocket - GREEN over RED over GREEN.
WHITE Very Lights, three in succession, will be fored when the objectives have been gained.

11. Orders as to the synchronisation of Watches will be issued later.

12. Zero Day and Hour will be notified later.

13. A copy of Group Organisation Charts will be forwarded to Battalion H'Q.by Group Commanders on the 18th: inst:.

14. ACKNOWLEDGE.

(Sd) R.H Cutting

Issued at 11.pm.
Lieut-Colonel,
Commanding 5th:Battalion Machine Gun Corps.
16/6/18.

ATTACHED. Appendix "A" (Communication)
Appendix "B" (Administrative Arrangements).
Barrage Map.

Copies to:-
1. 5/Division.
2. C.R.A.
3. 13/Inf:Bde:
4. 15/Inf:Bde:
5. 95/Inf:Bde:
6. O.C.A.Company.
7. O.C.B.Company.
8. O.C.C.Company.
9. O.C.D.Company.
10. O.C.B.Coy:39/Bn:M.G.C.
11. O.C.C.Coy:39/Bn:M.G.C.
12. O.C.,39/Bn:M.G.Corps.
13. O.C.29/Bn:M.G.Corps.
14. C.M.G.O.XI Corps.
15. Army M.G.Officer.
16. Office.
17. War Diary.
18. File.

Appendix "A" to accompany No. 5 Battn:M.G.C. O.O. No: 8.

COMMUNICATIONS.

1. RIGHT SECTOR.   Telephone. - "A" Battery is connected to Battalion H.Q. J.24.d.9/2. by armoured Cable.
"B" Battery is connected to Battalion H.Q. - J.24.d.9/2. via the Support Company H.Q.
VISUAL. -   Visual Communication has been established between "A" Battery and Battalion H.Q. - J.24.d.9/2.

2. LEFT SECTOR.
TELEPHONE. - The Right Group will be connected to the 13/Infantry Brigade H.Q. and the Left Group via the forward Exchange near CHAPLE BOOM. The Group H.Q. will be connected direct to "D" - "E" - "F" - and "G" Batteries.
The Left Group will be connected to 95/Infantry Brigade H.Q. and the Right Group via the forward exchange near CHAPLE BOOM. The Group H.Q. will be connected direct to "H" - "I" - and "K" Batteries.
VISUAL.- Visual Communication will be established between
(a). Group H.Q. and Inf:Bde: H.Q.
(b). Right Group H.Q. and "F" Battery.
(c). Left Group H.Q. and "I" Battery.
RUNNERS. - Two runners per Group will be at their respective Bde:H.Q., and Two runners per Battery at their respective Group H.Q.

3. The Personnel and instruments for the Stations in the Left Sector will be found as follows:-
RIGHT GROUP.
Personnel to man 5 Stations and 4 Lucas Lamps, 2 Fullerphones, 8 D.3's., and 1 Buzzer Board will be found by "B" and "C" Companies, 39/Bn:M.G.C..

LEFT GROUP.   Personnel and instruments for Group H.Q. and "H" Battery will be found by "B" Company, No:5 Bn.M.G.Corps.
Personnel and instruments for "I" and "K" Batteries will be found by "D" Company, 5/Bn:M:G:Corps.
The whole will be under the command of The Battalion Signalling Officer who will arrange the necessary details and will report to Battalion H.Q. when all the necessary Lines are laid.

4. CODE CALLS.   Right Group.   ROMU
                      Left Group.   HANK.
                      "A" Battery.   ALEC.
                      "B" Battery.   SCOT.
                      "D" Battery.   MGD.
                      "E" Battery.   MGE.
                      "F" Battery.   MGF.
                      "G" Battery.   MGG.
                      "H" Battery.   MGH.
                      "I" Battery.   MGI.
                      "K" Battery.   MGK.

A List if Code Calls for Units will be isued to all concerned.

Appendix "B" to accompany. No: 5 M.G. Bn: O.O.No: 8.

ADMINISTRATIVE ARRANGEMENTS

1. **SUPPLIES.** The normal system will continue, "B" and "C" Companies of the 39/Bn:M.G.Corps will be rationed by H.Q.,5/Bn: M.G.Corps. "A" and "B" Companies will draw their allowances of Solidified Alcohol from the 13/Inf:Bde: and 95/Inf:Bde: respectively.

The greatest care must be taken to salve all empty Petrol Tins.

All ranks will go into action with one complete days ration in addition to the Iron Ration.

2. **WATER.** The Water at MEREDITH STATION - K.8.c.30/15. will be given an added capacity of 800 gallons by the addition of 4 protected Tanks to the preseny system. The Sterilizing Lorries will be operating at BOESEGHEM I.14.c.20/80. and at I.34.a.60/70.. The latter is for the Water Carts and Water Train.

3. Two Advanced Divisional Dumps will open on Zero Day. Written Demands will be accepted from any Officer:-

"A" Dump at J.13.a.5/6.   South of VIA ROMA.

"B" Dump at J.16.b.10/80. South of BALLOON Line.

These Dumps will each contain the following:-

S.A.A., M.G.	30. Boxes.
S.A.A. - Bandoliers.	20. "
Grenades, boxes, No: 5	10. "
" " No:25.	10. "
Sandbags.	5000.
Picks,	50.
Shovels.	100.
Petrol Tins.(Full of Water).	50. (Issued in exchange for empties.

4. **AMMUNITION.** The following M.G.,S.A.A. Dumps have been formed:-

80 Boxes at K.14.b.70/50.
80   "   at K.9.c.60/90.
50   "   at K.3.d.45/25.

Each Battery Position will have 32 filled belts per gun at the Position. Also 5 Boxes per Gun in Emplacements these Boxes can be drawn from the above mentioned Dumps.

Each Group will maintain a Reserve Dump of 150 Boxes of S.A.A. The sites for these Dumps will be selected by O.C's, Groups. The Map Location of the Dumps will be reported to Battalion H.Q.

5. **WATER & OIL.** Will be arranged for by Company Commanders concerned. 2 Gallons of Water must be kept in reserve at each Gun Position.

6. **TRANSPORT.** All Pack Animals and any other Tactical Transport required by Companies may be quartered in the WOOD west of the Line NORTH and SOUTH through EDITH STATION J.23.a.10/55.

7. ARMOURERS SHOP. An Advanced Armourers Shop will be established at DOLLS HOUSE, J.23.c.05/95. (H.Q."C" Company, 5/Bn: M.G.C. All Guns and Gun Parts for Repair or Exchange will be forwarded to this Shop.)

Complete Guns will be available for immediate exchange at this Shop.

8. MEDICAL ARRANGEMENTS. Two Stretchers per Battery will be provided under arrangements to be made by the Medical Officer.

Line Of Evacuation.

(a). All lying cases will be cleared from R.A.P's. by R.A.M.C. Bearers by Hand carry to TANKARD FARM, thence by push Truck to ELANK FARM, from there by Light Railway via A.D.S. at J.16.d.7/2. to M.D.S.I.17.c.5/1.

(b). Walking Wounded will be directed to the VIA ROMA along which they will be carried by returning empty supply Trains and Wagons. From FOREST CORNER J.23.a.10/55. Horsed Ambulances will take them to J.21,d.2/5.

Map Locations of R.A.P's will be notified later to all conccerned.

60 Sets of S.D. Clothing will be kept at the DOLLS HOUSE J.23.c.05/95., under the charge of the MEDICAL orderly of Battn: H.Q.

This Clothing will be issued for the immediate replacement of Gassed Clothing.

SECRET.   W23/11.

To O.C.Detachment,39th Bn.M.G.C.

    Please arrange to fire on Target K.5.c.65/05 to K.5.c.50/50
from 10.30 p.m.27th instant to 3a.m.28th instant. Rate of fire 30
rounds per gun in bursts once every five minutes.

    Two guns to be used a time.

                                    Signed by Major Kydd
                                        for LT.COL.
27/6/18.   Cmdg.5thBn.M.G.C.

SECRET   W.23/8

1. The Divisional Commander wishes everyone, especially the personnel of T.Ms. and M.Gs. to be reminded to be extra careful about movement after dawn tomorrow, 28th instant.
   <u>No one is to move.</u>
   Officers are to see that the men go to the latrines before daylight and use them as little as possible after.

2. Certain L.Gs. are to be told off to fire at low flying E.As. so that the volume of fire shall be normal. Remainder not to fire. But all E.As. must be engaged at once to keep them high up.

3. Bayonets will not be fixed until the artillery barrage opens.

(Sd) R.H Cutting
Lieut. Colonel
Cmdg 5th Bn. M.G.C.

27th June, 1918.

Copies to O.C. "D" Company
       O.C. Det 39th Bn.M.G.C.
       O.C. "B" Company do
       O.C. "C" Company do

SECRET   W.23/5

           Reference No 5 Machine Gun Battalion, No.8.

1.   The initial Machine Gun Barrage will be applied from Zero plus 1 to Zero plus 5 and not as shown on the Barrage Map.

2.   The duration of all subsequent barrages remains unchanged and therefore one minute will be added to the times laid down for the commencement and completion of each barrage.

3. ACKNOWLEDGE.

                                    (sd) R.H Cultiup

12 Noon   Lieut. Colonel,
26/6/18.   Commanding 5th Battalion Machine Gun Corps.

Copies to all recipients of O.O.No.8.

5th Battalion Machine Gun Corps.

SECRET

Copy No

Warning Order No 6.

Reference Map 36A.N.E.1/20 000.Ed.7.

Previous Warning Order No   is cancelled.

1. On a date and at an hour to be notified later the 5th Division will attack and capture the enemy positions N.W. of the PLATE BECQUE between the SWING BRIDGE at K.15.d.55/66 and LE CORNET PERDU.

2. One Section of "A" and "B" Companies and the whole of "D" Company will be employed on Barrage work. In addition to these Companies "B" and "C" Companies of the 39th Bn.M.G.C. will be employed on Barrage work.

3. The following preparations will be taken in hand forthwith:-
"B" Company, 39th Bn.M.G.C. will prepare emplacements for 2 - 8 Gun Batteries, one on a Line K.9.c.9/6 to K,9.c.9/9, and one on a line K.9.a.7/5 to K,9.a.75/75.
"C" Company, 39th Bn.M.G.C. will prepare emplacements for 2 - 8 Gun Batteries. One on a line K.14.d.8/8 to K.14.b.7/2. (in trench) and one on a line K.14.b.5/5 to K.14.b.40/75 (just east of footpath along the edge of wheatfield).
"D" Company will prepare emplacements for one 8 Gun Battery on line K.9.b.6/6 to K.9.b.65/90. Also one 8 Gun Battery on line K.3.d.4/6 to K.3.b.6/0.

4. Working parties can be drawn from the Sections in the Divisional Line if necessary. "T" Bases will be sent up as soon as available: use will be made of local material to cover the work.
Three men per Gun Team must always be kept in the Divisional Line.

5. This work is urgent and must be completed by the night of the 17/17th instant. Reports will be sent to this Office each morning saying what progress has been made during the last 24 hours.

6. "B" Company, 5th Bn.M.G.C. will dump 50 boxes S.A.A. at K.3.d.4/2. This dump can be drawn on by the forward Guns during operations.

7. ACKNOWLEDGE.

Issued at 9 p.m.

14th June, 1918.

Captain & Adjutant,
for Lieut, Colonel
Commanding 5th Battalion Machine Gun Corps.

SECRET. W.23/7.

O.C."A" Company.
~~O.C."B" Company.~~
~~O.C."D" Company.~~

Reference No:5 Machine Gun Battn:O.C.No: 8.

1. The Guns of "A" and "B" Companies mentioned therein come under the orders of O.C."D" Company forthwith.

2. O.C."D" Company will issue the necessary orders to these Sections.

26/6/18.

Major,
for Lieut-Colonel,
Commanding 5/Battn:Machine Gun Corps.

SECRET.   W.83/4/1.
----------   --------

            The following Position Calls will be
substituted for those given No:5 Bn: M.G.C.
O.O. No: 8, Appendix "A":-

    Right Group H.Q.   SLAT instead of   ROMO.
    Left Group H.Q.   STAG instead of   HAWK.

            The following additional Calls are
allotted for temporary use:-

    O.P. Exchange   K.2.d.5/4.   BRAT.
    1/Inf:Bde: K.2.a.99/15.   CHOP.
      (forward station).
    95/Inf:Bde;   K.3.b.9/6.   SLIP.
      (forward station).
    Signal Office.   K.14.a.5/6.   DRAB.

            In the event of the Machine Gun
Communications breaking down Batteries will make use
of the Brigade Forward Stations for transmitting
messages to Group H.Q. via the O.P. Exchange at
K.2.d.5/4.

    12/6/18.   Lieut-Colonel,

                    Commanding 5th:Bn; Machine Gun Corps.

            Copies to all recipients of O.O. No: 8.

S E C R E T.   Reference 5th: Machine Gun Battalion   W.23/3.
              Operation Order No: 8.

1. The attention of the various Commanders is called to S.S.192, Section 17, para 5. Where practicable the duties laid down in the paragraph should be performed.

2. During the first phase of the operation full teams will be required in the vicinity of the Guns, (i.e. 1 N.C.O. and 5 men per Team). After the consolidation is complete it will only be necessary to keep two men per gun and a proportion of N.C.O's: actually with the Guns. The remainder should be accomodated under cover somewhere close to the Battery Positions but ready to "stand to" immediately on an S.O.S. Signal being given.

3. Care should be taken to oil the barrels after every two belts have been fired, during normal barrage fire. This will not be possible during an S.O.S. period.

4. The following reports will be rendered by Group Commanders to O.C.5th:Battn:M.G.Corps at Advanced Divnl: H.Q. - First Report to be despatched two hours after Zero:-
   (a). Number of Casualties (Officers and Men).
   (b). Number of Gun Casualties.
   (c). Expenditure of S.A.A.
   (d). General Report on the local Situation.

A similar Report will be rendered every eight hours, until ordered to cease, These Reports will show at what time S.O.S. Signals were responded to, and will embrace the period since last Report.

5. All empty S.A.A. Boxes containing empty cases etc: will be dumped by Coys: near their respective S.A.A. Dumps. These Dumps must be marked "Empty Boxes". Boxes of S.A.A. not used will be dumped at their respective S.A.A. Dumps. After the completion of the operations a list of such Dumps & their contents will be sent to O.C.5th:Bn:M.G.Corps.

17/6/18.
                                        Major,
        Commanding 5th: Battalion for Lieut. Colonel,

Reports will be sent by Cyclist Orderly.

— CONSOLIDATING GUNS —
ROBERMETZ (2nd Edition) Enemy Organization up to 8-6-18

Enemy Work done between 8-6-18 & 25-6-18, shown in Green.

APPROX: DISPOSITION MAP
5TH BATTN M.G.C.   28-6-18

"A" COMPANY'S GUNS SHEWN THUS ✗
"B" COMPANY'S GUNS SHEWN THUS ✗

SECRET

Scale 20000

L.M.154

SECRET.   No.5 Machine Gun Battalion   Copy No.
          Operation Order No.11.

1.   On the night of June 30th/1st July the 31st Division are relieving that portion of the Divisional Front which lies NORTH of a line drawn from K.11.b.8/4 (Bridge inc:to 31st Division)bto K.4.a.7/0.

2.   "A"Company of 31st Bn.M.G.C. will relieve the following Guns of "B"Company,5th Bn.M.G.C.

        2 Guns at about K.5.c.9/3
        2 Guns at about K.6.c0/3

        On completion of this relief the remaining 8 Guns of "B"Company North of the line mentioned in para (1) will be withdrawn without relief.
        Guides for "A"Company 31st Bn.M.G.C.will be at "B" Company H.Q. K.5.b.7/4.at 9 p.m.
        Details of relief to be arranged between Companies concerned.
        Completion of this relief will be reported to the O.C. Left Group by O.C."A"Company.

3.   (a) On completion of the relief of the Guns of "B"Company by the 31st Bn.M.G.C. "H" and "I"Batteries and 4 Guns of "K" Battery will withdraw under orders of O.C.Left Group.

        (b) The sections of "A" and "B"Companies in "I"Battery will rejoin their Companies on withdrawal.

        (c) H.Q. and 2 Sections of "D"Company will take up positions in the Divisional Line vacated by them previous to "BORDERLAND".
        1 Section of "D"Company will withdraw to Divisional Reserve at THIENNES.

4.   "A"Company will arrange to relieve the following Guns of "B"Company:-

        4 Guns at about K.10.b.9/8
        2 Guns at about K.11.b.2/2

OO/11.(cont)

5. On completion of relief "B" Company will withdraw 3 Sections to Divisional Reserve and billet in reserve billets at I.16.a. One Section of "B" Company will take up the position in the BOIS DES VACHES area of the Divnl. Line. This Section will come under the orders of O.C. "D" Company.

6. The Section of "D" Company remaining in "K" Battery will come under the orders of O.C. "A" Company. The S.O.S. Line for this Battery will be from K.11b.3/2. to K.12.a.3/4.

7. Completion of movements referred to in the various paras: of this order will be reported to this office in Code as follows:-

    Movement detailed in para: (2).   By Code Name   SHOE.
    (3 -a)   do: BOOT.
    (3- c)   do: FLUTE.
    (4).   do: COOT.
    (5).   do: BANG.

8. ACKNOWLEDGE.

30/6/18.

(Sd) R.H. Gillman

Lieut-Colonel,
Commanding 5th Battalion Machine Gun Corps.

Copies to:-

1. 5/Divn: "G"
2. 13/Inf:Bde:
3. 95/ " "
4. O.C. "A" Company.
5. O.C. "B" do:
6. O.C. "C" Company.
7. O.C. "D" Company.
8. O.C., Det; 30/Bn:M.G.C.
9. O.C. 31/Bn:M.G.C.
10. O.C. "B" Coy: Rear.
11. Office.
12. War Diary.
13. do:
14. Spare.

B/11

SECRET
5th BATT.
1/6/18.

MACHINE GUN
MAP.

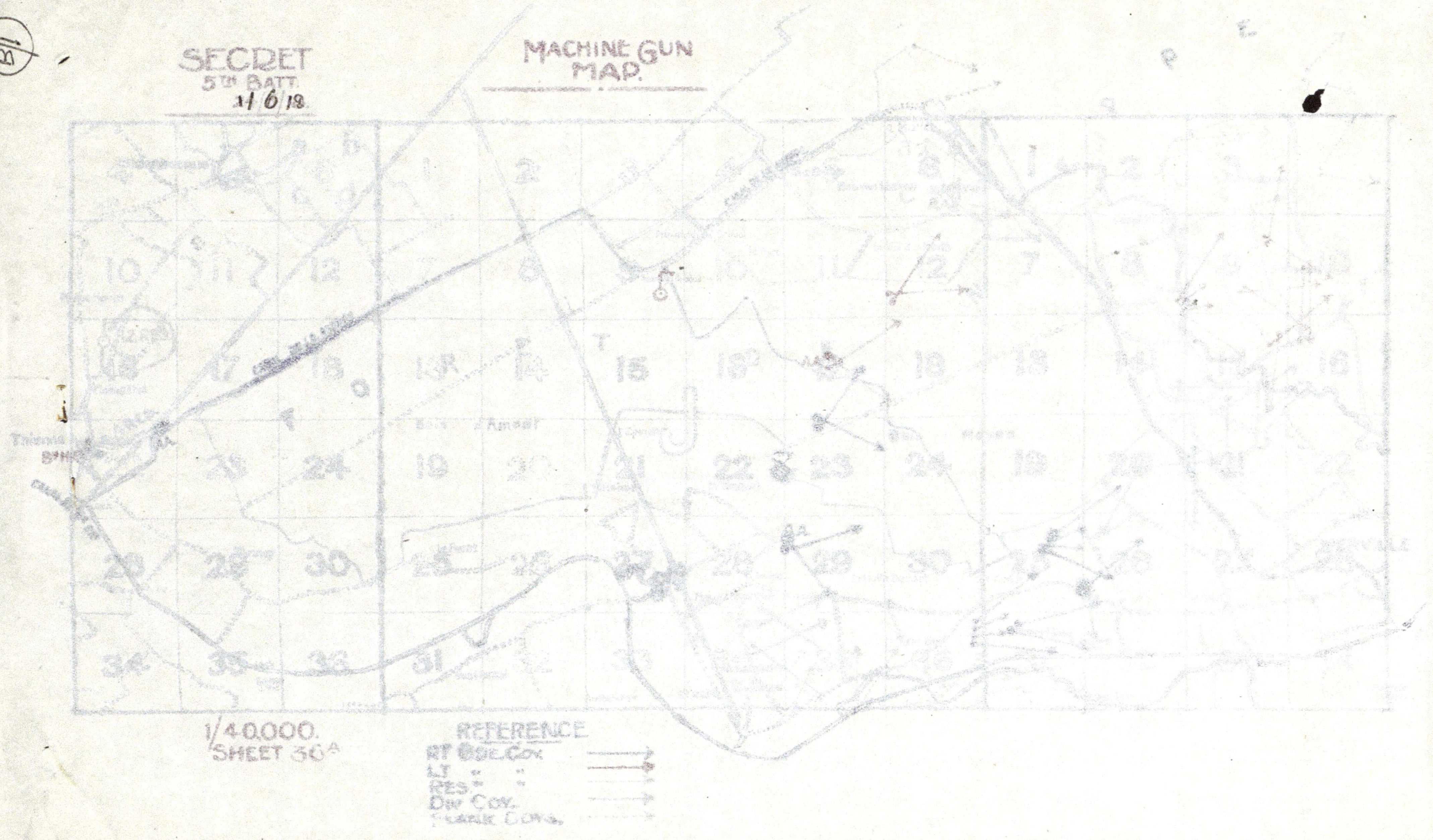

1/40,000.
SHEET 36A
REFERENCE
RT BDE. COY.
LT " "
RES. " "
DIV COY.
FLANK COYS.

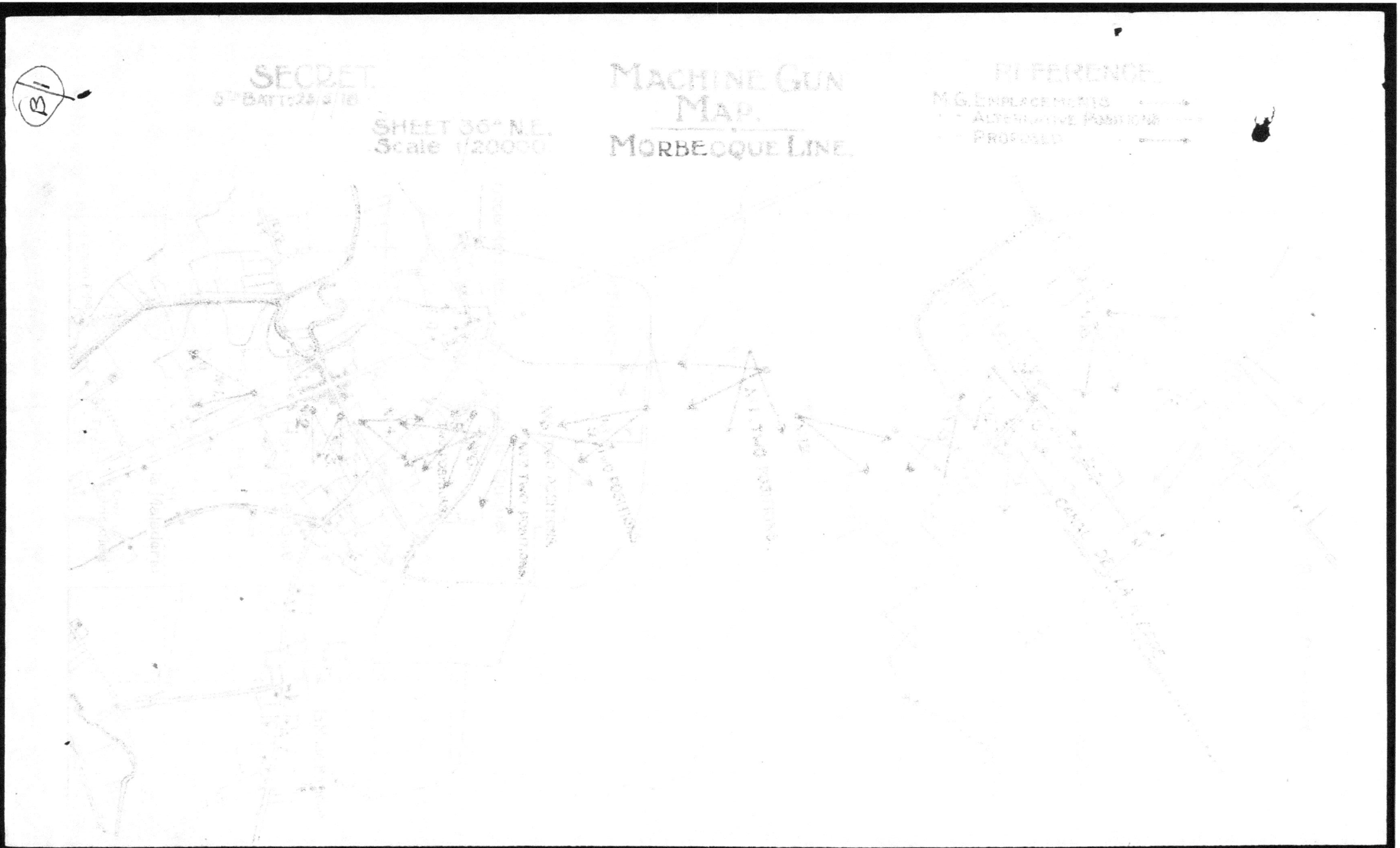

SECRET

MACHINE GUN MAP

MORBECQUE LINE

SHEET 36c NE.
Scale 1/20,000

REFERENCE
M.G. EMPLACEMENTS
ANTI-AIRCRAFT POSITION
PROPOSED

Syllabus of Training carried out by Companies when in Divisional Reserve at I.C.a. near THIENNES.

"A" Company.   Period 1st: to 5th: June, 1918.

June 1st: Refitting and close order Drill under Section Officers.

June 2nd: Physical Training - Immediate Action - Barrage Drill - Stripping.

June 3rd: Physical Training - Immediate Action - Barrage Drill.
            Lecture by Lt:Col; CUTTING, D.S.O., M.C.
                    Subject: (1). Use of Ground and Cover.
                              (2). Camouflaging Positions.
                              (3). Aerial Photography.

June 4th: Physical Training - Practical use of Ground and cover with Limbers in action.

June 5th: Physical Training - Section Drill - Lecture by Section officers to Men - N.C.Os' under the Se gt:Major. - Lecture by Lt:Col; R.H.CUTTING, D.S.O, M.C. on "Machine Gun Tactics".

"C" Company.   Period 7th: to 10th: June, 1918.

June 7th: Progressive methods of Advance.

                    (1). Single Gun Teams.
                    (2). Complete Sections.

                Action of Section Officers.

June 8th: The Advance continues:-

                    (1). The capture of the first Objective.
                    (2). The Infantry temporarily held up - Machine Gun support, how applied.
                    (3). Consolidation.

            Study of the Course with Maps.

June 9th: Sunday.

June 10th: (1). The completion of the Attack.
                (2). Final Dispositions of Machine Guns.
                (3). Consolidation in Depth.

June 11th:
  and   Sections attached to Battalions for Practice over the Taped Course
June 12th:

      (Training Areas for the 7th:, 8th:, and 10th, insts: I.8. - 9, 14 and 15.
            Sheet 36.A. 1/40000.)

5th Division

5th M.G.C.

July to December
1918

May 1919

C O N F I D E N T I A L.

Regd: No: W.
Volume No: 1
Part No: 4

Vol 4

D U P L I C A T E

W A R   D I A R Y   F O R   M O N T H
OF
J U L Y, 1918.

31st: July, 1918.

R H Cutting
Lieut: - Colonel,
Commanding No: 5 Battalion Machine Gun Corps.

Map Reference 36A NE 1/20000 Ed.Y.
Duplicate July 1918

WAR DIARY
or
INTELLIGENCE SUMMARY
(Erase heading not required.)

Army Form C. 2118.

Place	Date	Hour	Summary of Events and Information	Remarks and references to Appendices
Orchard	1st July 1918		Weather fine. Our heavy artillery especially active on MERVILLE & NEUF BERQUIN area. Hostile artillery shewed active on VERTBOIS at noon, registration very desultory. At 11.20am. ROBERT DE NIEPPE & VIETES were lightly shelled for short period. The SCHOOL & WINEBRIDGE in K.5.d were subjected to periodic bursts of light H.E. & gas shells. M.E. gas shells for 2 mins return and the vicinity of Bn pay Hdqrs at DOLLS HOUSE was shewed from 11.0pm to 2.30am. Hostile M.Guns were active and our located at J.20.d. & J.20.a. were troublesome throughout the night. Adrift of 5 off and 2.30 ok 20. 70m. Batt. fav. base depot. Casualties -- Nil. Battalion Strength offrs -- O.Rs 40 -- 806	Bn. of fr. are to take the line, the letter A.1. between the letter a and the l of L'Epinette the first approaching by way of FORÊT de NIEPPE to VIEPPE to NIEPPE CRN. (hardships in detail) see appendix A/8.
do	2nd.		Weather fine. Our arty. active on SACHET FARM -- LES PURESBEQUES, a short burst fire on MERVILLE at 3 pm. Hostile guns were quiet during the day but their activity increased at night. At 9-10pm. a large no of light shells fell about CORBIE Rd and the corner of WOOD at K.26. also at K.11.c. J.11.d.pm. M.Gun. were active on both sides all night -- the enemy M.Gs harassed the edge of the WOOD at K.19 & K.20. by direct fire a. d. along our frequently	

WAR DIARY
INTELLIGENCE SUMMARY

Page 2

Place	Date	Hour	Summary of Events and Information	Remarks and references to Appendices
Meches	2nd cont'd		traversed between the BOURRE RIVER & TAXI FARM. The two Companies of 39/Batt. M Gun Corps (B & C) attached for tactical purposes report their own unit. The attached HQ of A Company move to K 8 c 50/5. Casualties — Nil	See Appx A/1 for withdrawal of B & C Coys on rejoined 39 Bn MGC
do.	3rd		Weather fine. Our artillery was much greater than usual in concentration took place at 4.45 p. the object of which was to locate hostile Trench Mortars near GARNARD CROSS. The enemy was quiet in forward areas during the day. Hostile Machine Guns were very active during night and early morning fire from K.16d, 22a, 21b. The enemy's T.M.s showed lively activity at 3-30am causing some casualties to our Infantry at K15d b/3. MAJOR DG KYDD (2i/c) proceeded to ALDERSHOT on demobilisation of senior officers Course. MAJOR H TUFNELL (at C Company) proceeded to GRANTHAM (MGTC) for tour of duty there.	
do.	4th		Weather fine. Hostile artillery much in reaction — day & night — BOIS MOYEN HAVERSKERQUE WICTES and the vicinity of DOLLS HOUSE all being shelled at intervals with H.E. and Gas shells. Our artillery was active as ever fire at K 21b at 3.40 am. Trench Mortars also. Hostile M Guns were engaged as M 20 from —— Our Machine Guns were active firing on enemy tracks as approaches	

WAR DIARY
INTELLIGENCE SUMMARY

Army Form C. 2118.

Page 3

Place	Date	Hour	Summary of Events and Information	Remarks and references to Appendices
Dickebusch	4th	11.30pm	Hostile Machine Guns were generally most quiet. A few rounds of Grn. artillery shot at 11.30pm. Casualties — Nil	
— do —	5th	—	Weather fine. Situation Normal. Enemy were active shelling CAUDESCURE JUNCT. Road and the ORCHARD K.14.a.40.20 at intervals. CHAPEL ROAD & CAUDESCURE Road were shelled at 3.30am. by M.G. guns. ST VENANT — BOIS des VACHES & HAVERSKERQUE were shelled at intervals. Enemy Machine Guns enfilade the road in K.14 during the night. Also the track running from K.14.c.80.80 to K.14.c.60.70 gun. Also fired from left of BOIAR FARM. Our M. Guns fired 2600 rounds on target around K.26.8.9/5. Capt. R.H. DADD & 21 O.R. KITCHEN and 21 O.R. proceed on leave.	
— do —	6th	—	Weather fine. Hostile artillery active on the SOUTHERN edge of FORET DE NIEPPE intermittently during the night. Le BOIS & VIA ROMA were shelled with gas shells at 10.30pm the vicinity of Company HQ at K.8.5.9/5 at 9pm. M. Guns active on both sides on guns at K. 24. 1/8 was very troublesome throughout the night. A large fire was observed in MERVILLE at 2.30pm by our artillery. 40 O.Rs proceed on leave. Casualties Nil	

WAR DIARY
INTELLIGENCE SUMMARY.
(Erase heading not required.)

Page 4.

Place	Date	Hour	Summary of Events and Information	Remarks and references to Appendices
Dickebush	7th	—	WEATHER DULL. "B" Company relieved "A" Company in the LE SART SECTOR. Our Artillery were active day and night especially on RENNET & SINEAD FARMS. Hostile artillery was active and paid particular attention to the PILL BOXES in K.25.a. throughout the day and night. The WOOD around LES LAURIERS shelled by S.A.S. A few shells + flare lights fell at D.30o.Y.O. Our Machine Guns carried out a little harassing fire firing 1000 rnds. Casualties 1 O.R. wounded. Weather set in cool.	For relief of "A" Coy see App. A/2
do	8th	—	Artillery Field APPENDAGE & CRUDESAYE thought (?) the day. Our right Company M.G. at K.7.b.30/40 were shelled during the night, the vicinity of "B" Battery (MG) at K.25.b.30/33 was shelled from 11:45pm to 12:15am. Our Rocket Guns fired 3000 rounds on various enemy targets. Casualties Nil. Lieuts L. OVERSTALL & GLEDHILL & 2nd Lt WHITE & WILSON proceeded on leave to UK.	
do	9th	—	Weather fine. Enemy was quiet. Was in view during the day, although Hydroplane took from DOLL'S HOUSE to COPSE was shelled intermittently during the night. Mach. + Guns were unable on both sides. The G.O.C. found inspected the Transport Lines of Company (A & E) Casualties 1 O.R. accidentally wounded	

WAR DIARY
or
INTELLIGENCE SUMMARY

(Erase heading not required.)

Army Form C. 2118.

Place	Date	Hour	Summary of Events and Information	Remarks and references to Appendices
Hrendes	10th		Weather wet. The enemy artillery shelled CROIX-MARRAISE and HAVERSKERQUE during the day. Company HQ at J.27d.4.8 was shelled at 9.30 for a period of the shell containing Gas. Our Vickers Guns fire 3500 rounds on K.22.a.6.0 on COURTFROIE — CURN — TRAFLE SHOYTON FARMS. Casualties — NIL —	
— do —	11th		2/Lieut R.F.O. DARE joins from Base and is posted to "C" Company. Weather dull. Hostile artillery was fairly quiet. ITCHEN FARM was shelled at 9pm by 5.9's. The enemy's Mobile Guns were active opposite the LE SART Sector but quiet on ARREVAGE Sector. Vickers Guns of Platoons were active during night. Combs being dropped in vicinity of ST VENANT and FORET de NIEPPE. Casualties — 1 O.R. wounded. —	
— do —	12th		Weather wet. Hostile artillery shelled the vicinity of our support trenches in the vicinity of K.25.b. Our Vickers Guns fired 4000 rounds on the harassing targets. Casualties Nil.	
— do —	13th		Weather wet. Situation Normal. Relief of "A" Company by "C" Company on the ARREVAGE Sector. "A" Company returning to Divisional Reserve on completion of relief. Our artillery active both day and night carrying	

WAR DIARY

INTELLIGENCE SUMMARY

Page 5.

Place	Date	Hour	Summary of Events and Information	Remarks and references to Appendices
Treclos	12th	—	Concentrated shoots at 9.30, 9.38, 11.0 p.m.; 8.12.30 a.m. Our enemy approached and Headquarters. Hostile artillery quiet during day - during night our front and support lines and back areas were shelled freely. NA ROMA received much attention. Our section HQ at J30d 9/2. (B Co. pn.) were shelled enemy obtaining 2 direct hits. Our machine guns were active firing 13250 rounds harassing fire & also firing in conjunction with the artillery on areas around K25B & K28B. The enemy's guns replied vigorously. Guns fire sweeping areas K25b regularly throughout the night. Casualties Nil.	30 relief of "C" Company see App: 9/3
—do.—	14th	—	Weather wet. Situation normal. Hostile artillery active on our support line - K20 central. Quite a house was collapsed on M. Gun shelter in support line - 19 guns being badly damaged - the RUE des MORTS and BOIS des VACHES were heavily shelled during early morning. Our machine guns fired 9000 rounds on forms, tracks and roads in the enemy's forward area. Hostile M guns fired repeatedly on K and BK 15 during the night. Our aircraft were fairly quiet on both sides. Casualties — 1 OR Wounded	

Army Form C. 2118.

WAR DIARY
INTELLIGENCE SUMMARY
(Erase heading not required.)

Instructions regarding War Diaries and Intelligence Summaries are contained in F.S. Regs., Part II. and the Staff Manual respectively. Title pages will be prepared in manuscript.

Summary of Events and Information

Page 6

Place	Date	Hour	Summary of Events and Information	Remarks and references to Appendices
Hinges	15th		Weather – Westerly winds, cold, heavy showers. Our artillery were very active. Attacks normal. Our artillery engaged during the day MERVILLE, PENNET FARM and LES PURESBECQUES all being engaged during the day. Harassing fire was maintained from 9pm to 4.30am. Our H. Guns fired 7080 rounds of tracks. Shows in the enemy's lines & our H. Guns fired action on B.R. sides day and night. A number of enemy aircraft were active on both sides during the day & the night. Several of them were bombing planes engaged on lines during the night. Hostile flares were very active opposite APPENAGE SECTOR firing at our aircraft during the day and at night swept our parapet. Hostile gun were located firing from forward of K 26.d. 4/7 & 1/6. Casualties — 1 O.R. acc'd. Wounded.	
— do. —	16th		Weather few situation normal. Our arty. very active especially at night applying a small barrage on certain risk road by Left Battalion. The enemy was very active at night in the vicinity of LA MOTTE LES GRAND DEVISE were heavily shelled, at 3.30am. The area around K 26.b – K 31.a & WOOD at K 25.d received machine gun & light shell bursts at K 10 & the BOHIR FARM. Our arty. fired 18950 rds. Hostile harassing fire & c.o.— operations with artillery Hostile M.G.s very active. Casualties — Nil.—	

D. D. & L., London, E.C.
(A8004) Wt. W14771/M2 31 750,000 5/17 **Sch. 52** Form/C.2118/14

Army Form C. 2118.

Page 4

WAR DIARY
or
INTELLIGENCE SUMMARY.
(Erase heading not required.)

Instructions regarding War Diaries and Intelligence Summaries are contained in F.S. Regs., Part II. and the Staff Manual respectively. Title pages will be prepared in manuscript.

Place	Date	Hour	Summary of Events and Information	Remarks and references to Appendices
Yperles	10th	—	Weather warm & occasional thunderstorms. Situation — very abnormally quiet. Hostile artillery was fairly active during night, & during the day the shelling was lightly shelled. LA MOTTE SUC. by P.M. Gun posted in FORCE at J.23d 5/4. a.d. Jordaing B Battery of M. Garwick K.25b 50/33. Our artillery were not active though the enemy registering a d. enterals too ladies t of FAL FARM a d. society a d. fire actual harasing fire. Our Machine Guns expended 5000 rou ds principally on MERVILLE — LA MOTTE Road. a d. area about RENNET FARM. The enemy Machine Guns were active during the night. N of &y. Our Snipers. a d. K.10.c continuously Captn. HO COLLYER join from Base 2p.b. also Gother sh — Casualties — NIL —	carried outduring period see app. B/11
— do —	11th	—	Weather fine. Situation Normal. Our artillery very active on LES PURESECQUES FAL FARM area also on MERVILLE. The enemy guns shelled ARDEWACE a d. LES LAURIERS reinforcementstein Ord Machine Guns expended 17500 rounds long fired from 9:30 pm. to 1:30 am. on Road junctn at K.23b 7/5 — K.22b — K.23a. a.d. from K.22 a 4/4. to K.22 w 84/55 Hostile M Guns were very active as were usual A Battery at K 31a 50/60. Casualties — NIL —	

WAR DIARY

INTELLIGENCE SUMMARY.

(Erase heading not required.)

Place	Date	Hour	Summary of Events and Information	Remarks and references to Appendices
Trenches	18th	—	Weather fine. Shells North of our artillery into LES PUISIEUX a L FAY. Front the enemy artillery shelled ARRANGE at far and front line attention to LES LARGIERS. Our Hotch Gs. fired 19,500 rounds between 9.30 p.m. & 11.30 a.m. on the following targets K.21.d.5/90 (tripoder) — Road at K.21.b.70/95 — K.22.b & 23.a — K.22.d.4/0 to K.22.a.8/45. Hostile Hotchkiss Guns were active about the area in front of "Pastry" were silenced (Rifle Safto)	[illegible margin notes]
			Casualties — Nil.	
– do. –	19th	—	Weather fine. Stand to relief completed. A Coy.—Fray relief B in the LE SART Sector. Our artillery wore active all night a.d. L/Cpl Rowe with one a Lewis Guns flange covered as seldom in support of various operations. Our Hotchkisses carried out numerous shoots throughout the day. Hostile guns were fairly active TANKERD FARM and ARRIVANCE very heavily shelled 1600 rounds were expended by our Hotchkiss Guns on various targets behind the enemy lines. Our aircraft very active bringing down 2 Observation Balloons & 1 E.A. during the day. Major F.H.	

PETRIE HAY MC came on duty at 2.15. Capt. M°COLLIER became L. of Coy.

WAR DIARY
or
INTELLIGENCE SUMMARY.
(Erase heading not required.)

Army Form C. 2118.
MACHINE GUN

Page 9.

Place	Date	Hour	Summary of Events and Information	Remarks and references to Appendices
Trenches	20th		Weather fine. Our artillery active on SINBAD FARM and also on rest billets on the NEUF BERQUIN — ESTAIRES ROADS. A dump near MERVILLE was set on fire at 3-30 pm. Наmourgh's was manned throughout the night. Hostile guns were active on ACREVAGE & BONAR FARM and BOIS de VACHES at irregular intervals day and night. Hostile Machine Guns were active and harassed out tracks in the ARGENTRE Sector: gun fire from kind of ad K 1901 S/8 & from direction of PURESERVE. Our Machine Guns fired 6000 rounds on MERVILLE Cross Roads during early hours of morning. Casualties — Nil —	
do	21st		Weather fine. Situation normal. Hostile artillery was much more active than usual at 10 am. One of our working parties was shelled on the LA MOTTE — MERVILLE Road. BEDFORD FARM & LA MOTTE were shelled with 5.9's during the day. Our Machine Guns fired 2,750 rounds on following targets behind enemy lines. K 22 Central — Road Junction K 228 SINBAD FARM — J K 22 B to K 23 a. Hostile Machine Guns were fairly active during night. Casualties — Nil —	

WAR DIARY or INTELLIGENCE SUMMARY

Page 10.

Place	Date	Hour	Summary of Events and Information	Remarks and references to Appendices
Trenches	22nd	—	Weather wet. Situation Normal. Hostile artillery generally quieter, the neighborhood of CAUDESCURE CHURCH - STATION INN and the MORBECQUE - ST VENANT Road was shelled. From 12.15a to 1.15a about 300 gas shells fell about K.25a S.E. Our Mach & Guns carried out the usual harassing fire on enemy back areas, 18500 rounds being fired. The enemy attacked Gun harassed our trench etc. One gun believed to fire from K.26b 7/10. Casualties — Nil.	
Trenches	23rd	—	Weather fine. Situation Normal. Our artillery very active carrying out usual harassing fire on enemy's communications, LOXTON HOUSE and CANAL BANK receiving attention during the day. No enemy guns were active on BOIS des VACHES — LE TOUQUET — HAVERSKERQUE and L'HAMOTTE. In particular attention paid to the cross roads running S.E. from K.9 a & 10. Our Machine Guns fired 3000 rounds on K.21c 69/81 and 1900 rounds on K.22 a&b, K.28, K.28 b (road junction) and K.22 b, between hours of 10p. and 11.30p. Hostile M.Gs were active on areas around J 30d 90/64 and K.25 a 58/28. Casualties — 1 O.R. Wounded.	

No. 5 BATTALION,
Army MACHINE GUN CORPS.
No. 2/9/1918
Date ....

WAR DIARY
or
INTELLIGENCE SUMMARY
(Erase heading not required.)

Page 11

Place	Date	Hour	Summary of Events and Information	Remarks and references to Appendices
The chat	24th	—	Weather fine. Situation normal. Our Heavy artillery active on LES PURESBECQUES, BRONCHO FARM — ATOM FARM and the COLLEGE. Much harassing fire on enemy communications. Hostile activity during the day, the HAIESKERQUE - ST VENANT Road receiving considerable attention. 12am & neighborhood received numerous gas shells. Hostile guns were generally inactive after 2am. Our Machine Guns fired 5000 rounds on what English looked enemy lines. Hostile Machine Guns were unusually quiet. Casualties. 1 OR Wounded.	For situation of front line Battalions Refer Appendix a/5.
-do-	25th	—	Weather fine. Situation normal. Our artillery carried out their normal harassing programme on enemy's communications. Hostile artillery shelled CAPLE ROAD and the vicinity of CROIX MAKEAISE. Was shelled by heavy Calibre guns at 2am. The ST VENANT - HAVESSKERQUE Road received unusual attention. Machine Guns were active on both sides. Our front 2000 rounds on the following at crossroads at K.28c.70.11. - R.2.4. 20/10 and K.29c.20/00.. hostile burst on our trajectory area, on gun fired on roads about K.9b.7/2. Casualties - 1 OR Wounded. —	For appreciation of situation on the Oril. Front see app. a/4.

WAR DIARY / INTELLIGENCE SUMMARY

Army Form C. 2118

Page 11

Place	Date	Hour	Summary of Events and Information	Remarks and references to Appendices
Ine. Shed	26th	—	Weather wet. Started Normal. The completed carrol of Les positions about — CAUDESCURE & ARPENIECE during the day. ST VENANT a.d. H.S. CROIX MARMUSE Road was heavily shelled from 10.30 to 11.30am also K.33 central & a teering field on NEUF BERQUIN — VIERHOUCK & Pereonel L.13d. Carried out Harrowing fire as usual on M. Gun field track at intervals throughout the night on enemy back areas up to 4000 round. With the exception of 6 left battalion own guns covered the BERKENAGE Sub. Section fired half a belt per gun on their SOS lines from 9.30 – 9pm at 5 minute intervals for test purposes. Officer observed report guns not located & no flashes from guns opposite the company's Np. Saw above. On our front sand area. — Casualties 3 o.r. wounded. —	For training carried out see Appdix 8f.
do	27th	—	Weather fine. Situation Normal during the day. CROIX MARMUSE & ST VENANT were shelled, a number of gas shell were used of CAUDESCURE. Our Machine Gun Sections again tested satisfactorily on their SOS lines also carried out Harrowing fire firing 12,750 rds. Our artillery very active as usual. NEUF BERQUIN — VIERHOUCK — MERVILLE & LE SART — Casualties 1 o.r. —	

WAR DIARY
or
INTELLIGENCE SUMMARY

(Erase heading not required.)

Army Form C. 2118.

Page 12

Place	Date	Hour	Summary of Events and Information	Remarks and references to Appendices
Trenches	28th	—	Weather fine. Situation Normal. Our artillery shelled PONT-RONDIN and the vicinity of MERVILLE — LE SART and carried out vigorous harassing fire during the night. The enemy was active on our old front line in the vicinity of PARMENPLE and CHAPEL ROOM. 8" Shells fell about J.28.B at 11.15p. The CROIX MARRAISE ST VENANT received a great deal of attention. Our M.Guns fired 1500 on various targets in enemy's lines. A fire was observed in the enemy's lines at K.29.c.40/19 at M.45a.m. also 1½ a dump and caused by our artillery fire. — Casualties — Nil. —	
- do -	29th	—	Weather fine. Situation Normal. Our arty action on whole front is fairly heavy. Barrage was put down in conjunction with a raid by the 13th Bgde. in which our Machine Guns fired 240,250 rounds. Hostile artillery fairly active. ST VENANT — CROIX MARRAISE — AMONT WOOD and the ST VENANT road being shelled. 2 large fires were observed in the enemy lines to the right of LE CORBIE. One of our ammunition Dumps at J.27.a.c. 85/60 shelled & set fire to our ammunition Dumps at J.27.a.c. 85/60. Casualties — 2 O.R. —	

WAR DIARY
INTELLIGENCE SUMMARY

Page 13

Place	Date	Hour	Summary of Events and Information	Remarks and references to Appendices
Dreschen	30th	—	Weather fine. Our artillery active carrying out vigorous harassing fire. Enemy artillery very active after dark fr shelling on large scale during early morning on areas around J.29 — J.34 — J.35. Considerable shelling of Bois des VACHES and LA MOTTE au BOIS during day and the area East of HAVERSKERQUE for half an hour with heavy shells. Our M.Guns fired 10,000 rounds on usual targets. Casualties 1 O.R. wounded.	For I eneur Absence of Strength see App B/2
— do —	31st	—	Weather fine. Hostile Artillery was very active from 11am to 2am principally on J.28 — J.29 — J.34 — J.35 most of shells being Gas shells. Our day Werkerhack from CROIX MARAISE — FOREST CORNER, BRISTOL, FORET de NIEPPE and K.18.a were all gas shelled during night. Hostile aircraft very active at night bombing. Our Machine Guns were active firing on usual targets. Casualties 3 O.Rs wounded. Officers 4-5 O.Rs 862	For relief by A Coy by E. Coy of the 5th Battn Retn see App. A/6

Battalion Strength

Lieut Colonel
Commanding No 5 Bn M.G. Corps

SECRET

No. 5 BATTALION.
MACHINE GUN
CORPS.

Copy No. 9/1

No 5. Machine Gun Battalion.

Operation Order No. 12.

Reference Map 36 A. 1/20 000

1. On the night of 1st/2nd July "B" and "C" Companies of 59/Bn.M.G.Corps will withdraw from "D" - "E" - "F" and "G" Batteries without relief and will proceed to billets at I.20.c. and c.d.

2. Withdrawal will not commence before 10.30 pm.

3. STORES.

    (a). All empty S.A.A.Boxes will be dumped at MEREDITH STATION - K.6.c.5/2.
    (b). Location of all dumps of S.A.A. left near Battery Positions will be notified to H.Q., 5/Bn.M.G.C.
    (c). All "T" Bases will be left in positions.
    (d). The vacated Positions will be carefully covered with Camouflage before withdrawal.
    (e). Positions and Emplacements will be left clean and all tools etc. will be brought out.

4. Completion of withdrawal will be reported to this office by the Code Word "Blighty".

Issued at 11.30 a.m.

1/7/18

Captain & Adjutant
for Lieut. Colonel
Commanding 5th Bn. Machine Gun Corps.......

Copies to:-

1. 5/Divn "G"
2. 13/Inf. Bde
3. C.M.G.O.
4. 59/Bn.M.G.C.
5. O.C. Det. 59/Bn.M.G.C.
6. "B" Company. 30th Bn. M.G.C.
7. "C" Company do
8. Office
9. War Diary
10. do
11. Spare.

SECRET.   No: 5 Machine Gun Battalion

Operation Order No: 13.

Reference Map 36.A. 1/20000.

1.   On the night of the 6th:/7th/July "B" Company will relieve "C" Company in the LE SART Sector. Details to be arranged by Company Commanders concerned.

2.   On completion of relief "C" Company will withdraw 3 Sections into Divisional Reserve. The fourth Section will take up the positions vacated by "B" Company in the BOIS DES VACHES.

3.   The 3 Sections of "C" Company in Divisional Reserve will be accommodated in the Billets vacated by "B" Company in I.16.a.

4.   Completion of relief to be reported to Battalion H.Q. in the B.A.B. Code.

5.   ACKNOWLEDGE.

Issued at 2.pm.   (sd) A.C.W.U. STANLEY.
                                        Captain & Adjt;
                                        for Lieut-Colonel,
                            Commanding 5/Battalion Machine Gun Corps.

Copies to :-   1. 5/Division.
               2. 13/Inf;Bde;
               3. 15/Inf;Bde:
               4. 95/Inf:Bde:
               5. O.C."A" Company.
               6. O.C."B" Company.
               7. O.C."C" Company.
               8. O.C."D" Company.
               9. File.
              10. War Diary.
              11.   do:
              12. Office.

No: 5 Battalion Machine Gun Corps.
Operation Order No: 14.
-o-o-o-o-o-o-o-o-o-o-o-o-o-o-o-o-o-

Copy No: 13.

Reference Map 36.A, 1/40000.

1.	On the night of the 12th:/13th: inst: "C" Company will relieve "A" Company in the ARREWAGE Sector. Details to be arranged between Company Commanders concerned.

2.	On completion of relief "A" Company will withdraw 3 Sections into Divisional Reserve. The fourth Section will take up the positions vacated by "C" Company in the BOIS DES VACHES.

3.	The 3 Sections of "A" Company will be accommodated in the Billets vacated by "C" Company in I.16.a.

4.	Completion of relief to be reported to Battalion H.Q. in the B.A.B. Code.

5.	ACKNOWLEDGE.

Issued at 9.pm.   (sd). A.C. STANLEY, Capt: & Adjt:,
                                            for Lieut: Colonel,
9.7.18.   Commanding No: 5 Battalion Machine Gun Corps.

Copies to -   1. 5/Division.
               2. 13/Inf: Bde:
               3. 15/   do:
               4. 95/   do:
               5. O.C. A. Company.
               6. O.C. B.   do:
               7. O.C. C.   do:
               8. O.C. D.   do:
               9. File.
              10. War Diary.
              11.   do:
              12. Office.

O.C., "C" Company.

No. 5 BATTALION, MACHINE GUN CORPS.
N.25/21.

      Please arrange to relieve the Section of "D" Company occupying Positions Nos: 35 - 36 - 37 and 38 by your Section which is in Nos: 23 - 24 - 25 and 26 Positions, in order to facilitate relief vide my Operation Order No. 15., attached.

16/7/18.

(sd). A.C. Stanley.
Captain & Adjutant
for Lieut-Colonel,
Commanding 5th Battalion Machine Gun Corps.

No. 5 BATTALION, MACHINE GUN CORPS.

Reference No: 5 Machine Gun Battalion Operation Order No:14.

Amendment.

Paras 2 and 3 are cancelled and the following substituted:-

Para 2. On completion of relief "A" Company will withdraw into Divisional Reserve and billet in the accommodation vacated by "C" Company M.T.M.C.

Para 3. The section of "B" Company at present in Divisional Reserve will relieve the section of "D" Company in the WIPPE BETTINGER on the night of the 12th/13th:inst:.

Signed A.T.D.B.
                                            Captain & Adjutant,
                                               for Lieut-Colonel,
11th:July,1918.   Commanding 5th:Battalion Machine Gun Corps.

Copies to :-   1.   5/Division.
               2.   13/Inf:Bde:
               3.   14/Inf:Bde:
               4.   95/Inf:Bde:
               5.   O.C."A" Company.
               6.   O.C."B" Company.
               7.   O.C."C" Company.
               8.   O.C."D" Company.
               9.   File.
              10.   War Diary.
              11.   do.
              12.   Office.

SECRET. No: 5 Battalion Machine Gun Corps.   Copy No:

Operation Order No: 15.
-o-o-o-o-o-o-o-O-o-o-o-o-o-o-o-o-o-o-

Reference Map 36.A. 1/40000.

1.   "A" Company will relieve "B" Company in the LE SART Sector on the night of the 18th:/19th:inst:. Details to be arranged between Company Commanders concerned.

2.   On relief, 3 Sections of "B" Company will withdraw to the Divisional Line and relieve 3 Sections of "D" Company. The fourth Section will relieve the Section of "D" Company at GRAND DAM LOCK, and come under the orders of O.C. "C" Company.

3.   On completion of relief "D" Company will withdraw to Divisional Reserve and will be accommodated in the Billets vacated by "A" Company in I.16.a.

4.   The Working Party detailed in W.16/3. of the 15th:inst: will be provided by "D" Company on the night of the relief. This Party will withdraw to Billets in I.16.a. on the completion of their Task.

5.   Completion of relief will be reported to Battalion H.Q in the B.A.B. Code.

6.   ACKNOWLEDGE.

Issued at 3.pm.   (sd). A.C. STANLEY, Captain & Adjutant
                                            for Lieut: Colonel,
16/7/18.   Commanding No: 5 Battalion Machine Gun Corps.
----------   ---

Copies to 1. 5/Division.
          2. 13/Inf: Bde:
          3. 15/   do:
          4. 95/   do.
          5. O.C. A. Company.
          6. O.C. B.   do:
          7. O.C. C.   do:
          8. O.C. D.   do:
          9. File.
         10. War Diary.
         11.   do:
         12. Office.

SECRET.   No: 5 Battalion Machine Gun Corps   Copy No:

Operation Order No: 18.

Reference Map 36.A. 1/40000.

1. "D" Company will relieve "C" Company in the ARREWAGE Sector on the night of the 24th/25th:inst:. Details to be arranged between Company Commanders concerned.

2. On relief 3 Sections of "C" Company will withdraw to the Divisional Line and relieve 3 Sections of "B" Company. The fourth Section will relieve the Section of "B" Company at GRAND DAM LOCK, and come under the orders of O.C."D" Company.

3. On completion of relief "B" Company will withdraw to Divisional Reserve and will be accommodated in the Billets vacated by "D" Company in I.16.a.

4. The Working Party detailed in U.16./3. of the 15th:inst will be provided by "B" Company on the night of the relief. This Party will withdraw to Billets in I.16.a. on Completion of their task.

5. Completion of relief will be reported to Battalion H.Q. in the B.A.B. Code.

6. ACKNOWLEDGE.

Issued at 10.30am.   (sd) A.C.Stanley
                                            Captain & Adjutant,
23/7/1918.   for Lieut-Colonel,
                              Commanding 5th;Battalion MachineGun Corp

Copies to :-
1. 5/Division.   7. O.C."B" Company.
2. O.C.,24/Bn:M.G.C.   8. O.C."C" Company.
3. 13/Inf:Bde: 9. O.C."D" Company.
4. 15/Inf:Bde;   10. War Diary.
5. 95/Inf:Bde: 11.   do:
6. O.C."A" Company.   12. Office.

SECRET.   No: 5 Battalion Machine Gun Corps.   COPY No:

Operation Order No: 10.

Reference Map 36.A. 1/40000.

1. "B" Company will relieve "A" Company in the LE SART Sector on the night of the 31st:July,/1st: August. Details will be arranged by the Commanding Officers concerned.

2. On relief 3 sections of "A" Company will withdraw to the Divisional Line and relieve 3 sections of "C" Company. The fourth section will relieve the section of "C" Company at GRAND DAM LOCK, and come under the orders of O.C."D" Company.

3. On completion of their relief "C" Company will withdraw to Divisional Reserve and will be accommodated in the billets vacated by "B" Company in I.16.a.

4. The working Party detailed in W.1 /6 dated 28/7/18., will be supplied by "C" Company on the night of 31st:July,/1st: August.

5. Completion of relief will be reported to Battalion H.Q. in the B.A.B. Code.

6. ACKNOWLEDGE.

Issued at 11.am.   (sd) F.W.Petrie Hay, Major,
28th:July, 1918.   for Lieut:-Colonel,
                    Commanding 5th:Battalion Machine Gun C.

Copies to -
1. 5/Division.   8. O.C."B" Company.
2. O.C.74/ Bn:M.G.C.   9. O.C."C" Company.
3. O.C.51/ Bn:M.G.C.   10. O.C."D" Company.
4. 13/ Inf: Bde: 11. War Diary.
5. 15/ Inf:Bde: 12. do:
6. 95/Inf: Bde: 13. Office.
7. O.C."A" Company.

Annexe to 5th Divisional Intelligence Summary.

Appreciation for week ending 26th July.

1. DISTRIBUTION OF ENEMY FORCES.

 (a) Order of Battle.
 There has been no alteration in the enemy's order of Battle opposite this Army front during the past week.
 (b) Reserves.
 There are 8 Divisions, 7 fresh and one moderately fresh, in reserve in the Sixth German Army.
 In Prince Rupprecht's Group of Armies there are 29 fresh Divisions available for immediate operations.

2. BRIDGES.
 A new heavy transport bridge has been built over the LYS (East of ESTAIRES) and another, also for heavy transport, is under construction (at ERQUINGHEM). Near MERVILLE two badly damaged heavy transport bridges have been replaced, one by a footbridge, the other by a light transport bridge, and, in addition, two extra footbridges have been placed across the BOURRE and one across the LYS.

3. GAS.

 Gas shelling was slight till July 24th since when it has increased. On that day Blue and Yellow Cross shell were included in the shelling of our front and support lines East of ROBECQ and in a concentration of 300 rounds on LES AMUSOIRES. Of 300 rounds fired on HAVERSKERQUE 100 were Yellow Cross. On July 25th some Blue and Yellow Cross were included in the shelling of LA MOTTE-au -BOIS, HAVERSKERQUE, and the area South of ROBECQ. A further increase in gas shelling occurred on July 26th. The HAVERSKERQUE area again received most attention, CROIX MARRAISSE in particular being subjected to a concentration of 500 Yellow Cross. The area North of LE PARC was shelled with H.E. and Yellow Cross for one and a half hours.

4. STRENGTH OF ARTILLERY.

 Fifty-nine new locations have been reported during the week. It is not considered, however, that this represents any real increase in strength of the enemy's artillery ; he is probably frequently changing the positions of his batteries to escape observation and the effects of our counter-battery fire. Most of the locations are opposite the centre of the Army front and it is possible that a re-grouping of portions of the enemy's artillery is taking place.

5. ENEMY'S INTENTIONS.

 The evidence from prisoners captured by this Army continues to be negative. None of the prisoners captured during the past week have seen any indications of a hostile offensive opposite this Army.
 Prisoners of the 16th Division, under special examination, stated that the 25th Division, whom they relieved on the night of 14th/15th July, expected to return into line on the night of July 27th/28th to support an attack further North, this attack might extend as far

/South

South as MERVILLE or be supported by a demonstration in the MERVILLE Sector.

Prisoners captured by the Army on our right state that no offensive action is contemplated in their Sectors. The attitude of the troops opposite the Army on our right is apparently entirely defensive.

Prisoners captured by the Army on our left state that an offensive in the BAILLEUL - KEMMEL area was to have taken place on the 18th inst, but has been postponed three times for unknown reasons.

A N.C.O. of a foot artillery battalion captured by the FRENCH in CHAMPAGNE states that heavy T.Ms had left the CHAMPAGNE front for the KEMMEL area.

6. APPRECIATION.

There has been some change in the enemy's attitude during the past week. After three weeks of exceptional quiet, raids have been attempted, patrols have become more active, and arty. fire has considerably increased.

Except for this somewhat apprehensive attitude on the part of the enemy the situation is unchanged.

There are no further indications of an offensive against this Army front, and it appears that the French counter-stroke has made the enemy postpone his FLANDERS offensive. But as long as the Crown Prince Rupprecht retains his large reserve of 29 Divisions this offensive must be reckoned with.

-:-:-:-:-:-:-:-:-:-

ANNEXE TO 5TH: DIVISIONAL INTELLIGENCE SUMMARY.

Extracts from Army Summary.

1. ORDER OF BATTLE.   (a). The 187th: Division relieved the 39th: Division in the NEUF BERQUIN Sector on the night July 13/14th:.

The 16th: Division after 10 days out of the Line returned to the MERVILLE Sector and relieved the 25th: Division on the 16/17th: July.

There is no change in the Order of Battle of the remaiming four Divisions opposite the Army Front. These have all been identified by contact during the week.

RESERVES.   (b). There are 5 fresh and 3 tired Divisions in reserve in the Sixth German Army.

In Prince RUPPRECHT'S Group of Armies there are still a total of 26 fit Divisions available for active operations.

2. ENEMY'S INTENTION.   With one exception, none of the Prisoners captured during the past week, have any knowledge of, nor have they seen any preparations for an offensive opposite this Army.

A Prisoner of the 220th: Division under Special examination stated that he had seen much artillery moving forward at night on the ESTAIRES - LOCON Road, and that there were Dumps of YELLOW and BLUE Cross Shells on the roadside.

Several Prisoners had heard from Officers that an offensive was shortly to take place in the KEMMEL area. The usual Trench rumours to this effect have also been prevalent.

Evidence from the statements of Prisoners captured by the Army on our Left, continues to indicate that an attack in the YPRES area is iminent.

3. APPRECIATION.   Strong evidence points to the Attack on the YPRES - HAZEBROUCK front being iminemt, and it is uncertain how far South this will extend.

The return of the 16th: Division to its original (MERVILLE) Sector and the withdrawal of the 25th: Division which is an assault Division is significant. The 25th: Division had been doing a month's intensive training (somewhere with cars representing Tanks) previous to taking over the 16th: Divisional Front and is now probably destined for the offensive.

The enemy's rear organisation is complete and an Attack on the BETHUNE Front by fresh Divisions passing through tired Divisions now holding the line appears possible although there is no definite evidence that points to this.

4. NOTES ON THE HOSTILE DIVISIONS OPPOSITE OUR FRONT.   The 187th: Division, now in the NEUF BERQUIN Scetor, was withdrawn from the GAVRELLE Sector on July 6th: and rested until the 13/14th: July, It is a fairly fresh Division of average quality. The 16th: Division returned to the MERVILLE Sector after a rest of 10 Days at LILLE. It was withdrawn because of the epidemic of P.U.O. which had rendered it too weak to hold the Line. It has already done two turns in the MERVILLE Sector and suffered severly on both occasions. Prisoners have already said that this Division consisted of Position Troops.

SECRET.

MACHINE GUN MAP.

REFERENCE MAP 36A N.E. 1:20.000

W. 14/13
16-7-18

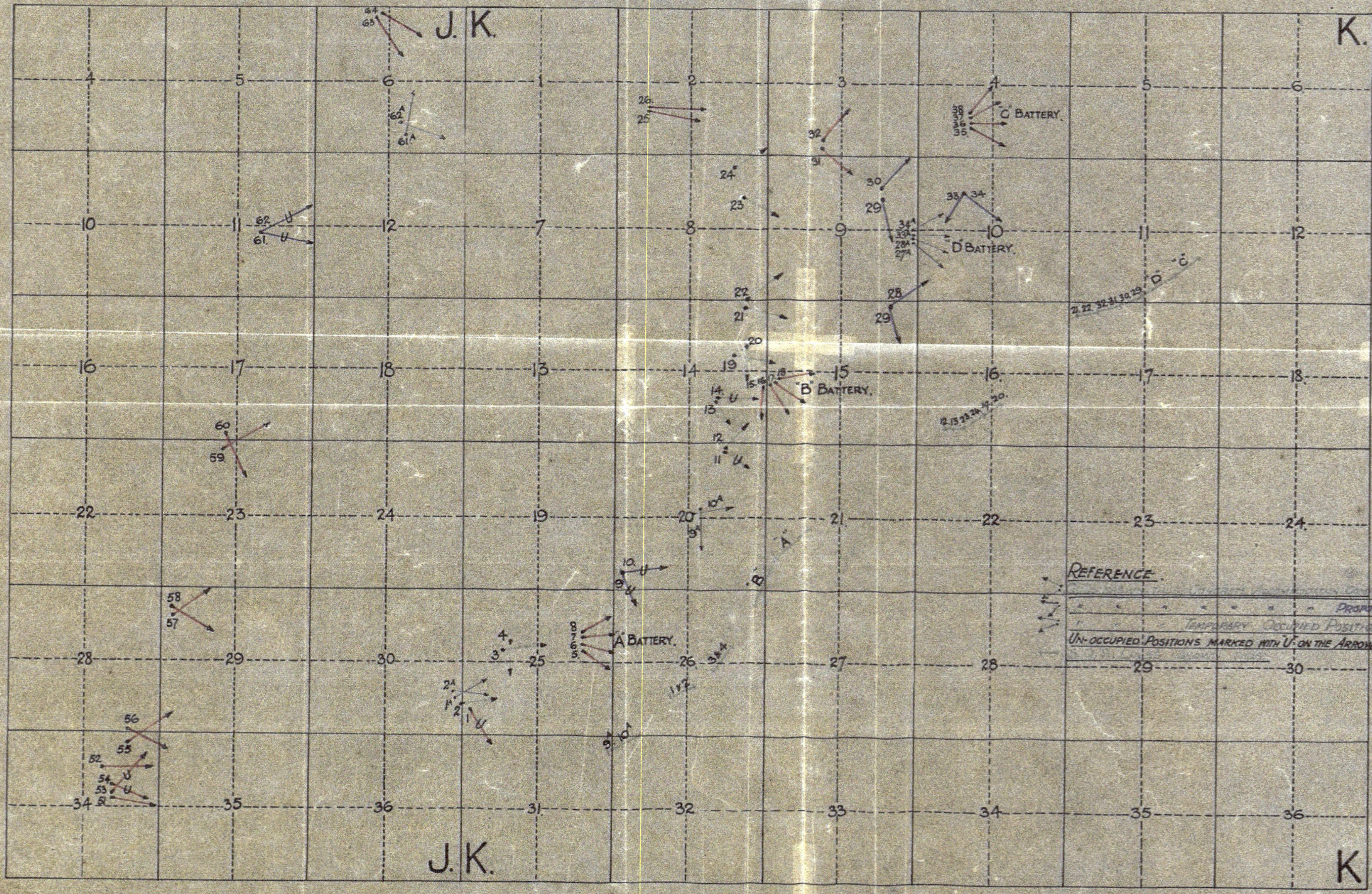
J.K.
K.
C BATTERY.
D BATTERY.
B BATTERY.
A BATTERY.
REFERENCE.
PROPOSED.
TEMPORARY OCCUPIED POSITIONS
UN-OCCUPIED POSITIONS MARKED WITH U ON THE ARROW.
J.K.
K

Army Form W. 3724.

TRAINING PROGRAMME FOR WEEK ENDING 21st July, 1918.

Corps.	Division and Location of H.Q.	Brigade and Location of H.Q.	Description of Training.	Approximate Date of Commencement and Completion of Training.	REMARKS. (Time and place of Divisional, Brigade and Battalion Exercises).
XI Corps.	5/Division. "D" Company, 5/Bn.M.G.C. (1.18.a.7/5) Sheet 36.A. 1/40000.		Physical Training - Arm Drill - Gun Drill. Instruction in Barrage work - Stripping and repairs. - Anti-Gas Drill - Immediate Action and Mechanism - Cleaning and overhauling of Guns - O.C., Company's Inspection - Kit Inspection - Advanced Gun Drill. Recreational Training - Parade of junior N.C.O's under the C.S.M.	21st July to 28th July.	
	"B" Company. 5/Bn.M.G.C. Advanced H.Q. at J.27.d.5/3.		NIL		Employed under the R.E's in the construction of concrete Emplacements.

(Sd) A.E. Healey,
Captain & Adjutant,
for Lieut-Colonel,
Commanding 5th Battalion Machine Gun Corps.

17/7/18.

Army Form W. 3724.

TRAINING PROGRAMME FOR WEEK ENDING July 28th

Map Reference Sheet 56. 1/40000.

Corps.	Division and Location of H.Q.	Brigade and Location of H.Q.	Description of Training.	Approximate Date of Commencement and Completion of Training.	REMARKS. (Time and place of Divisional, Brigade and Battalion Exercises).
XI Corps.	5/Division.				
		"B" Company, 5/Bn:M.G.C. Headquarters at T.16.a.7/5.	Cleaning of Gun Equipment & Limbers - Physical & Bayonet and Recreational Training - Gun Drill - Stripping and assembling of Guns - Tactical Schemes (M.Guns in Attack & Defence and Advanced Guards) - Company Drill - Anti Gas Drill - Infantry Drill by Sections - Lecture to N.C.O's on Trench Duties - Training of Rangefinders & Signallers - Lectures by Section Officers on Compass & Map Reading.	25th: to 30th:July.	To Trenches on 30/31st: July, 1918.
		"C" Company, 5/Bn:M.G.C. Headquarters at T.16.a.7/5.	Inspection of Guns & Equipment - Combined Gun Drill - Immediate Action - Range with M.G's, firing and stoppages - Physical Training & Bayonet Fighting - Lectures by O.C. Company on Discipline - Lectures to N.C.O's on Discipline and Duties.	31st:July, to 5th:August.	From the Line to Divisional Reserve on 30/31st:July, 1918.
		"A" Company, 5/Bn:M.G.C.	Stripping and assembling of Guns and Equipment - Mechanism - Musketry - Anti-Gas Drill - Indication & Recognition of Targets - Range Cards.	31/July, to 5th:August.	From Line to Divisional Line 30/31st:July, 1918.

(sd) A.E.Stanley Captain & Adjutant,
for Lieut-Colonel,
Commanding No: 5 Battalion Machine Gun Corps.

24/7/1918.

INCREASES AND DECREASES IN BATTALION STRENGTH DURING PERIOD 1st: to 31st: JULY, 1918.

	Officers.	O.R's.		offrs:	O.R.
Strength on 1st: July.	39.	862.			
Nos: joining from Base Depot and rejoining from C.C.S.	9.	86.			
	48.	948.			
Battle Casualties &c:	3.	86.	Killed	-	2.
			Wounded	-	62.
			Missing	-	1.
			Evactd: to C.C.S. Sick.	-	15.
			To U.K.	2.	3.
Strength on 31st: July.	45.	862.	Transferred to Base Dept:	1.	-
				3.	86.

WR 5

C O N F I D E N T I A L.

Original Copy.

Register Number. W20/5/5
Part No: ....5....
Volume No: ....1....

No: 5 Battalion Machine Gun Corps.

W A R   D I A R Y.

for the Month of

A U G U S T - 1 9 1 8.

P.H. Cutting

Lieut: - Colonel,

Commanding No: 5 Battalion Machine Gun Corps.

Original

Army Form C. 2118.
Ref: Maps. 36 A. 1/40000
LENS. II. 1/20000
57. FRANCE. 1/40000

Sheet 1.

No. 5 BATTALION.
MACHINE GUN

No. W.20/5.
Date. 31 Aug: 1918.

WAR DIARY
INTELLIGENCE SUMMARY.
(Erase heading not required.)

August 1918.

Instructions regarding War Diaries and Intelligence Summaries are contained in F. S. Regs., Part II. and the Staff Manual respectively. Title pages will be prepared in manuscript.

Place	Date	Hour	Summary of Events and Information	Remarks and references to Appendices
In Line (with 3 Coys approximately) FORET de NIEPPE to CANAL de la LYS	1st.	—	Weather fine. Situation Normal. Our artillery particularly active during night causing several fires in the enemy lines. Hostile guns were very active the GRAND DEVISE area & also heavily shelled at 3am; principally gas shells active & slight during day. at 4pm. the road in K.15a & 20 was heavily gas shelled & VII ROMA received special attention. Our M.Guns expended 9000 rounds on various targets in the enemy forward area. One hostile M.Gun troublesome, firing on areas K.15a and K.14d. Casualties — NIL. —	For strength of Battalion see appended list.
-do:-	2d.	—	Weather wet. Situation Normal. Our Rum/Sec active on NEUF BERQUIN — K.25c — ANCHOVY FARM — LES PURESBECQUES and carried out harassing fire at night. Hostile artillery very active on area around K.P.6. 60/60. from midnight to 4am. (Gas), VIETES ad BRISTOL PARK received some attention 8" shells falling in the latter. Our M.Guns fired 13,500 rounds in half minute bursts on the following Targets: 4 guns on K.17b. 4/2 at 12-2am. 8 guns on K.22d. 1/4 at 12-2am. 4 guns on K.18.c. 3/6, 4 guns on K.17a. 30/20. 4 guns on tracks K.15d 60/60 & K.17a. 40/20. 4 guns on K.17.b. 3//30. at irregular intervals in cooperation with Left Battalion (D.C.L.I). Casualties — NIL —	Lieut. Col.; Comdg: No: 5 Battalion M.G. Corps

Sheet 2.

Army Form C. 2118.

No. 5 BATTALION
MACHINE GUN
CORPS.
W.20/5.
31/Aug/1918

WAR DIARY
INTELLIGENCE SUMMARY
(Erase heading not required.)

Instructions regarding War Diaries and Intelligence Summaries are contained in F.S. Regs., Part II. and the Staff Manual respectively. Title pages will be prepared in manuscript.

Place	Date	Hour	Summary of Events and Information	Remarks and references to Appendices
In line	3rd:	—	Weather wet. Situation Quiet. Usual activity by our artillery on MERVILLE and LES PURESBECQUE. The enemy's trenches in K.16.B.&c. were engaged and LE SART was shelled a Trench Mortar Dump being destroyed. Hostile guns were active on our back areas all day, and especially so at 1am. & 3am: when concentrated bursts of fire were put down on VIA ROMA, Support Batt. H.Q. (Right Sector) and the area K.23.a. A large percentage of shells being Yellow Cross (Gas). Our M.Gs. fired 13,500 rounds on the enemy forward areas and tracks as follows: 12 guns fired on K.17.a 80/20. from 9pm. to midnight, 12 guns on PURESBECQUES at 10.23 pm. 10 guns on COURTREFROIE FARM at 10·45 pm: 8 guns on GENET CORNER at 10·45 pm. 8 on K.16.a.1/9 at 11·25 pm: 10 guns on the Cross roads at K.22.a. 4/4. See app: A/3. All guns fired half minute bursts. Casualties NIL. Hostile fired occasionally during night on our tracks etc: in K.21.b 85/90. Warning Order received from H.Q. 5/Divsn: re relief of Divsion by 61st Div: commencing 5/3/8.	For Warning Order re Relief see app: A/2. For dispositions notated over to the 61 Divn: See app: A/3.
– do: –	4th:	—	Weather fine. Our artillery active both day and night. Hostile flashes Guns active especially opposite LE SART Section where a heavy barrage put down about 1am. Our's carried out harassing fire on the usual	

A7092 Wt. W128.9/M1293. 750,000. 1/17. D.D & I. Ltd. Forms/C2118/14.

Sheet 2.

Army Form C. 2118.

No. 5 BATTALION,
MACHINE GUN
CORPS.
N/ 20/5.
31 Aug 1918

WAR DIARY
INTELLIGENCE SUMMARY.
(Erase heading not required.)

Ref. Sheet 36A. 1/40000.

Place	Date contd.	Hour	Summary of Events and Information	Remarks and references to Appendices
Ineches HK.			Targets in the enemy's forward area. "E" Company move from Divl. Reserve in 1.16.a.7/8. to ROCQUETOIRE Sub-area moving under orders of B.G.C. 13th J. Bde.... Casualties — NIL —	
— do: —		5h.	Weather wet. Situation Normal. Our guns very active shelling NIEPPE — RENNET FARM — LES PURES BECQUES and enemy tracks in the vicinity of K.16.a.&.7. the enemy guns were active on CROIX MARRAISE — INFANTRY ROW — DOLLS HOUSE Vicinity throughout the night. Our M.Gs active on enemy ar..? during the day and at night expended 13,500 rounds on the following Targets:- Bridge at K.29.a.4/8. — Cross roads K.24.a.0/6. — Cross roads K.22.d.1/7. — CORNER COTTAGE — ATOM FARM and the usual harassing of enemy tracks. "A" Comp. withdrawn from Divisional line on relief by the 65th. Bn. M.G. Corps. and march to Bicrets in PECQUER 1.20.c. "B" Company from line on relief by Company of the 66th. Bn. M.G. Corps. withdrawing from line to bivcets in 1.16.a. Casualties NIL	
— do: —		6h.	Weather wet Situation Normal. "E" Company move to HEURINGHEN with the 13th J. Bde. and under Rear orders. "A" & "B" Companies move under orders of B.G.C. 93/J/B.?	

A7092 Wt. w125 9/M1293. 750,000. 1/17. D. D & I. Ltd. Forms/C2118/14.

Sheet H
Army Form C. 2118.

No. 5 BATTALION.
MACHINE GUN
No. W.S. 20/5.
Date 31/Aug/1918.

WAR DIARY
or
INTELLIGENCE SUMMARY.
(Erase heading not required.)

Place	Date	Hour	Summary of Events and Information	Remarks and references to Appendices
WARDRECQUES Area. 36 A 1/40000	6th	—	"D" Company from ARRENAGE relieves section to PECQUES on relief by Company of the 6bh: Bn: M.G. Corps. Casualties — NIL —	
	7th	—	This Companies move into WARDRECQUES area. Battn H.Qrs: situated in BLARENCHEM, Companies situated as follows. A Company WITTES, "C" Company at RACQUINGHEM, "B" Company at RACQUINGHEM, D Company at BLARENGHEM.	For details see Appendix a/2.
	8th	—		
— do: —	—	—	Resting —	
	13th	—	Training carried out see Appendix B/1.	
	14th	—	This Division now to FREVENT — DOULLENS area. Battalion HQrs: and 4 Companies billeted in FREVENT.	Details of Entrainment.
FREVENT 15th Sheet 57D 1/40 000.	15th	—	This. Battn. Relieg. Lieut. WARNER and 10 O.R. from Base Depot. Training carried out by Companies. 8-30 to 9am: Arm Drill. 9-9.30am P.T. 10.- 10.30am: Gas Drill. 10-45 to 12-30pm: Route March - 5 Miles introducing simple tactical schemes. 2-3pm: Explanation of Tactical scheme by O.C. Companies to Officers and N.C.O.'	Present N.C.O. Off: P/4.

Sheet 5.

Army Form C. 2118.

WAR DIARY
OF
INTELLIGENCE SUMMARY.
(Erase heading not required.)

Place	Date	Hour	Summary of Events and Information	Remarks and references to Appendices
FREVENT.	16th		Weather fine. Training as follows:- Physical Training. 10am to 12pm Tactical Scheme, Attack & Defence including Fire Direction – Method of Advance – Concealment of positions and approaches. 2-3pm Limber Drill. Citron Poles etc by N.C.O's. Companies to Officers and N.C.O's Lieut. FITCH proceeds on leave.	See Appendix a/5.
do	17th		Weather Dull. The Battalion inspected by the G.O.C. 5th Division. Lieuts. FOSKETT and GOULD report off leave.	
do	18th		Weather Showery. Orders received at 2pm to be prepared to move at short notice. Battn: Noved to DOULLENS, marching via BOUQUEMAISON app w/o/6 and billeted in the CITTADELLE DOULLENS.	Appendix w/o/6
DOULLENS	19th		Weather fine. Battn: move to Brulart area as follows:- Ref: Sheet 57D/NE 1/20000 1/80000 {"C" Company to Bayencourt Area wk 15/8/4/40. (7.Inf.4/5) 30. w/18 wk/ "A" Company to COUIN Area wk 13/H/Bde. (Incl. 94) received. "B" Company to COIGNEUX Area wk 95/Inf. Bde. (7.30.9/5). op. 7 "D" Company to COUIN Area wk 13/Inf. Bde. (U.26.31)	

Sheet 6.

Army Form C. 2118.

No. 5 BATTALION MACHINE GUN
W.20/5.
Date 31 Aug: 1918.

WAR DIARY
or
INTELLIGENCE SUMMARY.
(Erase heading not required.)

Place	Date	Hour	Summary of Events and Information	Remarks and references to Appendices
FONQUEVILLER SECTOR.	20th	—	Weather fine. Battn. reaches forward area in lorries & marches to assembly point. Battn. near Hd Qrs. at BULLS or Gap.	
	21st.	—	Weather holding temporarily. Battn. near Hd Qrs. at BULLS or Gap. Marching to SUASTRE via AUTHIE & COUIN.	
			Weather fine, subsequently. Attack by K. 37/ Bde. on BUCQUOY & vicinity successfully accomplished ad 5/55am. Battn. through to Bn. Ob. "Leichtar" near 1st objective. Lt. F.N. ROBSON M.C. wounded. (Died of wds 27/8/18) Also 5 J.E.F. PACKER. 2/Lt. A WARNER wounded. Also 2/Lt. A.S. RICHARDSON 1.8 Major O.COOPER	Casualties Hs. 21/8/18 tote 21/8/18 to 31/8/18 see appx. c/-8
	22nd.	—	Weather fine. Reorganisation of the units of Bn. take place. No attack. Little Shelling against enemy	
	23rd.	—	Weather fine. 95/3f. Bde. & 15f.J. Bde. carry oih attack commency at 11am. Lieut. P.C. COUTTS killed in action.	
	24th.	—	Weather fine. Reorganising of Companies. B Company established their forward guns to Coy. H.Q. of L Co. 15f.J.C. to Coy H.Q. at L. Hd. 5020.	
	25th.	—	Fine. One status of Companies will Rue Brigade Groups "A & D" Companies with 13/J.5. Bde. R Company with 95/J.F. Bde. and C Company with the 15/J.F. Bde. B Echelon transport moved to BUCQUOY.	

Sheet 4.

Army Form C2118.
MACHINE GUN CORPS.
No. Y. Coy
Date 3/9/18

WAR DIARY
or
INTELLIGENCE SUMMARY.
(Erase heading not required.)

Place	Date	Hour	Summary of Events and Information	Remarks and references to Appendices
	26th		Weather fine. Attack carried out by the 13/Inf.Bde. "A" Company taking part in operations.	For details of operations See Appx. of 8
	27th		Fine. Interp. Section relief carried out by "B" Company.	
	28th		Weather fine. Preparations made for attack on the enemy positions in l.14.b.8d. 2 Sections of 'D' Company co-operated with 7th No 8 K. on the attack. Intermittent hostile shelling of our backwaters.	
	29th		Fine. The 95th Inf Bde relieved the 13/Inf Bde in the Echelon B. Transport of Bn this move to S.16a. Hostile aircraft very active.	
	30th		Fine. A Company withdrawn to reserve in G.12.d.95. B Company relieved the former guard of D in the enemy lines & came back & issued the SHRIKE - Batn. HQ. moved from ETRICOURT to SAPIGNIES.	
	31st		Fine. Notable arty fairly quiet except for good deal of gas shelly on our back areas. A.A. Was successfully dropped by the R.A.F. on all M.G. positions at Hill 120. NZ Divin. on right flank attacked W.452. reached their objectives.	

A.H. Catters Lieut-Col.
Comdg: No: 5/Bn. M.G.Corps

Original

Appendix "A"
War Diary
5/Battn: Machine Gun Corps
August 1918

		Officers	O.R's.
Battalion Strength on 1.8.18.		45.	883.

		Officers	O.R's.
INCREASE. during the Month.	From C.C.S.	-	16.
	From M.G.Corps Base Depot..........	7.	85.

		Officers	O.R's.
DECREASE. during the Month.	Casualties.		
	Killed............................	3.	9.
	Wounded...........................	2.	57.
	Missing...........................	-	7.
	To C.C.S. Sick....................	1.	63.
	To U.K..............duty.........	1.	4.
	Total Decrease.	7.	140.

		Officers	O.R's.
Battalion Stemgth on 31.8.18.		45.	844.

No: 5 Battalion   Machine Gun Corps.

Officer Reinforcements from Base Depot during the Month of AUG: '18.

2/LIEUT: J. HOLLOWAY.   joined 25/8/18.
2/LIEUT: A.F. FROST.   joined 25/8/18.
2/LIEUT: C. MASON.   joined 25/8/18.

2/LIEUT: T.D. PARRY.   joined 28/8/18.
2/LIEUT: H.E. PICKERING.   joined 28/8/18.
2/LIEUT: G. SHAW.   joined 28/8/18.

2/LIEUT: H. JONES.   joined 30/8/18.

No: 5 Battalion Machine Gun Corps.

List of AWARDS to N.C.O's and Men of the above Battalion during the month of AUGUST, 1918.

16209. Sgt: S. PRETTY. D.C.M.
22641. Sgt: B. RICHARDS., M.M.
31209. Cpl: G. GARFITT., M.M.
15356. Cpl: J. JACKSON., M.M.
149498. L/C. E. MEAD., M.M.
50557. Pte: W.M. Mc:FADYEN, M.M.
20412. Pte: S. STEER. M.M.
14328. Pte: J. STONE., M.M

        For gallantry and devotion to duty during the operations of the 5th: Division East of the FORET de NIEPPE on the 28th: June, 1918.

SECRET.   Copy No: 12.

5th: DIVISION OPERATION ORDER NO: 243.

Reference Sheet 36.A. 1/40000.   4th: August, 1918.

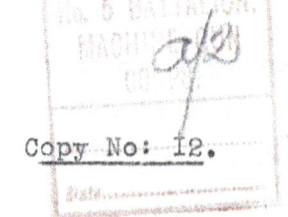

1. The orders for the relief of the 95th: Infantry Brigade in the Line by the 13/Infantry Brigade are cancelled.

2. The 5th: Division will be relieved by the 61st: Division in accordance with the attached Table.

3. Details of the relief of the Divisional Artillery and Field Ambulances will be arranged between C's R.A. and A.D.M.Ss concerned. Details of relief of Field Companies and Pioneers will be arranged between C's R.E.

4. All Defence Schemes. Maps. Aeroplane Photographs, and Trench Stores will be handed over to the incoming Units.

5. Units not mentioned in the attached Table will march under the orders of the A.A. & Q.M.G.

6. The Command of the Divisional Sector will pass to the G.O.C., 61st: Division at 10.am., 7th: August, at which hour 5th: Divisional H.Q. will open at WARDRECQUES.

7. ACKNOWLEDGE.

Issued at 5.pm.   (sd). GW.GORDON.HALL, Lieut;-Colonel,
                                              General Staff, 5th: Division.

Copies to   1. XI Corps "G"   2. XI Corps "Q"
            3. 31st: Division.   4. 74th: Division.
            5. 61st: Division.   6. 13/Inf: Bde:
            7. 15/Inf: Bde: 8. 95/Inf: Bde:
            9. C.R.A.   10. C.R.E.
           11. 1/6th: A. & S. Hrs: 12. 5th. Battn: M.G.C.
           13. A.D.M.S.   14. D.A.D.O.S.
           15. 5th: Division "Q"   16. 5th Divnl: Train.
           17. S.S.O.   18. 5th: Signal Company.
           19. War Diary.   20. War Diary.
           21. Office Copy.   22. A.P.M.
           23. Camp Commandant.

SECRET.

5th: Division No: C.C. /637.

Administration Instructions to accompany 5th: Division
Order No: 243 Ref: Sheet / 36. A. NE. and N.W. I/20000.
----

1. The Division on the move will be accommodated in the WARDRECQUES area with the Divisional Artillery in the NORRENT FONTES area.

2. SUPPLIES. The 13/Infantry Brigade will draw from (AIRE) to-morrow by Motor Transport. Change of Railhead for the Division will be notified later.

3. Transport Echelons will move full. The Grenade Limber to be packed half with Grenades and half with S.A.A.

4. TENTAGE. All Units, will, as far as the time permits, strike all Tentage not taken over by the 61st: Division and deliver it to the Area Commandant, BOESEGHEM or Town Major, TANNAY. Where this cannot be done Units will leave a note with the Area Commandant, BOESEGHEM or the Town Major, TANNAY saying where the tentage is and the numbers.

5. BILLETS, CAMPS and HORSE LINES. The greatest care will be taken to leave all Billets, Camps, and Horse Lines scrupously clean.

6. The Camp Commandant will arrange for the D.A.D.O.S. and "WHIZZBANGS" and the Canteen to be accommodated in the Divnl: H.Q. on the move.

7. BATHS. Baths together with the un-issued clothing will be handed over and receipts taken.

8. HARVESTING. All agricultiral implements issued to Units for the harvesting of crops will be handed over to the relieving Units of the 61st: Division and receipts taken.
   D.A. Officer will inform the D.A.O., 61st: Div; the location of Ricks and any crops cut in the area and not carried in order that the harvest may be completed by the incoming Units. Also the general Scheme for harvesting the area.

9. TRENCH and AREA STORES. All area and Trench Stores will be handed over and receipts obtained. Particular care must be taken to ensure the 1.000 petrol-tins for each Brigade on the Line are handed over.
   The anti-Gas Clothing recently issued and also stocks of S.D. Clothing to replace "Gassed" Clothing will be treated as Trench or area Stores.

10. AMMUNITION DUMPS. Ammunition Dumps will be handed over by the Unit in whose area the Dump is situated. The Dumps in the Corps Line will be handed over as follows:-

   At J.26.b.2/3. at present looked after by the Traffic control at that place, by the A.P.M. to A.P.M., 61st: Division.

   Dumps near JACKSON Siding (J13.b.9.2.) and in the Trench at J.I.d. and J.7.b. together with the ration dumps at VISNADELLA CAMP, will be handed over by the 1/6th; A. & S. Hrs: to the Battalion of the incoming Unit. taking over the VISNADELLA CAMP.

   Dump at the Town Major's Camp, NIEEPE FOREST (J.15.c.5.3.- will be handed over by the Area Commandant to Area Commandant, 61st: Division.

P.T.O.

11. RECEPTION CAMP.   Will close and be handed over at a date to be notified later.

12. CANTEEN.   Billets and Sheds will be handed over direct between Canteen Officers.

No Canteen Stores will be handed over.

13. SALVAGE.   Salvage Officer will hand over all Dumps to the Salvage Officer, 61st: Division.

14. LORRIES.   Lorries will be detailed to assist Brigades and Units moving. Detail will be published separately.

15. RECONNAISSANCE LORRIES.   One Lorry for each R.F.A. Brigade 15th: and 95Th: Infantry Brigades will report at H.Q., 5th: Divisional Artillery and Rear H.Q. of Infantry Brigades at 10.am., to morrow, to take Staff Captains and Parties to the new area to arrange Billeting.

ACKNOWLEDGE.   (sd). O.W. WHITE. Lieut:-Colonel, A.A. & Q.M.G., 5th: Division.

SECRET.

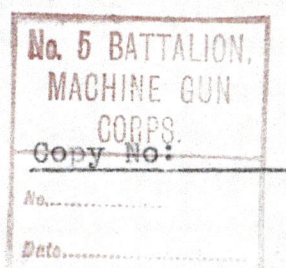

No: 5 Battalion Machine Gun Corps.

Operation Order No: 21.

Reference Map 36.A. 1/40000.

1. No: 5 Battalion Machine Gun Corps will be relieved by the 61st: Battn: M.G.Corps. in the Line in accordance with the attached Table.

2. Details of relief to be arranged between Company Commanders concerned.

3. All Defence Schemes, Maps, Aeroplane Photographs, and Trench Stores will be handed over to the incoming Companies.

4. The Working Party detailed in W.16/8 dated 28th:July,1918, is cancelled.

5. Completion of relief to be reported to Battalion H.Q. in the B.A.B. Code.

6. ACKNOWLEDGE.

Issued at 10.pm.   (sd) F.W. PETRIE-HAY,   Major,
                                                      for Lieut:-Colonel,

4th:August,1918.   Commanding No: 5 Battalion Machine Gun Corps.

Copies to 1. 5/Divn: 9. "B" Company.
           2. 61st:BN:M.G.C.   10. "C" Company.
           3. 74th:Bn: M.G?C.   11. "D" Company.
           4. 31st:Bn: M.G.C.   12. War Diary.
           5. 13/Inf:Bde: 13.   do:
           6. 15/Inf:Bde: 14. Office.
           7. 95/Inf:Bde:
           8. "A" Company.

Date.	Company.	From	To.	Remarks.
5/6th: August.	"A" Company.	Line.	PECQUER. 5/Bn;M.G.C. H.Q. £20c5/3	Rear H.Q. to take over Billets by 4.p.m. Gelules 1 Section attached "D" Company.
do:	"B" Company.	Line.	I.16.a.	Representative from Rear H.Q. to take over Billets from Company of 61st: Bn: M.G.Corps. before 4.pm.
do:	"C" Company.	ROCQUETOIRE Sub-Area.	HEURINGHEM Sub-Area.	March under the orders of the B.G.C., 13/Infantry Brigade.
6/7th: August.	"A" Company.	PECQUER. £20c5/3	RACQUINGHEM Sub-Area.	March under the orders of the B.G.C.,95/Infantry Brigade.
do:	"B" Company.	I.16.a.	do:	do:
6/7th: August.	"D" Company.	Line.	I.16.a.	Party from Rear H.Q. to take over Billets before "B" Company move.
7th: Aug:	Battalion H.Q.	PECQUER. £20c5/3	—	Destination will be notified later.

S E C R E T.

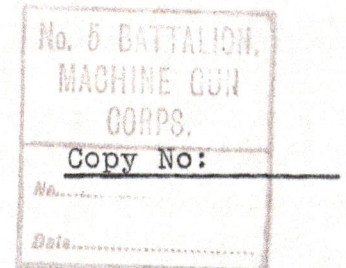

5th: Battalion Machine Gun Corps.

Operation Order No: 20
----

1.   "C" Company will move with the 13/infantry Brigade.
and No: 2 Company Train to ROCQUETOIRE Sub-area at 3.pm.

2.   The Company will be under the orders of the B?G.C.
13/Infantry Brigade and the order for the move will be issued
by the 13/inf:Bde:.

3.   One Officer to report to the 13/Inf:Bde: H.Q. at
STEENBECQUE. as a Billeting Representative at 3.pm. to day.

Issued at 2.pm. 3.8.18.   (sd). A.J.SHANKS., Captain & A/Adj

                                           No: 5 Battn: Machine Gun Corps.

Copies to O.C's Companies.
         13/Inf:Bde;
         War Diary.
         Office.

SECRET   Copy No. 11

No.5 Battalion. Machine Gun Corps,

Operation Order No. 21/I.

1. "D" Company on relief will come under the orders of the B.G.C. 15th Infantry Brigade. and will move to WITTES on 7th August under orders issued by that Office.

2. Battalion H.Q. will close at BECQUEUR (I.20.c.8.3.) at 10 7th August, and will open at BLARINGHEM (B.22.d) on arrival.

6.8.18.
Issued at 6 p.m.

                                                                       Major,
                                              for Lieut. Colonel,
                   Commanding No.5 Bn. Machine Gun Corps.

Copies to
1. 5/Divn.
2. 61st Bn. M.G.C.
3. 13/Inf. Bde
4. 15/Inf. Bde
5. 95/Inf. Bde
6. O.C. "A" Company
7. O.C. "B" Company
8. O.C. "C" Company
9. O.C. "D" Company
10. War Diary
11. do do
12. Office.

S E C R E T.

Copy No: a/4

5th: Division Operation Order No: 244.

12th: August.

The 5th: Division will move to-morrow by train.

Instructions for and the times of entrainment will be issued by 5th: Division "Q".

ACKNOWLEDGE.

Issued at II.pm.   (sd) G.W. GORDON. HALL, Lt; - Col;
-----------------   General Staff, 5th: Division.

O.C. "A" Company.
O.C. "B" Company.
O.C. "C" Company.
O.C. "D" Company.

W.23/34.

    Reference the Order for Entrainment please note the following amendment:-

St: OMER STATION.

  Train No: I................For "A" Company: read "C" Company.
  Train No: 7................For "D" Company: read "A" Company.
  Train No: 9................For "C" Company: read "D" Company.

    Brigade H.Qrs: will issue the necessary instructions to the Companies attached to their Group.

12th: August, 1918.   (sd) A.J.SHANKS., Captain & A/Adjutant
            for Lieut; - Colonel,
     Commanding Nº: 5 Battn: Machine Gun Corps.

SECRET.   5th: Division No: C.C./639.

ADMINISTRATIVE INSTRUCTIONS FOR THE ENTRAINMENT OF THE DIVISION.

Reference Sheet 36.A. - 1/40000.   12th: August, 1918.

1. The Division will entrain in accordance with the attached Tables).

2. ENTRAINING STATIONS.

   (A). ARQUES. Side and endloading Ramps. Water Troughs in the Station Yard. 5 Horses at a time.
Drinking Water in the Station.
In case of neccesity the yard and the small square in front of the Station can be used for concentration purposes.

   (B). St: OMER. Side Loading Ramps.(2). Water Troygh in the Station Yard. - good Supply.
Drinking Water in the Yard.
Concentration on the St: OMER Canal Bank.

   (C). WIZERNES. Side and endloading Ramps.
Water from the River South of Concentration Field.
Drinking Water in the Station.
Concentration Area - Field immediately South of the Station.

There are Latrines at each Station.

3. DETRAINING STATIONS. and the date and time of entrainment will be notified later.

4. GENERAL INSTRUCTIONS. Attention is directed to the General Instructions which accompanied this Office No: C.C./639 dated 8th: August, 1918.

With reference to para: 6. the per the parties for duty at each Entraining Station will be detailed as follows:-

ARQUES. By the 1/ th: A.& S.Hrs: Headquarters.
St: OMER. By the 1/6th: A.& S.Hrs: Headquarters.
WIZERNES. By the 15/Infantry Brigade.

The Trench Mortar Batteries(Medium) will supply any parties required by the Divisional Artillery.
In addition to the Officers detailed in para: 7 each Brigade will detail an Officer for duty at each Detraining Station. These will proceed by the Trains taking the first Units of the Brigade in each case.

5. POLICE. The A.P.M. will detail 1 N.C.O. and 6 men for Traffic Control at each of the Entraining Station.
Brigades will be responsible for the Police and Traffic Control, arrangements at Detraining Stations.

6. MOTOR TRANSPORT. The Motor Ambulances of the 3 Field Ambulances (less 6) will proceed by Road as one convoy. Destination and time of departure will be notified later.
Two Motor Ambulances with the necessary personnel will be on duty at each Entraining Station until the departure of the last train, when they will also proceed by Road as one Convoy.

All other Motor Transport will proceed by Road.

7. **LORRIES.** Lorries for the conveyance of Baggage and stores to the Entraining Stations will be detailed as follows:-

At 10.am., 13th: August.

Headquarters 13/Infantry Brigade. HEURINGHEM for Bde: H.Q. and
L.T.M. Battery.

H.Q., 2nd: K.O.S.B.A.28.a.4.5................I.
H.Q., 1st: R.W.Kents.........................I.
H.Q., 14th: R.Warwicks.......................I.
H.Q., 15th: R.Warwicks.......................I.

At 4.pm., 13th: August

Divisional H.Q..............................I.

At 2.pm., 13th: August.
H.Q. 95/Inf:Bde:, RACQUINGHEM for Bde: H.Q. and L.T.M.Batty:.2
H.Q., 1st: Devons...........................I.
H.Q., 1st: Bedfords.........................I.
H.Q., 1st: D.C.L.I..........................I.
16/ R.Warwicks. R...........................I.

The Lorries for the 15/ Inf: Bde: will load up and park with Units until time time to proceed to the Entaining Station.

On 14th: August (The lorries are required to report will be notified direct to O.C., 5th: M.T.Coy: by C.R.A.

Headquarters., 5th: Divnl:Artillery, NORRENT FONTES.......I.
" , 15th: Brigade R.F.A., WITTERNESSE............2.
" , 27th: Brigade,R.F.A. FONTES..................2.

In all cases lorries will deliver their loads at Entraining Stations One hour before the time fixed for the departure of the train.

8. **Y.M.C.A.** have been asked to arrange the Coffee Bars at entraining Stations.

9. **SUPPLIES.** On Entrainment, the situation as regards supplies will be:-

On the man Unexpired portion of the days rations. Following days ration. The Iron Ration.

On the Supply Vehicles, of the Divisional Train, 1 Days Rations.

To allow of this, a double refill has been made.

ACKNOWLEDGE.

(sd). O.W. WHITE., Lt; - Colonel,
A.A. & Q.M.G., 5th: Division.

SECRET.   5th: Division No: C.C.639/I.

ADMINISTRATIVE INSTRUCTIONS, ETC:-

In continuation of 5th: Division No: C.C./639 of to day:-

1.   The Division moves to the Third Army. Detraining Stations - FREVENT - BOUQUEMAISON - DOULLENS.

2.   Timings are on the Table issued to:-

Camp Commandant............... Camp Comtd: will entrain all Divisional H.Q.

Infantry Brigades............. One to each Brigade.
C.R.A......................... One.
Entraining Stations........... 3 Issued to the 13/ Inf: Bde: to be handed over.
Detraining Stations........... 3 issued to 13/ Inf:Bde: to be handed over.

Divisional Train.............. One.

The Infantry Entraining and Detraining Officers will be responsible that they hand over the Time Tables to the R.A. Officers entraining and detraining the Artillery.

3.   Supply Railhead moves to FREVENT on the 14th:inst:

4.   Lieut: C.M.DOUGLAS, 2nd.K.O.S.B. will remain at St OMER until the whole Division is entrained and will forward all the necessary reports to Corps and Army "Q".

He will keep in touch, by telephone, with the other entraining Stations.

5.   Billets.   All Unit Commanders will be resposible that all Billets are left clean and in proper order and clearance certificates from Area Commandants.

12th: August, 1918.   (sd). O.W. WHITE, Lt:-Col'
                                        A.A. & Q.M.G., 5th: Division.

Distribution to all recipients of C.C./639.

SECRET.　　　　　　　　　　　　　　　　5th: Division. C.C./639/2.

ADMINISTRATIVE INTRUCTIONS　　　Ref: LENS Sheet II.

1. Table of accommodation attached: Billeting Parties will apply to the Area Commandants for accommodation.

　　The 13th: Infantry Brigade Units marching from DOULLENS to "A" Group area can, if desired, stage in the BONNIERES area for up to 6 hours but 13/Infantry Brigade will ensure any accommodation required by the 95/Infantry Brigade will be available. 95/Infantry Brigade to allow of this staging will place Brigade Units last to arrive in BONNIERES.

　　The accommodation given in Table is the maximun to be expected.

2. LORRIES.　　3 Lorries will be detailed for each detraining Station.

3. Advanced Divisional H.Q. opens at REBREUVE at 8.pm. to-day where an Officer of this Branch will be on duty.

4. No: 5 M.T.Coy: will be quartered in PREVENT.

5. On detraining in the new area each Company of the 5th:Bn: Machine Gun Corps. will concentrate in PREVENT and come under the orders of the Officer Commanding the Battalion.

13th: August, 1918.　　　　　　(sd).　O.W. WHITE. Lt:-Colonel,
　　　　　　　　　　　　　　A.A. & Q.M.G., 5th: Division.

Copies to -　　13/Inf: Bde:
　　　　　　　95/　do:
　　　　　　　15/　do:
　　　　　　　CRA., 5th:Divn:
　　　　　　　CRE., 5th: Divn:
　　　　　　　I/6th: A. & S.Hrs:
　　　　　　　5th: Bn: M.G.Corps.
　　　　　　　ADMS., 5th: Division.
　　　　　　　A.P.M., 5th: Division.
　　　　　　　DADOS., 5th: Division.
　　　　　　　Camp Commandant.
　　　　　　　208th: D.E.Company.
　　　　　　　M.M.F.
　　　　　　　D.A.D.V.S.
　　　　　　　5th: Signal Company.
　　　　　　　5th: Divnl: Train.
　　　　　　　No: 5 M.T. Company.

ORDERS FOR ENTRAINMENT.

| Train No: | Unit. |

| X | X |

	I.	~~~~~~~~ I3/Infantry Brigade H.Q.
St: OMER STATION.		Brigade Signal Section.
		"C" Company, No: 5 Bn. M.G.Corps. at 7.I5.pm.
		I3/ T.M.Battery.
		One Company, Coy: Cooker and Team, 2nd: K.O.S.Bd:

| X | X |

| 7. | I3th: Field Ambulance. |
| | "A" Company, No: 5 M.G.Corps.   at I.I5.am. |

| X | X |

I9.	95/Infantry Brigade Headquarters.
	I5/T.M.Battery.
	Bde: Signal Section.
	"D" Company, No: 5 Bn: M.G.Corps. at I.I5.pm., I4/8/I8.
	One Company, Coy: Cooker and Team, Ist: NORFOLKS.

| X | X |

ARQUES STATION.

	H.Qrs: Divisional Train.
	H.Qrs: No: 5 Battn: M.G.Corps. at 6.27.am. I3/8/I8.
	208th: Divisional Employmeny Company.
I4.	5th: Mobile Veterinary Section.

| X | X |

WIZERNES STATION.

9.	95/ Inf: Bde: H.Q.
	Brigade Signal Section.
	"B" Company No: 5 Bn. M.G.Corps.
	95th: Trench Mortar Battery.
	I Company, Coy: Cooker and Team Ist: Bn: E.SURREYS.

O.C. "A" Company.
O.C. "B" Company.
O.C. "C" Company.
O.C. "D" Company.

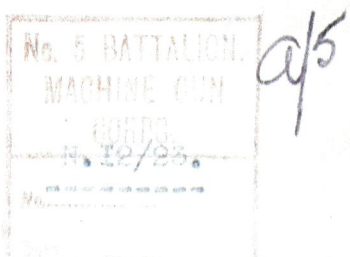

The Battalion will be Inspected by the G.O.C. tomorrow morning:-

Dress will be full Marching Order, Steel Helmets will be worn.

In order to obtain uniformity the following points are brought to notice:-

(1). Revolver Lanyards will be worn round the neck.

(2). This Office No: N.12/30. dated 11.8.18.

(3). Steadiness on parade. Men are inclined to talk and move about when standing at ease. It is intended to parade the Battalion in Line if a suitable ground can be found.

Transport.   All Transport will be cleaned this afternoon. If necessary the O's.C. Companies will provide Fatigue Parties to assist their Transport Officers.

The Second-in-Command will be on the Transport Field this afternoon and will issue any necessary orders re uniformity etc:.

Attention is drawn to the cleaning of Bicycles.

15th: August, 1918.   (sd) A.C. STANLEY, Captain & Adjutant.
                                 No: 5 Battalion Machine Gun Corps.

O.C. "A" Company.
O.C. "B" Company.
O.C. "C" Company.
O.C. "D" Company.

> No. 5 BATTALION,
> MACHINE GUN
> CORPS.
> No. H.12/23/I.

Reference the Inspection by the G.O.C. to-morrow

(1). OFFICERS DRESS. - Sam Browne, revolver on the right. Ammunition Pouch in the Left. Haversack on the left side. WaterBottle and Field Glasses on the Right. Packs will not be carried. Steel Helmets will be worn.

(2). MOUNTED OFFICERS. - Horses will be in full Marching Order.

(3). SIGNALLERS. - The Signalling N.C.O. - without Bicycle - and 4 Signallers with Bicycles will parade in front of their respective Companies.

(4). COMPANY COOKS. - Company Cooks will fall in behind the Travelling Kitchen. Dress - Full Marching Order.

(5). For further information refer to the Infantry Machine Gun Training.

(6). LIMBERS. - One Limber per Company will be left off Parade - they will be required as follows:-

I Limber from each of the following Companies to report to the Sanitary N.C.O. at 8.am. at the Town Major's Office.

"D" - "B" - "A" Companies.

4 O.R. for Sanitary Fatigue to be detailed by "D" Company reporting at 8.am. at the Town Major's Office.

"C" Company will detail One Limber for H.Q. Fatigue to report to the Q.Mr's: Stores at the usual time.

16th: August, 1918.   (sd). A.C. STANLEY. Capt: & Adjt:.

No: 5 Battalion Machine Gun Corps.

S E C R E T   No: 6 Battalion Machine Gun Corps.   Copy No:

Operation Order No: 23.
====================================

Map Reference LENS Sheet - 1/200000.

1.   The Battalion will move to the DOULIEU area to night.

2.   The Starting Point will be ½ of a mile SOUTH of the 2nd:
Railway Bridge on the PREVENT - DOULIEU. Road.

3.   Order of March - No: 8 Section, S/Signal Coy: Bn: H.Q.
"A" - "B" - "C" and "D" Companies.

4.   The head of Bn: H.Qrs: will pass the starting point at
6.10.pm.
        "A" Company will pass the starting point at 6.10.pm.
        "B"   do: do: do: 6.20.pm.
        "C"   do: do: do: 6.40.pm.
        "D"   do: do: do: 6.50.pm.

5.   March Order - Machine Gun Company in Column of Route -
Action not expected. A distance of 25 yards to be kept between
the rear of personnel and the head of Transport. 25 yards to be
maintained between every 6 vehicles and 150 yards between Coys:

6.   Company Commanders will arrange to carry Hot Tea on the
Travelling Kitchens which will be issued on arrival at DOULIEU.
"A" Company will arrange to provide hot tea for Battn: H.Qrs:

7.   Falling out States -(i.e. numbers of men falling out on
the line of March) - will be rendered to Battalion H.Q. on
reporting arrival in Billets.

8.   Strict March Discipline will be maintained.

9.   ACKNOWLEDGE.

10.   Dress: - Full Marching Order - Soft Caps to be worn.

Issued at 7.pm.   Captain & Adjutant,
                                                  for Lieut: - Colonel,
                                        Commanding No: 6 Battalion Machine Gun Corps.

SECRET.

No: 5 Battalion Machine Gun Corps.   Copy No:
Operation Order No: 25.

Reference Maps - LENS, Sheet 11 & 57D. N.E. 1/20000.

1. No: 5 Battalion Machine Gun Corps, less the Dumped Personnel, will move to night to the area GOUIN - COIGNEUX - BAYENCOURT.

2. Order of March:- "C" - "A" and "D" Company, - No: 5 Signal Section, 5th: Signal Coy. R.E., and H.Q. "B" Company will march under the orders of the 95/ Infantry Brigade.

3. Starting Point:- Junction of the DOULLENS - AMIENS and DOULLENS - ALBERT Roads, due South of DOULLENS.

4. The head of "C" Company will pass the starting point at 10.50.pm., "A" - "D" and H.Q. following it at 5 minutes intervals "C" - "A" and "D" Companies will move to the areas detailed in O.O. No: of even date and "C" Company will come under the orders of the 15/ Inf: Bde: on reaching the new area.

5. On arrival in the new area every precaution will be taken to ensure concealment. No bivouac fires or lights must be shown at night and movement by day will be restricted to the minimum

6. Personnel surplus to 8 Officers per Company and 6 O.R. (including N.C.O's) per Gun Team will report to Major COLLYER. at the 15/Inf: Bde: H.Q. in the CITADELLE. A Nominal Roll will accompany each Party.
    Rations for the 20th: will be brought by the men.
    O.C., No: 5 Signal Section will arrange for communications between Dumped Personnel and Battalion H.Q.
    The Qr: Mr: will arrange for the rationing of this Party. The O.C, Dumped Personnel will forward the ration strength daily.

7. Battalion H.Q. will close at the CITADELLE at 11.15.pm on the 19/8/18. and open at AUTHIE at 4.am., 20/8/18.

8. ACKNOWLEDGE.

19.8.1918.

(sd) A.C. STANLEY. Capt: & Adjt:
for Lieut: - Colonel,
Commanding No: 5 Battalion Machine Gun Corps.

S E C R E T.   Copy No: 14.

5th: Division Operation Order No: 247.

1. The 5th: Division (Less Artillery) will move to night to the COIUN - COIGNEUX - BAYENCOURT - SAILLY AU BOIS area, in accordance with the attached Table, "A".

2. Units will move in Brigade Groups as at present, with the exception that -

    13/ Field Ambulance will move under orders of 95/I.B.
    14th: do: "   "   "   13th: I.B.

3. Accommodation in the area is shown on the attached Table "B".

    "D" Company, M.G.Battn: will be accommodated in "C" Brigade Group area.

    Pioneer Battn: will be accommodated at J.8.d.8.9. with Transport Lines at J.8.d.6.4.

4. On arrival in th new area every precaution must be taken to ensure concealment. No Bivouac fires or uneccessary lights must be shown at night, and movement by day must be restricted to a minimum.

5. ACKNOWLEDGE.

19.8.18.   (sd). G.W. GORDON. HALL Lieut;Col

                                        General Staff, 5th; Division.

SECRET. 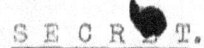 Copy No: 14.

5th: Division Operation Order No: 246.

Reference Maps - 1/20000 Sheets.   19th:Aug:
57.D.N.E. - 57.C. N.W. - 57.D. S.E. and 57.C. S.W.

1.   The Third Army has been ordered to press the enemy back towards BAPAUME without delay and to make every effort to prevent the enemy from destroying Road and Railway Communications.
   The 4th: and 6th: Corps will exploit the success by pushing through the Line IRLES - BIHUCOURT - GOMIECOURT and thence Northwards along the ACHIET le GRAND - ARRAS Railway.

2.   (a).   The initial attack on the 4th: Corps Front is to be made by the 37Th: Division, whose objective will be the BLUe Line.
   The 5th: Division on the right and the 63rd: Division on the Left will then pass through to the capture of the BROWN, RED and RED DOTTED Objectives.
   (b).   The N. Z. Divisions will advance in touch with the 5th: Division and the 42nd: Division will advance in touch with the N. Z. Division to a general Line L.29.b.central. - BEAUREGARDE DOVECOTE - R.2b. central forming a flank facing S.E. in touch with the 5th: Corps.

3.   The 5th: Division will attack with the 95th: Inf: Bde: on the right and the 15th: Inf: Bde: on the Left. The 13/ Inf: Bde: with Pioneers and R.E. Companies(less 4 Sections) and M.G. Battalion (less 2 Coys). will be in Divisional Reserve. One Company, M.Gun Battn: and 2 Sections R. E. will be attached to each of the 15th: Inf: Bde: and 95th: Inf: Bde:.

4.   The boundaries and objectives are shown on the attached Map (not attached).

5.   The 5th: Division will be formed up by Z plus 90 minutes under the final Barrage of the BLUE Line for the advance on the BROWN objective. The Final Barrage for the Blue Line will be commence to move forward at Z plus 90 minutes reaching the final position of the BROWN Line at Z plus 162 minutes. The rate of advance of the Barrage will be 100 yards in 4 Minutes.

6.   (a) One Company(12) Mk:iv Tanks will cover the advance of the 5th: Division to the BROWN Objective. 6 Tanks on each Brigade Front. The Tanks will be formed up ready to advance from the BLUE Objective at Z plus 90 and the Infantry will keep up close to them.
   (b). One Company (8) Mk: V Tanks will be formed up on the BROWN objective ready to advance at Z plus 162 Minutes for the attack on RED Objective. 4 Tanks on each Brigade Front.
   These Tanks will move quicker than the Infantry and will therefore not be followed so quickly.
   One Company (12) WHIPPETS and some armoured Cars will at the same time advance and gain ground in front of the Mk: V Tanks to an approximate distance of 1500yards, with a view to exploiting success beyond the GREEN Line, with the aid of Cavalry.
   (c).   The following signs are used by the Tanks:-

   (1). A GREEN and WHITE Flag denotes all clear and calls on the Infantry to advance.

   (2). A RED and YELLOW Flag means that the Tank is broken down and in this case the Infantry must continue the advance in a general direction and ignore the Tanks that have broken down.

   (3). A RED, WHITE and BLUE Flag flown by a Tank coming from the direction of the enemy is a sign that the Tank is BRITISH.

   (4). Where Infantry are held up and wish to attract the attention of a Tank they will place their Helmets on their Rifles and point them in the direction of the place that is holding them up.

7.   (a). ARTILLERY.   The Advance from the BLUE to the BROWN objective will be covered by a creeping Barrage of Field Artillery which will cease at Zero plus 162 minutes.
     (b). The 55h: Divisional Artillery (less 1 Brigade). will support the advance after the capture of the BROWN Objective.
          One 18. pdr: and one 4.5" How: Battery will be allotted to the 15th: Inf: Bde:.
          Two 18 pdr: Batteries to the 95th: Inf: Bde:.

8.   The Division will be assembled in depth as follows by Zero hour:-

     95th: Inf: Bde: In KEANE and CROSS Trench.
     15th: Inf: Bde: do:
     13/ Inf: Bde:)
     I/6th: A & S. Hrs:)   to be notified later.
     R. E. Coys, less 4 Sections.)

9.   MACHINE GUNS.

     One Machine Gun Company will be attached to 95/ Inf: Bde: and one to the 15th: Inf: Bde; the remainder of the Machine Gun Battalion will be in Divisional Reserve.

10.   On the night of the 19th: / 20th: August the 5th: Division will be closed up to the area COUIN - COIGNEUX - RED LINE - BAYENCOURT - and CHATEAU de la HAIE switch trenches.

     Dispositions of Brigades in this area will be issued separately.

11.   The following routes are allotted to the 5th: Division for approach to assembly positions,

For 95/ Inf: Bde;   COIGNEUX - SAILLY AU BOIS - HEBUTERNE - CRUCIFIX at
                     K.11.b.95.25. Southern Corner of BIEZ WOOD.

For I5/ Inf: Bde: CHATEAU de la HAIE Track - GOMMECOURT Mule Track -
                     GOMMECOURT - thence along the train Line to
                     Southern corner of RETTEMOY FARM enclosure.

For Divn: Reserve.   COIGNEUX - SAILLY AU BOIS - HEBUTERNE - CRUCIFIX at
                     K.11.b.95.25. - Southern Corner of BIEZ WOOD.
                     CHATEAU de la HAIE Track - GOMMECOURT Mule Track -
                     thence along the Train Line to the Southern Corner
                     of RETTEMOY FARM enclosure.

     The I5/Inf: Bde: will lead followed by the 95th: Inf: Bde: followed by the I3/ Inf: Bde:, Pioneers and Field Coys: R.E..
     Guides of the 37Th: Division will be at the Southern Corner of RETTEMOY FARM , E.30.d.8.1. at a time to be notified later.

12.   Time for the moves on the night of the 19th: / 20th: is being issued separately. Moves on the night 20th:/21st: August will comm commence at 8.30.pm.
     Troops must not show themselves during daylight 20th: August.

13.   (a). A Contact plane of the 59th: Squadron will call for fla flares at .

     Z plus 1 hour.
     Z "   3 hours.
     Z "   5 Hours.
     Z "   7 hours.

     (b). The 59th: Squadron will drop ammunition when called for and will arrange for a Contact Machine to be in the air from Zero onward

13. Contd: (c). The Signal to denote the assembly of the enemy for counter attack is the dropping of a RED SMOKE BOMB over the place where the enemy are seen.

14.   (a). 3 Gun Carrying Tanks have been allotted to the Division
The C.R.E. will arrange with Brigadiers for Engineer S ammunition, etc: to be taken up by these Tanks.
        (b). One Section of a Tunnelling Company R.E. will work under the orders of the C.R.E. for reconnoitring dug outs and looking out for Booby Traps.
        (c). The Pioneers and R.E. Companies (less 4 Sections) will receive orders from the C.R.E. as to the repairing of roads, exploiting the water supply and assisting the Infantry in Consolidation.

15.   Orders regarding the action of the Cavalry will be issued later.

16.   Watches will be synchronised as usual and in addition an officer will be sent round Brigades at 6.pm., 20th: inst:, to synchronise Watches.

17.   SIGNALS.

        (a). One VERY Light will be fired by order of the Company Commanders on the capture of the BROWN Objective, 2 in succession on the capture of the RED Objective.
        (b). The S.O.S. Signal will be RED over GREEN over RED.

18.   (a). Brigades will arrange for Liason Officers with Brigades on their Flanks.
        (b). The 13/ Inf: Bde: will arrange for Liason Officers with the 2 Leading Brigades. The Brigade of 5th: Divisional Artillery working with the 5th: Division will appoint Liason Officers with the attacking Inf: Bdes:.

19.   ACKNOWLEDGE.

20.   Divisional H.Q. in Dug-outs   (sd). G.W. GORDON. HALL.
        at E.21.b. FONQUEVILLERS.   Lieut; Col.
                                        General Staff, 5th: Division

Issued at 6.pm.

SUPPORTS and RESERVES.

Known Locations   (Sheet 57.c. N.W. and 57.d. N.E.)

   1 Battalion in Railway Cutting A.22.
   1 Battalion do: A.28.
   1 Battalion in LOGEAST WOOD.
   3 Battalions in LOGEAST WOOD G.10.c. to G. 15.d.
              (35 Feet Deep).

   1 Battalion in the vicinity of ACHIET le PETIT.
   1 Battalion in the QUARRY E. of MIRAUMONT.

   The possibility of a reserve Regiment (3 Battalions) in FAVREUIL has already been mentioned .

   The SUNKEN ROAD in G.8. central. is also suspected of harbouring a Support Battalion.

AREAS SHELLED. The Enemy artillery has not been abnormally active, areas chiefly shelled are shown on the attached Map.(to Bdes: and C.R.A. only).

   Hostile Artillery Fire usually comes from the Batteries firing from direction of G.20, 21 and 26. , also LOGEAST WOOD and from G.3, 4 and A.10. Areas which should be avoided are the ESSARTS and BUCUOY villages, PIGEON WOOD, BIEZ WOOD and SQUARE WOOD, RATTEMONT FME: L2.c., and d. , F.21.c. and 26.a.

   There have been a few cases of Hostile Shelling (Gas bombardments), the villages of BUCOUY and FONQUEVILLERS being chiefly affected.

OBSERVATION POST. Owing to the nature of the ground many good arty: and Infantry O.P's: are available, a few at present being manned by the Division holding the Line are located as follows:-

   F.25.c.85.85., 25.d., 30.95.,25.d.60.60.
   F.26.c.25.95.,26.a.55.60., L2.b.05.15.,L.1d.05.05., F.21.c.3,5.
   There is a very excellent O.P. E. of BUCOUY at L.4.a.4.2. from from which it is possible to see a distance of 25 Kilometres.

POSITIONS.

   The Line running N. and S. through L.5.b. to L.11.d. is a good Trench.
   The Trench running E. and W. through L.4.a. and B. and L.5.a. and b. contains many dugouts.
   The enemy has recently constructed small elements of Trenches in L.12a. which he occupies.
   The Sunken Road in G.1.d. and G.7b. is believed to be a close Support Position.
   The enemy has recently been doing work in L.10 b., L.11.a. and G.1.d.
   Sunken Roads are generally regarded with much suspicion and offer favourable defensive Positions of which the enemy has taken full advantage.

INTELLIGENCE NOTES TO ACCOMPANY 5th: Division O.O. No. 25.

ENEMY DISPOSITIONS.   Reference Sheet 57.D. N.E.

The Enemy is believed to hold this Sector with the following troops:-

2nd: GUARDS RESERVE DIVISION. From F.16. (N. of ABLAINZEVILLE) to L.3. (BUCUOY).

4th: BAVARIAN DIVISION.   From L./. to L.14. (PUISEUX.)

183rd: DIVISION.   From L.14. to about SERRE.

Order of BATTLE and COMPOSITION.   North to South.

    77 R.I. R.)
    15 R.I.R.)   2nd: Guards Reserve Division.
    91. R.I.R.)

    5th: Bav: I.R.)   4th: Bavarian Division.
    9th: Bav. I.R.)   Composition only, Order of Battle
    5th: Bav: I.R.)   unknown,

    418. I. R.)
    440. R.I.R.)   183 rd: Division.
    184. I. R.)

Dispositions in the Line.   The 2nd: Guards Reserve Division has all 3 Regts: in the Line, each with on e Battalion in the front , one in Support and one in Reserve. It is possible that the 4th: BAVARIAN Division may have taken over the same dispositions, in which case the Reserve Regt is proably located in Huts in the vicinity of FAVREUIL.

The 183rd: Division has all 3 Regts: in the Line, each with one Battalion in the front, one in support and one in Reserve.

MORALE.   The 2nd: Guards Reserve Division are considered a good Division, though they have seen a great deal of heavy fighting recently. They have been in this Sector since July 25th: and shown some offensive spirit. Their snipers have been active.

The 4th: Bavarian Division has a good reputation. It has come into the Sector within the last week and it may very likely have taken over some of the front of the Division N. & S. of it.

The 183rd: Division is very weak, its average Company Strength being about 20. It has been in the Line since July 25th and its morale is slow.

As far as is known there is only only one Division (the 185th:) in Reserve opposite the front of the British Army.

SECRET.

Copy No: _____

Refce Map.I/20000.57.C.N.W.

No: 5 Battalion Machine Gun Corps Operation Order No: 26.
....

1. At 11.am. on the 23rd: August the 5th: and 37th;Divns: will attack and occupy the ridge between IRLES and BIHUCOURT (both inclusive). The Attack of the 5th: Division will be carried out by the 95th: Inf: Bde: on the Right and the 15th: Inf: Bde: on the Left.

2. OBJECTIVE. The objective of the 5th: Division will be from IRLES inclusive to G.21.b.70.15..

3. On reaching the objective the Infantry will push out Patrols.

4. ACTION OF MACHINE GUNS. Machine Guns will support the Infantry of the 5th: Division with direct overhead fire from positions in G.14.c.,- G.20.a. - and L.23.b.. The Guns employed in this work will be :-

    8 Guns of "B" Company. from, L.23.b.
    4. Guns "C" Company from   G.20.a.
    8 Guns "D" Company from   G.14.c.

"A" Company will be in Divisional Reserve.

5. The Guns of "B" and "C" Companies employed on covering fire will cover the advance from the right Flank of the Division to G.26.b.8.4. and those of "D" Company from G.26.b.8.4. to the Left Flank of the Division.

If the advancing Infantry cannot be seen on account of smoke or mist the Guns employed on covering fire will shoot along the following Lines from Zero to Zero plus 40;

    8 Guns of "B" Company from G.31.b.1.4. to G.26.c.0.3.
    4 "   "C" "   " G.26.c.0.3. to G.26.c.3.6.
    8 "   "D" "   " G.26.b.8.4. to G.21.c.8.0.

6. SPECIAL INSTRUCTIONS.

(a). Care will betaken that clear accurate range Cards are prepared prior to the attack and that all Gun numbers are rehearsed in the tangent sight method of applying direct overhead fire.

(b). The trench system in G.20.d. will be kept under fire and close observation throughout the attack. If any movement is seen there concentrated fire will be brought to bear on it by "D" Company.

(c). The majority of the covering fire will be applied along the top of the ridge during the Attack. When the Infantry reach the Limit of safety guns will cease fire but will be prepared to open on any suitable target within the safety limit.

7. AMMUNITION There must be sufficient S.A.A. with the e Guns to allow of their firing about 40 minutes and leaving a reserv of 2000 rounds per Gun.
    O.C. "D" Company is forming a Dump of 80 Boxes Of S.A.A. on the South Edge of ACHIET le PETIT. Exact location of Dump will be notified to all concerned and can also be obtained from O.C. "D" Company.

8. HEADQUAUARTERS.

"A" Company. at E.29.c.8.8.
"B"   do: at L.16.c.75.65.
"C"   do.   at F.25.b.4.0.
"D"   do: at L.10.a.1.9.

9. ACKNOWLEDGE.

Issued at 4.am.

           (sd). A.C. STANLEY., Capt:
            for Lieut; Colonel,
23rd: August, 1918. Commanding No:5 Battn: M.G.Corps.

Copies to 1. 5th: Division.
     2. O.C. "A" Company.
     3. O.C. "B"   do:
     4. O.C. "C"   do.
     5. O.C. "D"   do:
     6. Office.
     7. War Diary.
     8.   do:

SECRET.   Copy No: 12.

5th: Division Operation Order No: 248.

&22nd; August?1918.

1.   The 5th: Division is yo attack to morrow 23rd: inst: in conjunction with the 37th: Division on the Left and the N. Z. Division on the Right.

2.   The 95th: Inf: Bde: will be on the Right and the 15th: Inf: Bde: on the Left, the 13/Inf: Bde: in Reserve.

3.   The Artillery will open a creeping Barrage at ZERO. This will be the Signal for the Infantry to advance.

4.   O.C., 5th: Machine Gun Battn: will arrange a M.G. Barrage in conjunction with the Field Artillery Barrage.

5.   The objective is the RED DOTTED LINE.

6.   Touch will be gained with the N. Z. Division at L.30.a.6.4. - L.35..b9.8. - L.35.b.3.1. - and with the 37th: Division at G. 15.c.6.7. - G.15.d.2.3. - G.21.b.9.6. - G.22.a.5.2.

7.   Orders for the Pioneer Battalion and the R.E. Companies as for the attack on the 21st: inst:.
     The C.R.E. will arrange for the tools to be carried forward.

8.   CONSOLIDATION.

   The Line of resistance on the reverse side of the slope of the Spur S. E. and parallel to the Railway will be consolidated, with Posts on the RED DOTTED Line.

9.   Advanced Brigade H.Qrs: will be established as follows:-

        13/ Inf:Bde: H.Q. .... L.11.d.5.2.

        15th: and 95th:Inf:Bde: H.Q...... L.9.b.8.7.

ACKNOWLEDGE.

                                  (sd). G.W. GORDON. HALL. Lt: - Col;.
                                       General Staff, 5th: Division.

SECRET.

5th: Division Warning Order No: 2.

&&&&&&&&&&&&&&&&&&&&&&&&&&&&&&&&&&&&&&&&

The 37th: Division is relieving the 63rd: Division to night. The 5th: & 37th: Divisions are to attack and occupy the RED DOTTED LINE from IRLES to BIHUCOURT (both inclusive) on a date and at a time to be notified later. The N. Z. Division and the 42nd; Division are to prolong the attack on the right and to clear the whole of the valley in L.24.c. - L.30.a. and c. and L.35.b. Tanks will support the Infantry till the Infantry have made good the ground beyond the Railway, but will not go beyond it.

ACKNOWLEDGE.

22nd; August, 1918.
            (sd). G.W. GORDON. HALL.
               Lieut; - Col;
           General Staff, 5th: Division.

SECRET.

No. 0 BATTALION, MACHINE GUN CORPS
No. a/8

ACTION OF MACHINE GUNS DURING THE OPERATIONS OF THE 5th Division from 21st August to 31st August.

ASSEMBLY for attack on 21st Aug.

On the 19th August orders were received for the 95th and 15th Infantry Brigades to carry out an attack on the 21st August. The 13th Infantry Brigade would be in reserve. The allotment of M.G. Companies for this attack was as follows:-
"B" Company was allotted to the 95th Infantry Brigade.
"C" Company was allotted to the 15th Infantry Brigade.
"A" and "D" Companies were in Divisional Reserve with the 13th Infantry Brigade.

The Companies marched from DOULLENS to join their respective Brigades on the night of 19/20th, leaving behind as dumped personnel one Company Commander and all section personnel in excess of 1 Officer, 1 Sergeant, 1 runner, and 1 batman per section, and 6 O.R. per team.

During the early morning of the 20th the Companies arrived in their Brigade areas which were about 8 miles behind the assembly trenches. A reconnaissance was made of the assembly positions during the morning.

The transport was divided into "A" and "B" Echelons before the Companies moved from this area.

"A" Echelon consisted of all gun limbers and 2 S.A.A. limbers per company, and a proportion of riding horses.

"B" Echelon consisted of Battalion H.Q. transport and the remainder of the Company transport.

After dusk on the 20th the Companies moved forward with their "A" Echelon transport to their assembly positions.

"A" and "D" Companies were able to take the whole of their "A" Echelon transport up to their assembly positions East of GOMMECOURT and keep it there.

"B" and "C" Companies made use of limbers and pack animals to take their equipment right up to their assembly positions. Ammunition was dumped by limber as far up as it was possible to go. After these Companies had got into their assembly positions their "A" Echelon transport with the exception of pack animals which were required to form forward dumps during the operation withdrew to FONCUEVILLERS.

"B" Echelon transport moved to SOUASTRE in the night of 20/21st.

Battalion H.Q. were established at FONQUEVILLERS on the night of 20/21st.

The Attack on 21st.

The attack by the 5th Division was carried out by the 95th Infantry Brigade on the right and the 15th Infantry Brigade on the left. These Brigades had to pass through the 37th Division after the latter had captured the first objective which was the high ground East of BUCQUOY.

Machine Guns.

RIGHT BRIGADE. The mist was very thick indeed during the morning and it was very difficult to maintain direction. The first objective of the 5th Division was soon captured and the machine gun sections of "B" Company were able to maintain their direction. By noon the forward guns had reached a line through L.17.central but were compelled to fall back a little owing to the Infantry falling back. During the afternoon the 12th Glosters attacked and captured the high ground at L.18.c. L.24.a. and c. and the machine guns were then distributed as follows:-

2 guns L.18.c.   2 guns L.24.a.1.8.
2 guns L.23.b.9.7. and 2 guns at L.23.d.5.7. These 8 guns were all on high ground and were able to give overhead direct fire if required.
4 guns were in support at L.16.d.5.3.
4 guns were kept in reserve at Company H.Q.L.16.c.7.7.

When the mist cleared the forward guns engaged a good many targets especially during an enemy counter-attack in the afternoon.

S.A.A. was taken up to the gun positions by limbers at dusk. The R.A.F. dropped a quantity of S.A.A. close to the positions. A lot of use was made of the captured machine guns thereby conserving our own ammunition supply.

LEFT BRIGADE. One section of "C" Company advanced in rear of each of the Battalions of the 15th Infantry Brigade. Nos.1 and 4 were with the attacking battalions and Nos.2 and 3 were with the support battalions.

No.1 section got into action East of ACHIET-LE-PETIT as follows:-

Two guns under a sergeant about G.14.d.central. The guns and teams were put out of action by enemy fire. The guns were found after our advance on the 23rd with the bodies of the teams. Two guns under the section officer came into action about G.14.c.8.3. When the line was adjusted after the battle these guns were able to cover the withdrawal of some of our forward posts. After the line was adjusted these guns were withdrawn to L.18.a.5.9.

No.2 section took up defensive positions West of ACHIET-LE-PETIT. Two guns were placed at L.18.a.3.7. and two at L.24.a.central. These guns were afterwards withdrawn to positions about L.17.b.9.5.

No.3. section advanced beyond ACHIET-LE-PETIT and came into action in a trench from G.14.c.30.05 to G.14.c.8.3.

No.4 section. Owing to the gun teams not keeping in close touch with the pack animals which were carrying their guns and tripods this section was delayed in getting into position. With the assistance of a party of Infantry these guns got into action at about G.13.d.central. From this position these guns were able to assist in covering the withdrawal of our forward posts when the line was adjusted later in the day.

RESERVE. During the evening of 21st two sections of "D" company took up positions commanding the valley running through L.16.b. and L.17.c. The guns were disposed as follows:- One section L.10.d. and one section in L.16.c.

August 22nd.

No attack was launched against the enemy on the 22nd and the day was spent in re-organising the sections, and pushing forward ammunition. S.A.A. was obtained from a supply tank and the R.A.F. dropped more near the gun positions.

Orders were received during the evening for the attack to be continued on the 23rd and the following distribution of Machine Gun Companies was made:-

"A" Company remained in Divisional Reserve
"B" Company remained with the 95th Infantry Brigade
"C" Company remained with the 15th Infantry Brigade
"D" Company. 2 sections remained in positions in
    L.10.d. and L.16.c.
    2 sections were moved forward to G.14.c. to
    support the attack next morning with direct
    overhead fire.

Attack on the 23rd.

The attack was carried out by the 95th Infantry Brigade on the right and the 15th Infantry Brigade on the left at 11 a.m.

Machine Guns.

RIGHT BRIGADE. One section of "D" Company went forward behind the attacking troops and got into position at about G.25.b.5.6. The advance was covered by machine gun fire. Direct overhead fire was employed. It was a splendid opportunity for this type of fire and it was taken advantage of. A thick barrage was first put down on the

railway embankment which was full of machine gun nests.
The result of this fire was fully proved, by the number of dead who were killed by bullets. At the end of the operation "B" Company was disposed as follows:-
    1 section about G.25.b.5.6.
    1 section about G.19.d.6.8.
    1 section (2 guns about L.23.d.8.4.
             (2 guns about L.23.b.8.7.
    1 section about L.16.d.5.3.

<u>Left Brigade.</u> After the objective had been gained on the left 6 guns were sent forward to assist in the consolidation of the captured area. They were put into position as follows:-
    2 guns about G.21.b.5.7.
    2 guns about G.21.c.4.8.
    2 guns about G.20.d.8.1.

The advance of this Brigade was also covered by direct overhead fire and several good targets were seen and engaged. There were three sections employed on overhead fire on the left, 2 from "D" Company and 1 from "C" Company. They expended about 20,000 rounds during the operation.

Re-organisation.
"D" Company relieved the forward guns of "B" and "C" Companies during the evening and "C" Company withdrew their forward guns to the vicinity of Company H.Q. at L.11.d.50.20. The forward section of "B" Company withdrew after relief to Company H.Q. at about L.16.c.7.7.

<u>Reserve Brigade.</u> The 13th Infantry Brigade was ordered to exploit the success of the morning's attack along the whole of the Divisional front up to LOUPART WOOD. "A" Company was allotted to the Brigade for this operation.

At 4 p.m. "A" Company was ordered forward to join the 13th Infantry Brigade and one section was detailed to each Infantry Battalion. The high ground running through G.32.central and G.29.central was gained and the machine gun sections were able to take up defensive positions by 11 p.m. without casualties. Four guns were placed on the left flank of the Brigade front as there was a gap between the left flank and the troops on the left.

At 4.55.a.m. on the 24th the New Zealand Division passed through the 5th Division to attack in the direction of GREVILLERS. The 13th Infantry Brigade were detailed to protect the right flank of this attack.

"D" Company assisted in the consolidation of the area occupied by the 13th Infantry Brigade and had its guns disposed as follows:-
    2 guns about K.20.d.7.2.
    2 guns about K.21.c.2.0.
    2 guns at   K.21.c.8.5.
    2 guns at K.21.b.4.2.
    4 guns in the trench system in G.25.a.
    4 guns in trench at L.17.b.

Company H.Q. of "D" Company moved to G.13.a.1.8.
"C" Company withdrew into reserve at L.11.d.5.2. and re-organised.

Concentration.
On the 25th the Companies concentrated with their respective Brigade Groups as the Division had been relieved.
"A" Company concentrated with the 13th Infantry Brigade at
                              G.29.central
"B" Company concentrated with the 95th Infantry Brigade at
                              G.23.b.
"C" Company concentrated with the 15th Infantry Brigade at
                              G.17.c.3.2.
"D" Company concentrated with the 13th Infantry Brigade at
                              G.29.central

"B" Echelon transport moved to BUCQUOY.
Battalion H.Q. was established at Advanced Divisional Report Centre at BIHUCOURT G.17.a.3.7.

At 11.20 p.m. "A" Company received orders to relieve the Machine Gun Company operating with the 111th Infantry Brigade who were holding the line between SAPIGNIES and FAVREUIL. The Company marched to the quarry at H.14.d.3.5. As the dispositions of the sections to be relieved were not known O.C. "A" Company sent one section forward to H.9.central, one section to H.14.a.central, one section to about H.14.a.2.4. and one section to the shrine in H.8.c.central.

Operations on 26th August.

At 6.30 a.m. on the 26th one section of "A" Company advanced with the 2nd K.O.S.Bs. and took up positions on the ridge at H.4.d. and H.10.b. The Infantry were held up on this ridge by hostile machine gun fire and one of our machine guns opened fire on the enemy position and succeeded in silencing their guns for the time. The enemy retaliated later and split the belt of one of our guns.

About midday it was decided to attack and capture the village of BEUGNATRE so as to assist the New Zealand Division operating on our right flank. The attack was timed to take place at 6 p.m. Machine Gun Sections were moved as follows to assist this attack:-

The forward section of "A" Company in H.4.d. and H.10.b. was moved up on the left flank to a position where the village of BEUGNATRE and the ground East of it could be commanded by direct enfilade fire.

At 2 p.m. "D" Company was ordered forward to assist the 13th Infantry Brigade. Company H.Q. was established at the SHRINE in H.8.c. 2 sections were in mobile reserve along the sunken road in H.7.b. and d. and 2 sections were disposed as follows:-

No.3 Section.

2 guns at about H.4.c.7.2.
2 guns at about H.10.b.2.8.

No.4 Section.

2 guns at about H.9.a.7.6.
2 guns at about H.9.d.3.8.

During the attack the forward Sections of "A" Company supported the attack with direct enfilade fire and were successful in silencing enemy machine guns and snipers. No.3 Section and 2 guns of No.4 section of "D" Company supported the attack with direct overhead fire on to the trenches in I.7.a. and H.18.c. 16,000 rounds were expended on this overhead fire.

After the village had been captured the forward Section of "A" Company was placed in positions to assist in the consolidation of the captured area. Two captured enemy Machine guns were also used for this work.

August 27th.

No alteration was made in the disposition of the machine guns on the 27th with the exception of an inter-section relief in "A" Company.

Advance of the 28th August.	On the 28th August preparations were made for an attack by the 13th Infantry Brigade on the enemy positions in I.14.b.and d. Two sections of "D" Company were to co-operate with Infantry in this attack. At about 5.30 p.m.on the 28th instant the 1st R.W.KENT R.advanced their line. The two left guns of "A" Company were pushed forward and got into action inflicting heavy casualties on the enemy as they tried to go from a trench to some dug-outs about H.12.b. They also fired on and silenced enemy machine guns. These guns fired about 15,000 rounds at various targets.

On the 29th "B" Echelon moved to G.16.c.

Attack of the 30th August.

During the night of the 29th/30th the 95th Infantry Brigade relieved the 13th Infantry Brigade in the line and at 12.30 a.m.on the 30th "D" Company received orders to co-operate with the 95th Infantry Brigade in the attack at 5 a.m. on the village of BEUGNY. "B" Company received orders at 2,30 a.m. to move forward at 5 a.m. to H.11.b.and to be ready to go forward should the attack on BEUGNY be successful.

Two sections of "D" Company moved forward in rear of the attacking battalions. Owing to the Infantry relief not being completed till one hour before Zero these two sections could not be advised of the exact location of the reserve companies of the Infantry. One section got well forward and took up positions on the high ground immediately in support of the 1st DEVONS as follows:-

2 guns at about I.14.b.2.4.
2 guns on HILL 120.at I.14.d.4.8.

The 1st D.C.L.I.had difficulty in getting forward owing to the village of FREMICOURT not being taken by the Division on the right and the Section moving in rear of this Battalion took up a position on the high ground in I.13.a FREMICOURT was captured later in the day and the 1st D.C.L.I. were enabled to advance their line. The machine gun section working in their area were able to move forward to a position at about I.13.c.4.7.

"B" Company arrived at H.11.b.at about 6.15 a.m. and O.C.,Company reported to 95th Infantry Brigade for orders As the attack had not been as successful as was anticipated this Company was not used.

At 2.50 p.m.the enemy counter-attacked our position and was driven off. The four guns on the left opened fire and vaused casualties to the enemy.

"C" Company moved under orders of the 15th Infantry Brigade to H.8.d.central.No.2 section was attached to the advanced guard and the remainder of the company moved with the main guard. At 1 p.m. orders were received from the 15th Infantry Brigade to attach 8 guns to the 1st NORFOLKS to hold the trench line from I.7.a.central to I.14.b.central for the protection of the left flank of the 95th Infantry Brigade. 8 guns were attached to the 1st CHESHIRES to hold a line H.11.a.30.60 to H.11.c.00.20.

Re-organisation.

On the 30th Battalion H.Q.moved with Divisional Report Centre to SAPIGNIES.

"A" Company withdrew into reserve at G.12.d.5.5.on the morning of the 30th.

"B" Company relieved the forward guns of "D" Company, during the evening of the 30th. The two sections of "D" Company withdrew to reserve at the SHRINE at H.8.c. The remaining two sections of "D" Company withdrew to the SHRINE on the 31st

August 31st.

The dispositions of "B" Company after relief were as follows:-
Company H.Q.at H.6.c.2.2.
2 guns at H.12.b.5.2.   2 guns at H.17.b.8.7.

2 guns at I.13.c.3.8.   2 guns at I.13.a.55.25
2 guns at I.14.b.50.45 2 guns at I.14.d.5.8.
2 guns at I.14.d.35.35. 2 guns at I.14.c.9.1.

The enemy made a counter-attack during the morning. He was beaten off on our front and our machine guns did a lot of useful work in repelling the attack. The Division on the right was pressed back slightly which left a gap in our line. The 2 guns at I.14.c.9.1. were swung round to cover the gap. In response to an application the R.A.F. again dropped a supply of S.A.A. at the gun positions. This was expended during the day. Some excellent targets were presented. All day long small parties of the enemy showed themselves and were shot at. S.A.A. was taken up to the positions by limber at night.

Orders were received to withdraw the two sections of "C" Company which were in position protecting the left flank of the Division. These sections withdrew after the infantry garrison had been relieved. One section remained in position till about 11 a.m. This section covered the retirement of the infantry on our flank from the ridge in L.2.c. and I.3.d.central to the trench line in which the guns were in position. Many good targets including enemy machine guns were observed and successfully engaged.

6th: Septr: 1918.

(sd).   R.H. CUTTING, Lieut: - Col:.
Comdg: No: 5 Batn: M. Gun Corps.

C O N F I D E N T I A L.

ORIGINAL COPY.

No. 5 BATTALION, MACHINE GUN CORPS.
REG: No:.......
Volume........
Part No:......

Vol 6

- W A R D I A R Y -

of

No: 5 BATTALION MACHINE GUN CORPS.

for the Month of

S E P T E M B E R 1918.

30th: September, 1918.

[signature]

Lieut: - Colonel,

Commanding No: 5 Battalion Machine Gun Corps.

No. 5 BATTALION
MACHINE GUN CORPS
Army Form C. 2118.

No. 11527
Date Septr. 1918.

WAR DIARY
or
INTELLIGENCE SUMMARY.
(Erase heading not required.)

Instructions regarding War Diaries and Intelligence Summaries are contained in F. S. Regs., Part II. and the Staff Manual respectively. Title pages will be prepared in manuscript.

Reference Map
57P.N.E. 1/20000.

Sheet. 1

Place	Date Septr. 1918	Hour	Summary of Events and Information	Remarks and references to Appendices
In Line. Divisional Frontage approx. from I.8.c.0/56 to I.20.c.95/00	1st.	—	Weather fine. Battalion in action. Battn. HdQrs. at SAPIGNIES, Rear Battn. & Company Headquarters situated near BIHUCOURT. Disposition of Companies as follows:- "A" Company 16 guns in Reserve with 13th J. Bde. at G.12.d.7.2. "B" Company 16 guns in the front system with 95th J. Bde. (8Hqs. with H.b.c.2.4.3) "C" Company 8 guns in H.10.2.H.11.11. and 8 guns Reserve at H.10.b. "D" Company 16 guns in Reserve at H.8.c. 4.4. Situation quiet. The enemy's artillery and aircraft were very active on our front and a large number of bombs were dropped in the Divisional area. "C" Company proceed to the line at dusk & relief of "B" Company.	
do.	2nd.	—	Weather fine. Relief of "B" Company completed. Operations were resumed the Division continuing to attack (15th J. Bde), the BRONEHIRES reached their objectives and was during Relief operations of C Companys guns were 4 guns with 1st CHESHIRES from I8 to I.8.c.95.00. 4 guns in support with the 16th R. Warwick R. from I.14.b.20/20 to I.14.d.90/30.	See app. A/1.

A7092 Wt. W123.9/M1293. 750,000. 1/17. D. D & I. Ltd. Forms/C2118/14.

No. 5 BATTALION
Army Form C. 2118.
CORPS.

WAR DIARY
or
INTELLIGENCE SUMMARY.
(Erase heading not required.)

Sheet 2

Place	Date	Hour	Summary of Events and Information	Remarks and references to Appendices
In line	2nd	—	4 gns with 1st NORFOLKS, 2 at 1.22.c. 4's and 2 at 1.28a.-2/3 about in support with the 1st BEDFORDS at 1.00a.3/3. Battn HQ moved forward to the village of FAMPOUX.	For details of operations refer to L.t.E. Col. Septimus Att L.4/1.
do.	3rd	—	Weather fine. Battn H.Q. now forward and established on FRESNES-ROEUX Road. Orders received to effect Relief. Bn would be relieved by the 3/6th Division.	
do.	4th	—	Fine. Relief of Battn by 3/[M]4th Battn. completed & Battn withdrew to area near BIHUCOURT to rest (G.234).	
G.23d near BIHUCOURT	5th	—	Weather fine. Lieut. R.M. WILSON to U.K. sick. Clean & refit.	
	6th	—	Weather wet. The following officers join from Base Depot. Lt. P.E. GORDON, Lt. L.G. CASTLE, Lt. J. PAGE.	
do.	7th	—	Weather fine. Lt. L.C. GOULD to C.C.S. sick. Lt. G. SHAW joins from Base Depot.	
do.	8th	—	Weather wet.	
do.	9th	—	Weather wet.	
do.	10th	—	Weather wet.	
do.	11th	—	Weather dull.	

WAR DIARY or INTELLIGENCE SUMMARY

Sheet 3.

Place	Date	Hour	Summary of Events and Information	Remarks and references to Appendices
G.23.d.		12h	Centerchill Order received to relieve Re bt N.Z. Divison.	For Master Boundaries see app: A/a.
G.23.d.		13h	Weather fine. "A" Company proceed to forward area (YPRES) in relief of R.E. support, N.Z. Division. (P20d.5.7.) Casualties 1 Officer Killed (2 Lt. PAYNE) 1 Officer wounded & 8 O.R. wounded during shelling of YPRES 2 vicinity	
In line		14h	Fine. "B" Co Company proceed to forward area 2 took Re 95 Fd. Coy. R.E. Group) to the YPRES area. "A" - "B" and "C" Companies relieve No. 2 (N.Z.) N.G. Battalion in the line, Battn. HQrs at C.23d. (Co. H.H. Stores etc)	
In line		15h	Fine Batt. HQrs move forward and were established in MILL ?? Situation Normal. Our artillery active at 2am. Enemy planes active over the lines, be Enemy Aircraft especially active over QUEENS Road & the vicinity. Aircraft especially active over looking E.A. saw large E.A. was though brought down	
		11.30pm	near BEUGNY. 2 of our Balloons were attacked at though down by enemy aircraft during the day. "C" Company move to Reserve in BARASTRE took Re 15Fd. R.E. Group and relieved the Reserve Company of the N.Z. N.R. Battalion	

WAR DIARY or INTELLIGENCE SUMMARY

No. 5 BATTALION MACHINE GUN CORPS
Army Form C. 2118.

Sheet 4

Place	Date	Hour	Summary of Events and Information	Remarks and references to Appendices
In line	10th.	—	Weather fine. "D" Company reconnoitre and take up position near front on the Hurd Line of Resistance. "B" Company reconnoitred look up positions for the defence of the Distressed at Northleaverskeven. Very active. Enemy artillery was very active carrying out one shoot on YPRES–INCOURT WOOD — WINCHESTER VALLEY — QUEEN'S CROSS. Fire was also on Kelly and Blue Dress. Crew of Q.25 a dummy by day.	
— do —	11th	—	Stormy weather. Orders received with regard to attack by 142 & 143/Bde. on our Right in which Divn. was to co-operate. "B" Company on a line in QUARRY at B.22.c.	
— do —	12th	—	Weather fine. Attack carried out by 1/7 & 1/8 Rgl. For 5/Div. when being protection of our L.h. of 38 Div. "A & B" Companies co-operated by covering the valley in front of Ypres, in front. Guns reported in positions at 5.20 a.m. 12-40 a.m. attack took place at 5.20 a.m. Lieut. H.A. WARNER proceeds to the U.K. on duty. Lieut. W. MITCHELL joined from Base for attached to D Company.	Forwarded details of the attack on GOUZEAUCOURT see app. 47.

WAR DIARY
INTELLIGENCE SUMMARY.
(Erase heading not required.)

Place	Date	Hour	Summary of Events and Information	Remarks and references to Appendices
In Line	19th	—	Weather fine. Situation Normal. Our Arty. active all day. M.Gs. & T.Ms. active on sunken road running thro' Q.26.d. & 2.GOUZEACOURT WOOD also on our forward Support system. Our M.Gs carried out night harassing fire on targets in Q.30.b.3/50, the valley in Q.24.b, Q.24.d/26.d Q.20.5/3 and the sunken road from Q.12.6.12.30 p.m. 8000 rounds being expended. Hostile snipers were active in the vicinity of tanks in Q.28.b. Lieut G.L. ATTEWELL S.M. extra-ordinary posted to his Regt depot.	To training cadre only. Copy per Readers App. a/5. 100 depot to app. apk. re.
—do—	20th	—	Situation Normal. Our artillery active all day especially from 11 a.m. to 7 a.m. Hostile arty active on GOUZEACOURT WOOD in Q.21 and the sunken road in Q.22.d, 4/1 and carried out retaliation, 570 O.R. for Lund patrolling from 4 a.m. to 6 a.m. Our M.Guns fired 9000 rounds on targets in the vicinity of Q.24.c, Q.30.B and the road at Q.7/3.80/20. Bombs were dropped by E.A. on HAVRINCOURT WOOD at 9.15A.	
—do—	21st	—	Weather fine. Situation Normal. Our Arty. carried out in an a shoot at intervals. The hostile artillery shelled area W. and S. of HAVRINCOURT WOOD at irregular intervals. METZ-EN-COUTURE was shelled with 5.9s.	

WAR DIARY or INTELLIGENCE SUMMARY.

(Erase heading not required.)

No. 5 BATTALION. MACHINE GUN CORPS.
Army Form C. 2118.

Place	Date	Hour	Summary of Events and Information	Remarks and references to Appendices
Trenches	21st	—	GOUZEAUCOURT, QUEENS CROSS 8Q.22 & R.24.b/z. HIGHLAND WOOD SH 62E. Our 11 Guns opened 13000 rounds on the Bn. Front 10.45.p.m. to 11.04.p.m. on No 1 & 2 M.G. Nobile Guns were quiet.	For relief see app A/1
do	22nd	—	Weather fine. Our arty very active. QUEENS CROSS and GOUZEAUCOURT were heavily shelled at 4 pm by 5.9. 10.p.m to 11.p.m. 5.9's to METZ received considerable attention. MACHINE GUNS were kept silent. Shelled with H.E. & Shrapnel. Our M. Guns fired 2000 rounds on Q.13, b, B.c. and Q.V.C.	
do	23rd	—	Weather fine. Situation normal. Hostile artillery active on back of the Sunken Villages on S. side of HAVRINCOURT WOOD. Q.26.d/B.3 and Q.3d, Q.14b, & Q.20a.'s received very careful day attention by 5.9. Hostile F.O were active bombing METZ, GOUZEAUCOURT, WINCHESTER VALLEY, HAVRINCOURT WOOD and our Battery Positions.	
do	24th	—	Weather fine. E/car Company relieved earned on. Orders received re attachments of 1 Company from 3/Bn M.G. Corps for future operations. 1st KITCHEN to H.Q. Sick. Hostile H.V. guns active on VILLERS-AU-FLOS.	

No. 5 BATTALION.
Army Form C.2118.
CORPS.

WAR DIARY
or
INTELLIGENCE SUMMARY.
(Erase heading not required.)

Instructions regarding War Diaries and Intelligence Summaries are contained in F. S. Regs., Part II. and the Staff Manual respectively. Title pages will be prepared in manuscript.

Place	Date	Hour	Summary of Events and Information	Remarks and references to Appendices
Inches	25th		2nd Inter Brigade relief carried out. 3/Rifle Brigade relieved by 95th/Rifle Brigade. Orders received for attack to be carried out on 27th instant.	See app. re 8 forward re attack
do	26th		Weather fine. Situation quiet. Attacked Batt. 16 Qrs moved to R.20.d.6/6	Situation quiet
do	27th		3 Company 3/Batt. M.G.C attached for operations. (party) Weather fine. Attack on Corps front took place. 2Lt Holder Barnet, wounded. 2Lt Mason and 2Lt J. Holloway killed and wounded.	see app
do	28th		Weather fine. 2Lt C.I Attewell, 2Lt - near B. Weristone wounded. Moved to Neuville. Enemy shelled Beaucamp Ridge, Companies now formed all behind. Hd.Qrs. established at Quarry at Q.20.d. 3/3 Remained Est. as before. to NEUVILLE	d/9
do	29th		Weather fine. Operations continued. B.E.D. Corps. pushed by out.	For strength during work see app: 9/11
do	30th		Weather fine. The Battn. relieved by the 3/Batt. W.Y.C. for orders issued, marched that Battn. to come into in BERTINCOURT by N.E. Railway.	

30th Sept. 1918.

D. Lottery
Lieut-Colonel
Comdg. 5 Bn. M. Gun Corps

Original

War Diary
Appendix "A".
for
Month. Septr. 1918

No. 5 BATTALION,
MACHINE GUN
CORPS.
No. 3
Date 30.9.18

A H Cutting
Lt Col.
Comm'g No 5 Batt. M.G.C.

SECRET.

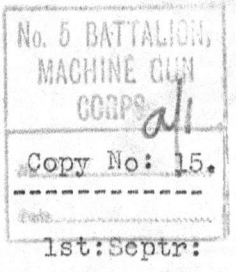
Copy No: 15.

5th: Division Operation Order No: 254.

1st:Septr:

1. The advance is to be resumed to morrow on the whole Army Front.

2. The 5th: Division is to capture BEUGNY and the ridge South and East of it, and establish connection with the N.Z. Division on the right of it at I.28.a.1/1.and with the 62nd:Division on the Left, at I.16.b.5/4.

3. The advance of the 5th: Division will be made by the 15th: Inf:F Bde:. This Brigade will relieve the 95/Inf:Bde: to night and the latter will withdraw into Support. The 13/Inf: Bde: will remain in its present position.

4. Zero Hour will be at 5.15.am. For the Division on the Left Zero Hour will be at 5.30.am.

5. (a). The advance of the 15th: Inf: Bde: will be covered by an Field Artillery Barrage which will dwell on the opening line for 4 minutes and then advance at the rate of 100 yards in 4 minutes.

(b). When the barrage has reached the objective line it will move forward for a distance of about 500 yards to enable patrols to push forward to secure Prisoners.

(c). If available, smoke will be fired by the Field Artillery on the Right Battalion Front for the first few minutes of the opening of the barrage.

(d). The Heavy Artillery will bombard the high ground in I.27.b. and I.28.a. and the village of BEUGNY within safety limits. of the Infantry Advance.

6. 4 Tanks will be available for the operation for mopping the village and running down any M.Gun nests or pockets on the ridge.

7. One M.G. Company will accompany the 15th:Inf:Bde: and 2 Sects of another Company will be available to cover the flank(left) of the Bde:.

8. Should the objective of the 5th: Division and the Divisions on the flanks be secured the success gained will be exploited. The 15th: Inf:Bde: will push forward to the line I.34.b.9.7. - cross roads at I.17.d.5.7. where touch with the flank Divisions will be gained.
The Signal for this advance will be the opening of the Field Artillery Barrage on the protective Line of the first objective. The Barrage will dwell on this Line for 4 minutes and then move forward at the rate of 100 yards in 4 minutes, this will be the signal for the Infantry to advance.

9. ACKNOWLEDGE.

Issued at 8.15.pm.

(Sd). G.W. GORDON. HALL.,
Lieut: - Colonel,
General Staff, 5th: Division.

Distribution as for O.O's.

Operations 1st to 3rd Sept. 1918   a/1.

Sept. 1st.
The Division on the right made an attack this morning which was successful and the gap on our right flank was closed up. The 2 forward sections of "B" Company supported this attack with covering fire. After the attack the two guns at I.14.c.9.1. were pushed forward to I.14.d.2.2. Small parties of the enemy were seen moving about and were engaged with Machine Gun fire

The attack on Sept. 2nd.
On the 1st September the 15th Infantry Brigade received orders to attack the enemy position at BEUGNY and the high ground to the East of the village.

"C" Company was allotted to the Brigade for this operation and "D" Company was detailed to assist in the protection of the left flank of the attack and also to apply a barrage on the high ground in I.27.b. and I.28.a. and c.

On the night 1/2nd September "D" Company relieved the forward section of "B" Company and also placed a section in position in I.8.c. "B" Company withdrew its H.Q. and three sections to reserve in H.9.d.

"C" Company moved forward to assembly positions as follows:-
1 section with the Norfolks)
1 section with the Cheshires) Attacking Battalions
1 section in support with 16 R.W.Regt.
1 section in reserve with 1st Bedfords.

Battalion H.Q. moved to FAVREUIL on the morning of the 2nd

The attack commenced at 5.15 a.m. and resistance was met with on the left flank. The Norfolks on the right captured the high ground in I.27.d. and I.28.a. and c.

The machine gun section with the Norfolks advanced in rear of the Battalion and when the first objective was gained the guns were placed in position as follows:-
2 guns I.22.c.8.2.
2 guns I.28.a.3.3.

During an enemy counter-attack the two left guns covered the retirement of the Infantry and then withdrew suffering heavy casualties. Both guns were withdrawn but one was damaged beyond repair by bullets. The remaining gun was placed in position about I.21.c.5.7. covering the valley and the opposite ridge. The two guns of this section on the right were surrounded by the enemy during the counterattack and neither of the Gun Teams survived. The R.A.F. dropped S.A.A. for this section in response to an application.

The machine gun section with the 1st CHESHIRES advanced from the Army line in rear of the support Company. As the Infantry were unable to advance into the village of BEUGNY the guns were employed to cover the left flank of the village. Two guns were placed at I.15.c.05.05. and two at I.15.c.70.35. A few targets were observed and engaged. This section suffered heavily from artillery fire and machine gun fire. At one period the four guns were manned by 10 men.

The machine gun section with the 16th R.Warwick Regt. moved behind the support company to defensive positions in the Army line, at I.14.b. and d. After the attack these guns were re-organised as follows:-
  2 guns at I.14.d.8.8.
  2 guns at I.14.b.3.6.

The machine gun section with the 1st BEDFORDS moved to positions in the Army line and took up the following positions:-
  1 gun about I.20.b.45.90
  1 gun about I.20.b.80.35
  2 guns I.27.a.2.8. covering the valley running North-east to the village.

From Zero to Zero plus 60 the right section of "D" Company applied a creeping barrage on the high ground in I.27.b. and I.28.a. and c. This barrage crept forward at the rate of 100 yards in 8 minutes and rested on its final barrage line which was along the reverse slope of the hill for 12 minutes. When the situation on the right had been cleared up this section withdrew into reserve. The 2 sections of "D" Company on the left flank of the 15th Infantry Brigade remained in position.

"B" Company withdrew its fourth section into reserve at midday.

Advance of 3rd Septr.

The 15th Infantry Brigade attacked at dawn on the 3rd September to capture the village of BEUGNY but finding that the enemy had withdrawn moved forward and eventually held the line of the railway through J.26.c.-J.32.a. and c. with a support line through J.28.a and c and J.34.a and c.

The machine gun Section of "C" Company with the 1st CHESHIRES moved forward under orders of C.O.,1st CHESHIRES, and remained with the Battalion until withdrawn to reserve in I.29.d.6.3. at 6 p.m.

The remaining sections of "C" Company concentrated in I.20.central and under the orders of the 15th Infantry Brigade moved forward to I.29.d.6.3.

Two sections of "C" Company took up defensive positions along the main line of resistance as follows:-
  4 guns from J.32.a.4.8. to J.32.a.6.2.
  4 guns from J.32.c.7.4. to P.2.b.05.80.

"C" Company was relieved during the night of the 3/4th by "B" Company of No.37 Battalion, Machine Gun Corps.

"A" Company moved forward with the 13th Infantry Brigade to support the advance of the 15th Infantry Brigade. This Company was relieved by "C" Company of No.37 Bn.M.G.C.

"B" Company moved forward in Reserve with the 95th Infantry Brigade to I.13.b.

"D" Company concentrated at I.20.b.2.5.

Battalion H.Q. moved with the Adv.Div.Report Centre to I.20.central.

Concentration.

On the 4th September the Battalion concentrated on the area North of BIHUCOURT with Battalion H.Q. at G.12.b.0.5.

(sd) R.H. CUTTING

7th September, 1918.
            Lieutenant-Colonel,
          No.5 Battalion, Machine Gun Corps.

SECRET.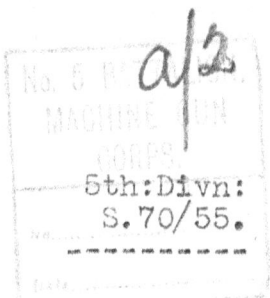

5th:Divn:
S.70/55.

....

The Divisional Boundary is being re-adjusted as follows:-

Northern Boundary. with 37th: Division will run along the existi boundary as far East as Q.8.c.0.8. - PLACE MONTMARTE (excl:) - BEAUCAMP (incl) - thence due East. This adjustment will be made at dusk to night by the 13/ Infantry Brigade, details being arranged direct with B.G.C., 111th: Inf: Bde:, before the relief of the 111th: Inf: Bde: by the 112th: Inf: Bde: takes place.

Southern Boundary. between the 5th: Division and 38th: Division will be a line running through East and West through Q.28.d.9.5. This adjustment will take place on the night 16th:/17th:, details being arranged direct with the between the 13/ Inf: Bde; and 113/ Inf: Bde:.

13th: Septr:

(sd). S. GORE-BROWN.
Lieut: Colonel,
General Staff - 5th: Division.

S E C R E T.   No: 5 Battalion Machine Gun Corps

Operation Order No: 27.

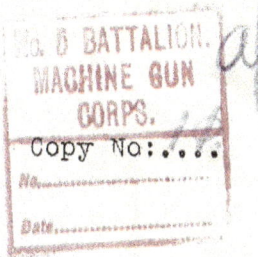

Ref: Sheet 57.C. 1/40000.

1.   No: 5 Battn: M.G.Corps will relieve the N.Z. Battn M.G.C. in accordance with the attached Table.

2.   Details of the relief will be arranged between Company Commanders concerned.

3.   Dumped Personnel will proceed to the 5th: Divn: Reception Camp, near ACHIET-LE-GRAND. The Dumped Personnel of "B" - "C" and "D" Companies will proceed to-morrow, 14th:inst:, parading at Battn: H.Q. at 10.am.. Transport will be provided by Battn: H.Q. commencing collecting at "B" Company at 9.am..
2 Days rations will be carried.
"A" Company Dumped Personnel will remain at "B" ECHELON till they receive further orders.

4.   All work in connection with defences etc: now in hand will be taken over and continued. All plans for projected work will also be taken over.

5.   Battalion H.Q. will open at 0.7.d.9.5. at 10.am., 15th: Septr:.

6.   ACKNOWLEDGE.

Issued at 9.30.pm.

13.9.1918.

Major,
for Lieut:-Colonel,
Commanding No: 5 Battalion Machine Gun Corps.

Copies to

1. 5th: Division.
2. N.Z., M.G. Battn:
3. 13/ Inf: Bde:
4. 15/   do:
5. 95/   do:
6. A. Company.
7. B. Company.
8. C. Company.
9. D. Company.
10. Quartermaster.
11. War Diary.
12.   do:
13. Office.

RELIEF TABLE TO ACCOMPANY OPERATION ORDER NO: 27.   13.9.1918.

Date.	Company.	From.	to.	Relieving.	Remarks.
"A" 13th:	"A"	BIHUCOURT area.	YTRES area		The N.Z.M.G.Coys.will remain in support and "A" Company will not relieve. The Coy: marches with the 13/Inf: Bde:Group under the orders of B.G.C.,13/Inf: Bde:.
14th:	do:	YTRES area.	Front System.	Wellington M.G. Coy: H.Q. at P.18.c. central.	
14th:	"B"	BIHUCOURT area.	YTRES area Battle Zone.	OTAGO M.G. Coy: Coy: in Support Location of H.Q. will be notified later.	The Coy: marches with the 95/ Inf: Bde: Group. under the orders of B.G.C., 95/Inf:Bde:
14th:	"D"	do:	do:	Auckland M.G. Coy: in Support.(H.Q. at P.20.c.50.55.)	do:
15th:	"C"	do:	BARASTRE area.	CANTERBURY M.G. Coy: H.Q.at P.21.d.4.2.	The Coy: marches with the 15th:Inf:Bde:Group. The Canterbury Coy: will move from their present location in Reserve when "C" Coy: No: 5 Bn: M.G.C. move in to Bivouac at BARASTRE. "C" Coy: will report their arrival in BARASTRE area immediately to Bn: H.Q.
15th:	H. Q.	do:	VILLERS-AU-FLOS.	H.Q., N.Z.,M.G. Battn: - O.7.d.9.5.	

No: 5 Battalion Machine Gun Corps

ADMINISTRATIVE INSTRUCTIONS.
----

1. **RATIONS.** Rations for the 15th:, 16th: and 17th:insts: will be issued as follows -

   15th:

   "A" Company......... Delivered by H.Q. Transport to "B" Echelon Lines, O.10.b.8.2., at 10.am. on the 14th: inst:.

   "B"-"C" and "D"..... Already drawn from the Q.M. Stores.

   16th:

   "A" Company......... Delivered to "B" Echelon with rations for the 15th:.
   "B" Company......... Delivered to "B" Echelon by H.Q. Transport on the 14th:inst:.
   "C" Company......... Drawn by Company from Q.M. Stores.
   "D" Company......... Delivered to "B" Echelon by H.Q. Transport on the 14th:inst:.

   17th:............... All Companies draw from the Q.M. Stores as usual on the 15th: inst:.

2. **Qr: Mr: STORES & SHOPS.** The Quartermaster and Staff, the Q.M. Stores and Shops will move to "B" Echelon to-morrow with Wagon proceeding with "B" and "D" Companies Rations. The spare G.S. Wagon will transport as much as possible of the stores and Shop equipment.

   These two Wagons will remain at the new "B" Echelon.

   The Wagon which transports "A" Coy: rations will return here on the 14th: inst: and transport the remainder of Battalion H.Q. on the 15th: inst:.

3. **ADVANCE PARTY.** An Advance Party of 1 Officer and 10 Men from "C" Company will proceed to morrow and report to H.Q: N.Z.M.G. Battn:. They will be shown accommodation in BARASTRE. This accommodation requires certain improvements which will be carried out by this Party.

4. **AMMUNITION.** The S.A.A. Section D.A.C. will take over existing Dumps and Trench munitions at HAPLINCOURT.
   The Battalion Reserve of Ammunition will be formed at "B" Echelon Transport lines on the 15th: inst: at which date the 2 S.A.A. Limbers per Company detailed in W.14/16. will come under the direct orders of Battalion H.Q.

5. TRANSPORT.	Units Transport will move and be accommodated as "A" and "B" Echelons. Cookers may be with "A" Echelon.
"B" Echelon of Battalion will be grouped together at O.10.b.8.2.

6. TENTAGE.	Tentage recently received by Companies from Division will be handed over to representatives of the N.Z. M.G. Battn:. Receipts will be taken and handed into this Office.

Issued at 9.30.pm.

13.9.1918.

Major.,
for Lieut: - Colonel,
Commanding No: 5 Battalion Machine Gun Corps.

Distribution as for Operation Order No: 27.

SECRET.

No. 6 BATTALION,
MACHINE GUN
CORPS

Copy No: 12.

5th: Division Operation Order No: 257.

13th: Septr: 1918.

1.   The 5th: Division (less Artillery) will relieve the N.Z. Division (less Artillery) in accordance with the attached Table.

2.   Details of the relief will be arranged between Brigade Commanders concerned. The respective C.R.E's will arrange for the relief of Field Companies and Pioneers. Details of the relief of Field Ambulances will be settled between the A.D.M.S's concerned.

3.   Dumped Personnel will proceed to the 5th: Divisional Reception Camp near ACHIET-le-GRAND. The Division Lewis Gun School will also remain at the Reception Camp.

4.   The two troops of the 3rd: Hussars at present attached to the N.Z. Division will pass under the Command of the 5th: Division on completion of the relief.

5.   The 5th Division will take over and continue all work on defences etc:, now in hand, and will take over any plans for any projected work.

6.   The Command of the Sector and of the Artillery covering the front will pass to the G.O.C. , 5th: Division at 10.am. on the 15th: Septr:, at which hour the 5th: Divn: H.Q. will open at O.8.a.6/4.(with an advanced report centre at P.20.d.8.2.)
        Up to this hour all 5th: Division Troops moving into the N.Z. Sector will be under the orders of the G.O.C. N.Z. Division.

7.   Completion of relief to be reported to this Office.

8.   Acknowledge.

Issued at 2.pm.

(sd) S. GORE- BROWNE.
    Lieut:- Colonel,
General Staff. 5th: Division.

Relief Table to accompany 5th: Division Operation Order No: 257.

Date.	Unit.	From	To	Relieving.	Remarks.
13th: Septr:	13/Inf:Bde: Group. (including "A" Coy:, 5th: M.G.Battn:)	FAVREUIL area.	YTRES area. (Support Bde:)	3rd: N.Z. Brigade Group.	(i). The forward Battn: 13/Inf:Bde: (14/Warwicks) in P.24 and 30 comes under the orders of the 1st: N.Z.Bde. in the Line for counter-attack purpose. (ii). Two N.Z. M.G.Coys: will remain in Support and "A" Coy:5th:M.G.BN: will not relieve.
14th: Septr:	do:	YTRES area.	LINE.	1st:N.Z Brigade Group.	(i). 3 Battns: in the front line, one in Support. (ii). "A" Coy:5/M.G.Bn: will relieve the WELLINGTON M.G. Co: in Line.
do:	95:Inf:Bde: Group including "B" and "D" Coys: 5/M.G.Bn;.	BIHUCOURT area.	YTRES area. (Support Bde:) One Battalion in P.24.& 30. under the orders of 13/Inf:Bde:for counter attack purposes.Other Bns: at NEUVILLE, RUYALCOURT, YTRES, Bde: H.Q.YTRES.	13/Inf:Bde: Group.	(i) 95/Inf:Bde: Group to be clear of BAPAUME by 12 Noon. (ii). "B" and "D" Coys:,5th; M.G.Bn:will relieve OTAGO &n AUCKLAND M.G. Coys: in-Support.

Date.	Unit.	From.	To.	Relieving.	Remarks.
15th:Septr:	15th:Inf:Bde: Group.	BIEFVILLERS area.	BARASTRE area. Reserve Bde: Battalions at VILLERS-AU-FLOS, HAPLINCOURT, HAPLINCOURT WOOD, BARASTRE, Bde: H.Q. at BARASTRE.	1st: N.Z.Bde: Group.	(i). 15th: Inf:Bde: Group to be clear of BAPAUME by 12 Noon (ii). "C" Coy;,5th:M.G.Bn: will relieve the CANTERBURY M.G.Coy
do:	5th: Divn:H.QRs: 5th:Signal Coy: H.Q.,5th:M.G.Bn:	BIHUCOURT.	VILLERS-AU-FLOS.	H.Q.,N.Z.Divn: N.Z.Signal Coy: H.Q.,N.Z.M.G.Bn:	Units not mentioned above, or in the attached O.O. will move under the orders issued through 5th:Division "Q"

SECRET.   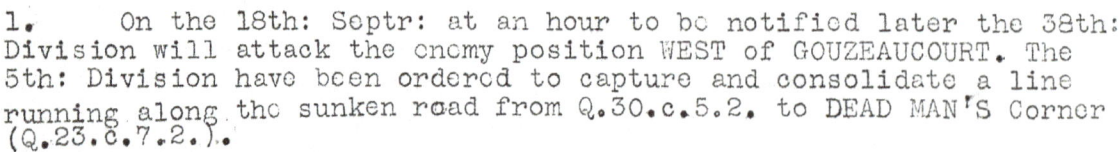 Copy No: .....

No: 5 Battalion Machine Gun Corps.

Operation Order No: 28.

Ref: Map - 57.c. S.E. 1/20000.

1.   On the 18th: Septr: at an hour to be notified later the 38th: Division will attack the enemy position WEST of GOUZEAUCOURT. The 5th: Division have been ordered to capture and consolidate a line running along the sunken road from Q.30.c.5.2. to DEAD MAN'S Corner (Q.23.c.7.2.).

2.   The 13/ Inf: Bde: will carry out the attack for the 5th: Division. "A" and "D" Companies, No: 5 Battn: M.G.Corps will co-operate in the attack by applying searching fire along the valleys in Q.30.b. - Q.24.b. - and Q.17.b..

3.   ACTION OF MACHINE GUNS. - The following Table shows the position of the Machine Guns and the tasks allotted to them.

No: of Guns.	Coy:	Location.	Target.	Remarks.
6.	"A"	About Q.28.b.2.2.	200 yds. each side of line from Q.24.b. 7.1. to Q.24.b.3.8.	Searching fire will be applied on the targets from Zero till the Artillery ceases. Fire will be re-applied on those areas in the event of an S.O.S. Call.
2.	"A"	At Q.22.d.45.70.		
4.	"A"	2 at Q.16.b.80.15. 2 at Q.17.a.15.10.	Enfilade sunken Rd: from Q.24.c. 4.2. to Q.30.b. 5.3.	
4.	"D"	About Q.28.c.7.5.	200 yds: each side of line Q.30.b.6.2. to Q.30.b.3.7.	
8.	"D"	About Q.21.b.3.8.	200 yds. each side of line Q.18.a. 3.1. to Q.17.b.8.8.	

All the guns mentioned above must be prepared to open fire on any area in range and within the safety limits of the gun on receipt of orders to do so.

The 2 guns of "A" Company at QUEEN'S CROSS must be ready to move forward to about Q.29.central. when the final objective has been gained these guns must be sited when they move forward so that they can command the valley in Q.30.a. with direct fire.

The 2 guns of "A" Company in Q.23.a. will keep the ground in Q.24. under observation and will open fire on all suitable targets within range.

4.   COMMAND.   The guns of "D" Company mentioned in para (3) will come under the command of O.C. "A" Company at Zero.

5.   HEADQUARTERS.

    Adv: Battn: H.Qrs:.   -   Divn: Report Centre.YTRES.
    Adv: Bde: H.Qrs:.   -   Q.26.b.7.7.
    "A" Company.   -   Near Q.26.b.7.7.
    "B" Company.   -   P.13.d.4.4
    "D" Company.   -   Q.13.d. central.

6.   COMMUNICATIONS.   O.C. "A" Company will establish a Report Centre at Q.20.c.9.6. and will connect it up by wire to "A" Coy: H.Q. about Q.26.b.7.7.

O.C. "D" Company will establish a Report Centre in the vicinity of Q.21.b. and connect it up to "A" Coy: H.Q. about Q.26.b. 7.7.

7.   When the situation becomes normal the Sections of "D" Company employed in this operation will withdraw to defensive positions in and in rear of the MAIN LINE of RESISTANCE. The order for this withdrawal will be given by O.C. "A" Company after consultation with the B.G.C. 13/Inf: Bde:.

8.   In the event of the 13/Inf: Bde: being able to exploit the success of the attack O.C. "A" Company will be prepared to move one Section forward to assist in the exploitation.

9.   "B" Company will be ready to move at short notice with its Echelon "A" Transport so as to be able to co-operate with the 95/ Inf: Bde: should that Brigade be ordered to exploit the success of the attack

10.   "A" and "D" Coys: will notify Battn: H.Q. when they are in position.

11.   Zero Hour will be notified later.

12.   S.O.S. Signal will be a Rifle Grenade Rocket GREEN over RED over GREEN.

13.   M.G. Coys: will please acknow;edge.

Issued at 7.30.pm.
17.9.1918.
                              Lieut: Colonel,
        Commanding No: 5 Battn: M.Gun Corps.

Copies to
1. 5th: Divn:
2. 38th: Bn:M.G.C.
3. "A" Company.
4. "B" Company.
5. "C" Company.
6. "D" Company.
7. 13/ Inf: Bde:
8. 95/ Inf: Bde:
9. O.C. Signals.
10. Qr: Mr:.
11. Office.
12. War Diary.
13.   do:
14. C.M.G.O
    IV Corps.

S E C R E T.   Copy No:12

5th: Division Operation Order No: 258.

17th: Septr:'18

1.   GENERAL INTENTION.

   (a).   On the 18th: Septr: at an hour to be notified later, the
V. Corps on our right is attacking in conjunction with the troops further
to the right.
   (b).   The 38th: Division on our immediate right has two
objectives, the BROWN Line (AFRICAN TRENCH - HEATHER TRENCH), and the
GREEN Line (Trench running just WEST of GOUZEAUCOURT).
   (c).   The duty of the 5th: Division is:-
          (i). To protect the 38th:Division from counter attack
               and from enfilade fire on its left flank.
          (ii).To exploit in conjunction with the 38th:Division
               any success gained.

2.   OBJECTIVES.

       First Objective,(BROWN Line) the trench from Q.29.c.9.6. to Q.29.b.
0.4. thence Sunken Road to DEAD MAN'S CORNER.
       Second Objective,(GREEN Line) the sunken road from Q.29.b.0.4. to t
the Divisional Boundary at Q.29.d.6.5. From this point our troops will
push forward along the sunken Road to Q.30.c.4.2. where they will join
hands with the left Battalion,113th: Inf: Bde:,38th: Division, and
establish a combined Post on the GREEN Line.
       There will be no pause on the first Objective.

3.   INFANTRY.

   (a).   The attack will be carried out by the 13/Inf: Bde:.
   (b).   The attacking troops on the front line will move out
before Zero from 50 - 100 yards in front of the line to avoid the enemy's
counter barrage.
               Troops in the present front line who are not taking
in the attack will also vacate their present positions before Zero,
bombing patrols moving forward from each Battalion, and the rest of the
Battalion withdrawing a short distance from the line in order to avoid
the enemy's counter barrage.
   (c).   Two Companies of the Support Battalion will be held in
readiness in, or behind, the present front line for immediate counter-
attack.

4.   ARTILLERY.

   (a).   An intense bombardment will be opened at Zero on the
trench running from Q.29.c.9.6. to the junction of LINCOLN RESERVE with
the sunken road in Q.24.c.0.9.. 4.5" Hows: will continue to bombard the
Northern portion of this Trench during the advance within the limits of
safety.
               3 Batteries of 6" Hows: will bombard the trench line
Q.30.c.4.5. to Q.23.d.75.60. and will lift to the sunken Road in Q.30.b. -
 - Q.24.c..
               4.5." Hows: will bombard the trench system around
Q.18. central.
   (b).   A Smoke screen will be established on BEACAMP RIDGE
(Q.23.b. - Q.18.c.) for one hour after Zero.
               The 37th: Division have been asked to establish a
similar smoke screen on the high ground in Q.5.central.
   (c).   The advance will be covered by a creeping barrage
synchronising with 38th: Division.

The Barrage will dwell on the the initial line for 3 minutes 300 yards East of the present line, the first two lifts will be at the rate of 100 yards in 3 minutes the remainder at the rate of 100 yards in 4 minutes. As soon as the protective barrage line has been reached the Barrage will creep forward and then die away.

5. MACHINE GUNS.

(a). 2 Companies of Machine Guns will work with the 13/ Inf: Bde:. Their principal tasks will be to enfilade the sunken road in Q.24.c. and Q.30.b. and to sweep the 3 valleys in Q.30.b., Q.24.b. & Q.17.b.
(b). A Machine Gun Company will be attacehd to the 95/ Inf: Bde: to move with this Brigade if required to exploit.

6. TRENCH MORTARS.

(a). 2 T.M's will fire on the Trench junctions Q.23.d.3.3. and Q.23.d.8.5. from positions near DEAD MAN'S CORNER.
(b). All available T,M's(Light) will be employed together with Rifle Grenade Sections to prevent the enemy bombing his way down old or existing trenches.

7. HEADQUARTERS.

Advanced H.Q. will be established at Q.26.b.6.8.. The Divisional Report Centre is at YTRES.

8. CONSOLIDATION.

(a). A front line will be established along the final objective Q.30.c.4.2. - Q.29.d.5.7. to DEAD MANS CORNER.
(b). A Support Line will be dug and consolidated from Q.29.d. 0.5. to Cross Roads Q.29.a.9.0. and back to the present front line about Q.29.a.4.5.
(c). Two Sections of a Field Company, R.E. will be available to assist the Infantry.

The 1/6th: A.& S. Hrs: willl be employe on mending Roads.

9. SIGNALS. (a). Flares will be called for by an Contact Aeroplane at one hour and two hours after Zero.
(b). A RED Smoke Bomb fired from an aeroplane denotes the assembly of a hostile counter attack and wwill be dropped on the place where the enemy is seen assembling.
(c). 3 WHITE STARS (Rifle Grenades), 38th: Division Front denotes arrival on final objective.

10. EXPLOITATION. After objectives have been taken patrols will be pushed out automatically to ascertain the position of the enemy along the whole front. No general advance will be made until definite orders have been made by Division, on information being received from the flanks. The first bound of the 13/ Inf: Bde; should be to the line of the sunken Road through Q.30.b. amd 24.c..
One Brigade R.F.A. will be deatiled by the CRA to move forward with the 13/ Infantry Brigade in the event of an advance.
The 95/ L.T.Battery will be placed under the orders of the 13/ Inf: Bde: for exploitation purposes.
A Section of Tunnellers will be at the disposa disposal of the 13/ Inf: Bde:.

11. ACKNOWLEDGE.

Issued at 5.30.pm.   (sd). G.W. GORDON.HALL Lieut; - Colone
                                 General Staff, 5th: Division.

Programme of Training for Reserve Company for 5 Days.

Hour.	1st: Day	2nd: Day.	3rd: Day.	4th: Day.	5th: Day.
8.30.am. to 9.15.am	P. T.	P. T.	P. T.		P. T.
9.30.am. to 10.30.am.	½ hour Gas Drill. ½ hour Gun Drill	½ hour Gas Drill. ½ hour I. A.	Mechanism.	Company Scheme. Details of Scheme will be issued by Battn:.	Fire Direction.
10.30.am. to 12.30.pm.	Section Scheme.	Section with Transport.	Section Excercise - changing from Limber Draught to Pack Draught.		Section Scheme.
2.pm. to 3.pm.	Map reading for Sergeants under an Officer.	- do -	Explanation of Coy; Scheme to Officers & N.C.O's by Company Commander.	Critism of Scheme to Officers & N.C.O's by Company Commander.	Map reading for Sergeants under an Officer.

NOTE. Gas Drill will be practised on all Parades.

22nd: Septr: 1918.

Major, for O.C.,

No: 5 Battalion Machine Gun Corps.

SECRET.

Disposition of M.G.'s at 9 A.M.

W.23/56

No. 5 BATTALION
MACHINE GUN
CORPS

a/6

Company and Coy. Gun
positions shewn
are at present
concentrated at
P.28.c.50.30.

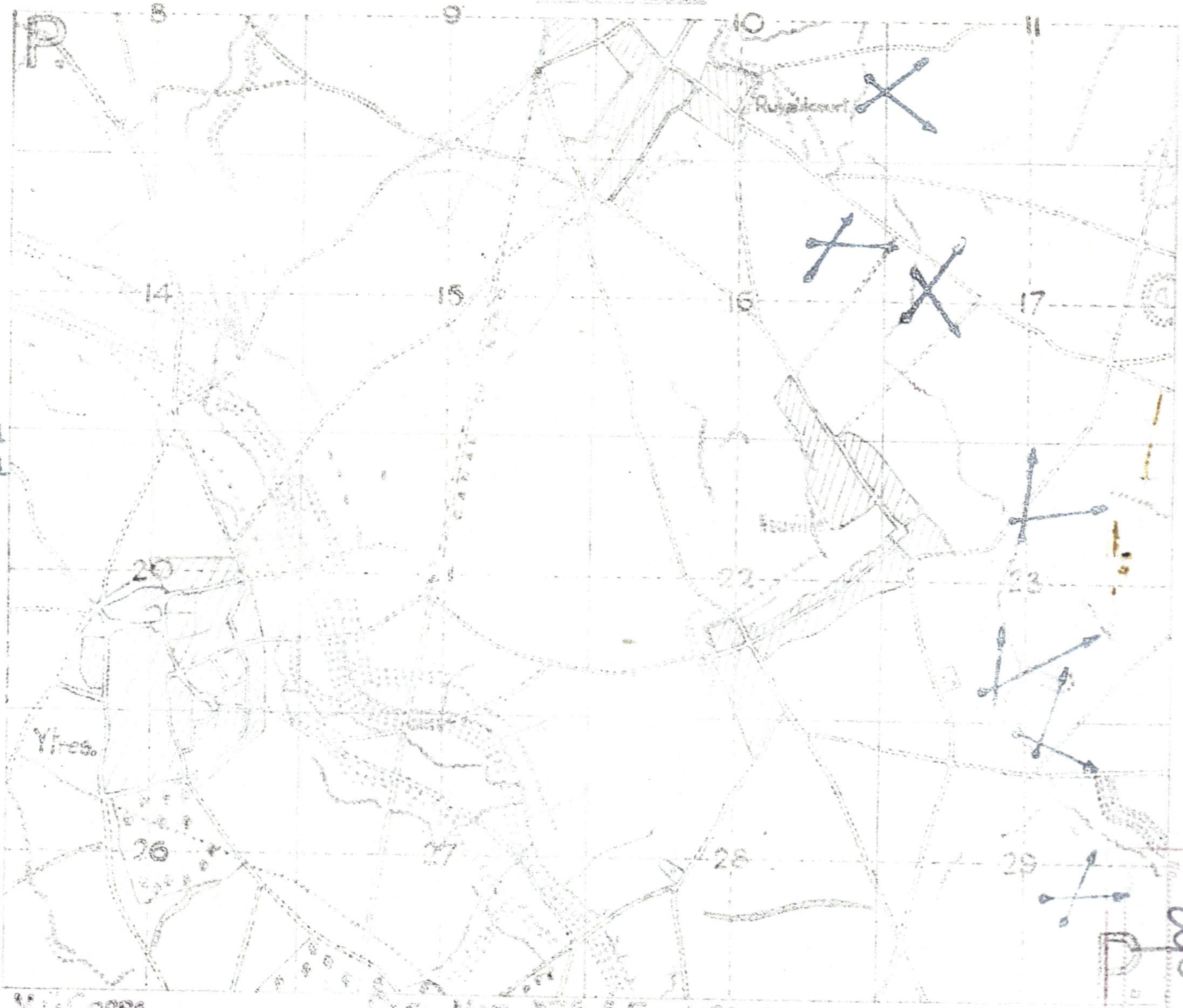

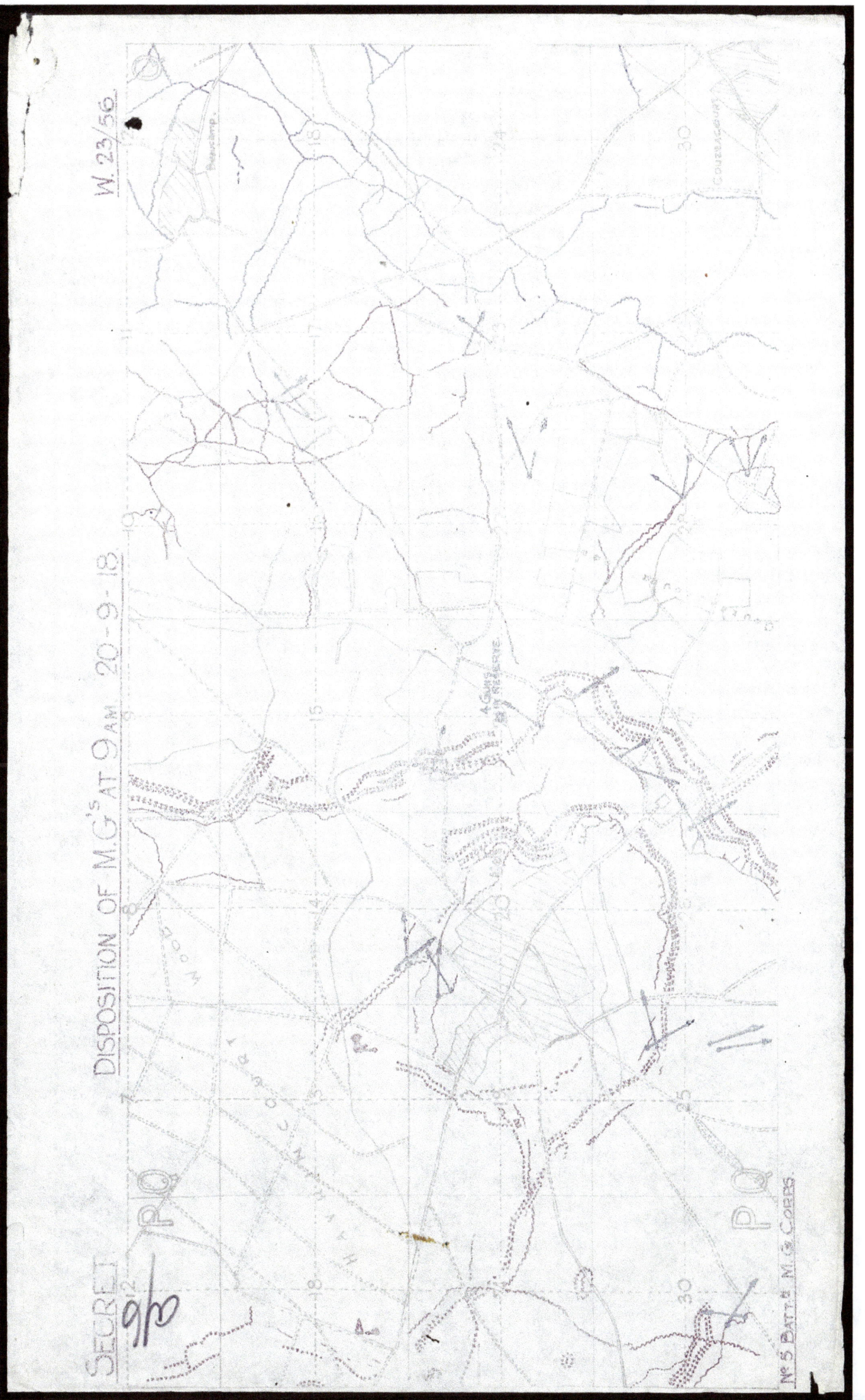

SECRET.   Copy No:..........

No: 5 Battalion Machine Gun Corps.

OPERATION ORDER No: 30.

Map Reference - Sheet 57.c. - 1/40000.

1. On the night 24th:/25th: Septr: Company reliefs will take place in accordance with the Table attached.

2. Details of the relief will be arranged between Company Commanders concerned.

3. All work in connection with the defence etc: now in hand will be taken over and continued. All plans for projected work will also be taken over.

4. Completion of relief will be notified to Battalion Headquarters by the Code Word "ROMA".

5. Machine Gun Companies will acknowledge.

Issued at 7.15.pm.   (sd) R.H.Cutting.   Lieut: - Colonel,

22nd: Septr: 1918.   Commanding No: 5 Battn: M. Gun Corps.

Copies to   1. 5th: Divn:
             2. 13/ Inf: Bde:
             3. 15/   do:
             4. 95/   do:
             5. A. Company.
             6. B.   do:
             7. C.   do:
             8. D.   do:
             9. Signalling Officer.
             10. Qr: Mr:.
             11. Intelligence Officer.
             12. War Diary.
             13.   do:
             14. Office.

P. T. O.

Table of Moves to accompany No: 5 Bn: M.G.Corps O.O. 30.

Company.	From.	To.	In relief of.	Remarks.
"A" 1 Section.	Reserve.	Q.25.b. & d.	Position vacated by "C" Company.	
1 Section.	Reserve.	Q.26.d.& Q.27.a.		
2 Sections.		Front Line	Right 2 Sections of "B" Company.	
"B" Company.	Front System.	BARASTRE.	"A" Company.	
"C" 1 Section.	Q.25.b.& d.	Q.21.central.	Reserve Section,"B" Coy.	
1 Section.	Q.26.d.& Q.27.a.	Q.16.b. & Q.17.a.	Left Section, "B" Coy.	
2 Sections.	Remain in present positions.			
"D" Company.	Remain in present position.			

"C" Company Headquarters will remain in present position.

"A" Company will take over the present Headquarters of "B" Company.

S E C R E T.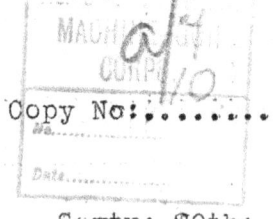

Copy No:........

No: 5 Battalion Machine Gun Corps.

OPERATION ORDER NO: 29.   Septr: 20th:

Reference Map - Sheet 57.c. - 1/40000.

1. On the night of the 21st:/22nd:Septr: Company reliefs will take place in accordance with the attached Table.

2. Details of the relief will be arranged between Company Commanders concerned.

3. **All work in connection with the defence** etc: now in hand will be taken over and continued. All plans for projected work will also be taken over.

4. Completion of relief will be notified to Battalion Headquarters by the Code Word "NILLA".

Issued at 12 Noon.

Captain,
for Lieut;-Col:,
Commanding No: 5 Battn: M. Gun Corps.

Copies to -
1. 5/Division.
2. 13/ Inf: Bde:
3. 15/   do;
4. 95/   do:
5. "A" Company.
6. "B"   do:
7. "C"   do:
8. "D"   do:
9. Signalling Officer.
10. War Diary.
11.   do:
12. Office.

TABLE OF MOVES TO ACCOMPANY 5/BN,M.G.CORPS O.O.,No: 29.

Company.	From.	To.	In relief of	Remarks.
"A"	Front System	Reserve in BARASTRE (O.16.d.)	"C" Company.	After relief O.C. "A" Company will reconnoitre the route to MAIN LINE of RESISTANCE and get in touch with O.C. "C" Coy: who will show him the disposition for the defence of the line.
"B"	Divn: Line Area P.22.	Front System.	"A" Company.	
"C"	Reserve BARASTRE,O16.d.	MAIN LINE of RESISTANCE. Q.13.d.	"D" Company.	
"D"	MAIN LINE of RESISTANCE. Q.13.d.	Divn: Line Area. P.22.	"B" Company.	"D" Company will take over the present location of "B" Coy; and will be ready to occupy positions in the Divn; Line in case of alarm. The Coy: will not be responsible for the defence of the ground in rear of the Divn: Line.

SECRET.   Copy No:........

No: 5 Battalion Machine Gun Corps.

Operation Order No: 31.

Reference Map - Sheet 57.c. S.E.

1. On a date to be notified later the IV Corps will resume the offensive. The objective of the 5th: Division will be the BEAUCAMP and HIGHLAND Ridges.

2. The attack of the 5th: Division will be carried out by the 13/ Infantry Brigade on the right and the 15/ Infantry Brigade on the left.

3. ACTION OF MACHINE GUNS.

"A" Company will be allotted to the 13/ Infantry Brigade to assist in the consolidation of the captured area.
"C" Company will be allotted to the 15/ Infantry Brigade to assist in the consolidation of the captured area.
"B" Company will be in Divisional Reserve and will be available for exploitation.
"D" Company will support the attack of the 13/ Infantry Brigade by enfilading the sunken road in Q.30.a. and b. with 8 guns from positions about Q.16.d.1.4.. This Company will also support the attack of the 15/ Infantry Brigade with direct fire on BEAUCAMP and the ridge EAST of BEAUCAMP from positions about Q.11.c.4.3.. The guns of this Company will remain in position ready to engage any target within range during the operation.
One Company of No: 37/Bn: M.G.C. will be in position about Q.16.b.9.3. and will apply a barrage on the high ground EAST of BEAUCAMP and on the slopes WEST and NORTH of VILLERS PLOUICH.
The V. Corps will arrange to enfilade the ground in the vicinity of the sunken roads running S.W. to N.E. in R.25.a. and also the area in the vicinity of GREEN SWITCH in R.31.b., R.32.a., and R.26.c..

4. AMMUNITION. "A" and "C" Companies will arrange to make Dumps of S.A.A. in the vicinity of their assembly positions or other convenient places well forward for the use of their forward guns.
Lieut: BROADFOOT will form a Dump of S.A.A. at about Q.16.d.7.0. for the use of the barrage guns. He will use the limbers forming the Battn: Reserve for this purpose.
Battn: Reserve of S.A.A. will move to NEUVILLE to-day and will be accommodated in the vicinity of the M.G. Company stationed there.

5. Further detailed orders will be issued later.

ACKNOWLEDGE.

Issued at 11.30. am.   Lieut: - Colonel,
                                     Commanding No: 5 Battalion Machine Gun Corps.
24th: Septr: 1918

Copies to:- 1. O.C. "A" Coy: 5. " " Coy:, 37/Bn: M.G.C.
             2. O.C. "B" Coy: 6. " "   do:
             3. O.C. "C" Coy: 7. War Diary.
             4. O.C. "D" Coy: 8. Office.

Account of Operations from 12th September, 1918,
to 30th September, 1918.

No. 5 Battalion, Machine Gun Corps.

No. 5 BATTALION, MACHINE GUN CORPS.

12th Sept. 1918.   Battalion concentrated at ACHIET-LE-GRAND.
Orders received to relieve the New Zealand Machine Gun Battalion in the line.

13th Sept. 1918.   "A" Company moved off to YTRES.

14th Sept. 1918.   "A" Company relieved one Company of New Zealand Battalion in the front line. Positions were taken up as follows:-

    Left Sect.   (2 guns Q.16.b.70/20.
                   (2 guns Q.17.a.30/40.

    Centre Sect. (1 gun   Q.23.a.50/40.
                   (1 gun   Q.23.a.95/20.
                   (1 gun   Q.22.b.80/40.
                   (1 gun   Q.22.d.50/80.

    Right Sect.   (2 guns Q.28.b.30/05.
                   (2 guns Q.28.d.30/20.

    1 Section.   4 Barrage guns at Q.27.b.60/05.

The left section had 3 other ranks wounded in taking over, also 2 casualties to horses.

"B" Company marched with the 95th Infantry Brigade to YTRES area and relieved the Divisional Line Company of the N.Z. Battalion.

Company H.Q. were established at P.13.d.4/4 and the Company concentrated in dug-outs and shelters in the vicinity.

"D" Company relieved Auckland Company, N.Z. Battalion as follows:-

    1 Section - PRATTLE TRENCH. P.29.b.
    1 Section - PONDER TRENCH. P.16.d.

Section in PONDER TRENCH concentrated at P.16.d.5/2.

2 Sections concentrated at P.22.c.7/3 ready to reinforce the Divisional line if necessary.

Company H.Q. were established at P.20.c.6/6.

15th Sept. 1918.   "A" Company. It was found that the three front sections had good positions and it was decided not to alter them. The Section employed on barrage work, however, was moved back to trench running through Q.27.a. and Q.21.d. Their guns were laid on S.O.S. lines, firing up sunken road leading from GOUZEAUCOURT. It was thought that this would be a probable assembly place for the enemy.

"B" Company. This Company was ordered to be responsible for the defence of the Divisional line, (PRATTLE TRENCH, POWER TRENCH, PONDER TRENCH, and PIRATE TRENCH.)

Sixteen positions were selected and constructed as follows:-

    2 guns P.30.c.7/5.
    2 guns P.29.d.15/65.
    2 guns P.29.b.0/9.
    2 guns P.23.c.55/20.
    2 guns P.23.a.9/2.
    2 guns P.16.d.35/65.
    2 guns P.17.a.2/2.
    2 guns P.10.d.9/5.

2.

These positions were not manned but Sections were kept ready to move out into position if necessary.

"C" Company. Moved from ACHIET-LE-GRAND and took over billets S.E.of BARASTRE O.16.d.70/30.This Company was kept in reserve.

"D" Company. 1 section from P.22.c.7/3 moved to position in PESTLE TRENCH P.30.a. and c.

16th Sept.1918.   The "A" Echelons of Companies were billeted as follows:-

"A","B",and "D" Companies near NEUVILLE in QUARRY at P.22.c.7.2.

Battalion "B" Echelon was formed N.of BARASTRE at O.10.c.9/9.

Battalion H.Q.were established at VILLERS-AU-FLOS.O.8.c.O/7.

"B" Company moved to QUARRY near NEUVILLE at P.22.c.7/2.

On night 16/17th 1 section of "D" Company in PESTLE TRENCH moved to positions in Q.25.b. and d.

Section of "D" Company in PONDER TRENCH relieved Section of "A" Company in QUOTIENT TRENCH in Q.27.a.

Section of "D" Company at P.22.c.7/3 took up positions in Q.14.c. and Q.20.c.

Section of "A" Company relieved by Section of "D" Company went into reserve at Q.21.b.3/2.

17th Sept.1918.   "D" Company H.Q.moved to Q.13.d.central.

Section of "D" Company at PRATTLE TRENCH moved to QUOTIENT TRENCH.

Section of "D" Company already in QUOTIENT TRENCH sideslipped to the left to positions in QUALITY and QUACK TRENCH, Q.21.c and d.

The Battalion was then established as follows:-

"A" Company. Front System.
"D" Company. Main Line of Resistance.
"B" Company. Divisional Line.
"C" Company. In Reserve.

18th Sept.1918.   The Division attacked in conjunction with the Division on the right. 2/K.O.S.B.were the attacking Battalion for this Division - first objective being a line from DEAD MAN'S CORNER,Q.23.c. to Q.29.d.90/30. The guns of this Battalion were employed as follows:-

"A" Company.   Centre Section of this Company at Q.28.b.and d. were ordered to be prepared to move forward and consolidate the first objective.

	Barrage Guns.	Target.
"A" Battery.	6 guns at Q.28.b.30/10.	200 yds.each side of a line Q.24.b.7/1 to Q.24.b.3/8.
"B" Battery.	2 guns at Q.22.d.45/70.	200 yds.each side of a line Q.24.b.7/1 to Q.24.b.3/8.
"C" Battery.	2 guns at Q.16.b.80/15.) 2 " " Q.17.a.15/10.)	Enfilade sunken road from Q.24.c.4/2 to Q.30.b.5/3.

"D" Company.	Barrage Guns.	Target.
"Y" Battery.	8 guns at Q.21.b.3/8.	200 yds.each side of a line Q.18.a.3/1 to Q.7.b.8/8
"X" Battery.	4 guns at Q.28.c.7/5.	200 yds.each side of a line Q.30.b.6/2 to Q.30.b.3/7.

Zero hour for the attack 5.20 a.m.
The attack was not a success owing to the Division on our right failing to take their objective.

"Y" Battery fired 13,000 rounds.
"X" Battery fired 6,000 rounds.

At 2.30 p.m. "D" Company's barrage guns returned to their original defensive positions.
Consolidating section of "A" Company also returned to its original position.

"B" and "C" Companies. In same position carrying on training.

19th Sept.1918. News received that the enemy were carrying out a relief. 3 Sections of "A" Company carried out harassing fire - S.A.A. expended - 4,000 rounds per gun. Barrage section of "A" Company withdrawn to Company Reserve.

20th Sept.1918. All companies now in original positions - day passed quietly.

21st Sept.1918. Inter-Company Relief. Disposition of Companies now as follows:-

"A" Company. In reserve at BARASTRE.
"B" Company. Front line.
"C" Company. Main Line of Resistance.
"D" Company. Divisional Line.

22nd Sept.1918. Day passed quietly - enemy quiet.

23rd Sept.1918. ------------------------------

24th Sept.1918. Inter-Company relief as per Operation Order attached. Disposition of Companies after relief as follows:-

"A" Company. Echeloned in depth in Right Sector.
   i.e. 2 sections. Front Line.
        2 sections. Main Line of Resistance.
"B" Company. In reserve at BARASTRE.
"C" Company. Echeloned in depth in Left sector.
   i.e. 2 sections. Front Line.
        2 sections. Main Line of Resistance.
"D" Company. Divisional Line.

25th Sept.1918. Companies in same positions. Enemy quiet.
Operation Order issued for attack to be carried out on the 27th. See O.O.32 attached.

26th Sept.1918. Companies in same positions. Enemy quiet. Advanced Battalion H.Q. moved to Div. Report Centre at P.24.b.6/6.
"B" Company, No.37 Battalion, M.G.C. attached to this Battalion for the operation. This Company billeted at RUYAULCOURT.
No.16193 Cpl.W.MUNCEY. "A" Company, did excellent work in getting his limbers right up to the front line in daylight and making a dump of S.A.A. for the ~~coming~~ attack.

27th Sept.1918. "A" Company. On the morning of the 27th the 5th Division attacked in conjunction with Divisions on its right and left flanks; the task allotted to the 13th Infantry Brigade was to capture and consolidate LINCOLN RESERVE TRENCH from Q.18.d.10/40. to Q.29.c.95/50. This Company was attched to the 13th Infantry Brigade. Two sections to consolidate objective gained and two sections to remain in depth. The 1st R.W.Kent Regt. who attacked on the right of the

Brigade front failed to gain their objective; they dug in some 200 yards in front of their original front line. No.2 Section, who were to consolidate the objective with them, if gained, was ordered to take up the following positions, in the old front line:-

        2 guns Q.29.a.10/20.
        2 guns Q.29.a.40/80.

These guns came in for some very heavy shelling during the day.

The 14th R.Warwick.Regt. gained their objective, this Battalion being on the left of the Brigade front. No.3 Section moved up into the following positions:-

        2 guns approximately Q.23.b.70/40.
        2 guns approximately Q.23.b.95/50.

The infantry had failed to complete their tasks, in that the communication trench leading from SMUT TRENCH to LINCOLN RESERVE was not cleared of the enemy. Also the communication trench running from DELLA POST to MIDLAND RESERVE was not cleared. During the early part of the morning from about 10.a.m. the enemy organised strong bombing parties working up communication trenches into MIDLAND RESERVE placing the four guns in a very critical position. During attack 2/Lieut.G.SHAW, O.C. No.3 Section and Sergt.YOUNG W. got out of the trench with the Infantry reconnoitring for gun positions. They captured 30 prisoners some being captured in the dugout and some in a trench. These prisoners were marched to Battalion H.Q. (Infantry)

About 4 p.m. the enemy organised a counter-attack, and drove in our left flank. Enemy worked down DUNRAVEN and got right behind No.3 Section, and worked down SOOT AVENUE. A bombing party which was organised by the 14th R.Warwick.Regt. managed to beat him back and established a post about Q.23.b.60/60. Two of No.3 Section guns which were situated about Q.18.c.40/50 had to retire owing to a strong enemy bombing party working right up to their position. These guns were subsequently mounted in SOOT AVENUE and inflicted casualties on the enemy. The remaining two guns of No.3 Section were mounted in communication trench running from MIDLAND TRENCH to SOOT AVENUE in Q.23.b. These two guns inflicted very heavy casualties on the enemy.

It was during this operation that Sergt.W.YOUNG and Sergt.S.THOMSON, "A" Company, did excellent work both in the initial attack and in the GERMAN counter-attack of the afternoon. These N.C.Os. kept their guns in action until the enemy were only 30 yards from their positions and then having to withdraw because of the heavy hostile bombing attack managed to bring their guns back to another position, having completely covered the withdrawal of the Infantry. Private JOUGHIN of the same Company did especially good work as No.1 of his gun.

"C" Company. On the morning of the 27th three sections went forward and one was in reserve at BATTERY POST Q.23.a.

Owing to the enemy machine guns and snipers the infantry were unable to quite reach their objective and the front line was established just West of the first objective. Owing to casualties only 9 guns were able to come into action out of the 12 which had gone forward and these 9 helped in the consolidation and covered the exposed left flank.

Owing to the enemy getting in behind our front line on the right about 5.30 p.m. on the same day after several local counter-attacks, the whole line withdrew and was again established on the road running from BEAUCAMP through Q.17.b. to Q.17.d.50.30.

During this withdrawal two of the guns of this Company fell into the hands of the enemy after functioning as long as possible, and one was put out of action by a direct hit of a shell.

The two guns were afterwards retaken by the 95th Brigade.

The remaining six guns then helped in the consolidation of the road mentioned above and remained there during the night of the 27/28th.

Owing to casualties this Company was re-organised into 3 Sections.

"D" Company.   Barrage guns fired 57,785 rounds.
               Two guns were put out of action by enemy shell fire.
               At 12 noon two sections of "D" Company at Q.15.c. and
Q.11.c.were ordered to move forward.
               These two sections took up positions as follows:-
               1 section at Q.11.a.3/5.
               1 section.(2 guns Q.17.b.4/3.
                         (2 guns Q.17.b.2/6.
               During the counter-attack at about 4 p.m.these two
sections obtained good shooting causing casualties to the enemy. About 5,500
rounds were fired.
               During this attack 19 belt boxes were sent forward to
"C" Company and one gun of "C" Company was attached,to a section of "D" Company.
               During the night 27/28th Company H.Q.of "D" Company
moved to Q.17.a.0/5 and "A" Echelon Transport was brought forward to Q.15.d.
as these sections were warned to be prepaped to move forward at 3.30 a.m.
to consolidate WELSH RIDGE should the 95th Brigade attack be successful.
As the attack during the day had not secured the objective the 95th Brigade
were ordered to complete the capture of BEAUCAMP RIDGE.
               "B" Company operated with the 95th Infantry Brigade for
this attack.
               The Company moved at 2 a.m.(28th inst.)to take part
in the attack.No.1 Section to go forward with the 1st East Surreys
attacking VILLERS PLOUICH. No.3 Section with 1st DEVONS to attack
LINCOLN RESERVE. No.2 Section on right flank in MIDLAND RESERVE at Q.23.b.
90/80,to assist in consolidation. No.4 Section in reserve at BATTERY POST.
The attack on the left went well but little progress was made on the right.
               During the attack No.1 section captured 30 prisoners
and 3 Machine Guns.
               At conclusion of attack the dispositions were as follows:-
               Company H.Q.at Q.17.a.0.5.
               Reserve section   do
               1 section in MIDLAND RESERVE(2 guns at Q.12.a.6.1.
                                           (2 guns at Q.18.b.7.9.
               1 section in sunken road Q.17.d.6.5.
               1 section(2 guns Q.23.b.9.6.MIDLAND RESERVE.
                        (2 guns Q.17.d.3.2.
"B" Company,No.37 Bn.M.G.C. fired 111,000 rounds. Three guns of this
Company were put out of action by enemy shellfire.
28th Sept.1918. On the morning of the 28th it was found that the enemy
                had vacated his positions in the BEAUCAMP RIDGE.
                "A" Company was ordered to rest in its present position.
                "C" Company was withdrawn to bivouac at Q.14.c.& Q.20.a.
                Advanced Battn.H.Q.moved to QUARRY at Q.20.d.3/3.
                "B" Echelon moved to NEUVILLE P.22.c.7/2.
                95th Infantry Brigade had orders to push forward with
15th Infantry Brigade in support.
               The right Battalion(1st DEVONS) were able to feel their
way forward to objective LINCOLN RESERVE after which orders were received
for the SURREYS to attack SURREY ROAD as first objective and GONNELIEU
ROAD R.10.c. R.16.a and c.as final objective. 1st DEVONS were to attack
same objectives on the right.
   "B" Company.   No.4 Section from reserve was ordered forward on left
and No.3 section on right. The first objective was taken.
               No.4 section reached their objective NEW YEAR TRENCH
in good time.
               No.3 section got as far as the trenches in R.13.c.6.7.
when the order of attack was again changed.
"D" Company.   At midday this Company received orders to theeffect
that they were at the disposal of the B.G.C.15th Infantry Brigade,and were
ordered to be disposed as follows:-

1 section at Q.29.b.3.5.
1 section at Q.24.central.
2 sections concentrated at BATTERY POST.
Company H.Q.at DEAD MAN'S CORNER Q.23.c.
The sections used limbers to get into their positions.

The two forward sections of this Company were ordered to give covering fire during the advance of the Infantry to the Railway in R.19.d. The Infantry moved forward at 1.30 p.m. but owing to orders being received late by this Company, the sections were not then in position.

These sections fired off 15,000 rounds in direct overhead fire.

The Section of "D" Company in Q.24.central owing to casualties were only able to man two guns.

During the night 28/29th sections were disposed as follows:-

1 section at Q.30.b.4.5.
1 section at Q.24.a.6.8.

2 gunteams of reserve section went forward and made a complete section with the 2 guns already at Q.24.a.6.8. Pack transport was used right up to position.

This Company was then reorganised into 3 sections owing to casualties.

29th Sept.1918. For the attack by the 15th and 95th Infantry Brigades "B" and "D" Companies' operations were as follows:-

"B" Company. Sections Nos.4 and 3 were employed to go forward, the other two sections to go forward and consolidate in depth. The intended dispositions were

4 guns in JAMT TRENCH R.21.c and d.
4 guns in FERN TRENCH R.27.a.
4 guns in HOLLY TRENCH R.20.d.
4 guns in PRENTICE TRENCH R.14.d.

The 15th Infantry Brigade was to pass through the 95th Infantry Brigade and attack a further objective. Information was received that the objectives of the 95th Infantry Brigade had been taken and the rear sections were moved forward with limber transport. On reaching FLAG RAVINE R.14.d.8.4. one section complete with limbers was heavily fired on by Machine Guns and rifles and it was discovered that the objectives had not been taken.

This section had moved up with limbers to within 200 yards of the enemy position. The Division on the right had not taken their objective either so final dispositions of the Company were

4 guns in NEWPORT TRENCH R.14.d.
4 guns in trenches R.13.c.6.7.
4 guns in DUNRAVEN TRENCH R.19.a.8.3.
4 guns in sap of DUNRAVEN TRENCH R.19.a.2.7.

The sections remained in these positions overnight.

"D" Company.

Two forward sections (nos.1 and 2) were ordered to move forward with pack animals to R.19.a.5.3. to cover the advance of the 15th Infantry Brigade and to follow them up on to the ridge in R.30 and 26. No. 2 section covered the advance with indirect fire from R.19.c.2.7. on R.22.c. and 28.a. 2,000 rounds being fired.

No.2 section then moved to R.19.a.7.4. O.C.Company had established a report centre with Brigade H.Q. during the night 28/29th at Q.29.b.1.2.

No.1 section early on the 29th reached R.19.d.3.7. but 3 mules were hit crossing the Railway in R.19.

The situation was very obscure and the enemy were sweeping the valley with machine guns from GONNELIEU.

2,200 rounds were fired by Nos.1 and 2 sections on GONNELIEU.

During the 29th No.1 section moved to R.20.b.7.5.

PRENTICE TRENCH and No.2 section moved to positions R.20.c.HOLLY SUPPORT and R.20.a.GANE TRENCH being in position by 3 p.m. These two sections did not advance further from these positions.

On night 29/30th Reserve section moved by way of limbers to R.25.b.06.65.and then by pack mule to positions at R.26.a.1.9.

They fired indirect on to GONNELIEU from 4.30 to 4.50 p.m.. As it was getting light the section moved to the trench R.26.a.5.5. and continued to fire direct on GONNELIEU expending in all 19,250 rounds. The sections withdrew on orders at 4.30 p.m.(30th inst)by which time a Company of No.37 Battalion,M.G.C. had passed through.

During the night 29/30th the Company H.Q.were gassed and all except the O.C. and the C.S.M. became casualties.

30th Sept.1918.   The Battalion was relieved by No.37 Battalion,M.G.C.

1st October,1918.   Battalion concentrated in BERTINCOURT.

During the period 12th/30th September,1918,the total casualties to this Battalion were

Officers.		Other Ranks.	
Killed	Wounded.	Killed.	Wounded.
3	3	16	67.

Lessons Learnt from these Operations.

1. That it is sometimes necessary to re-organise Companies into 2 Sections after heavy casualties have been suffered. If possible the Company should be withdrawn into reserve to carry out the re-organisation but if this withdrawal is not practicable the Company should be re-organised while in action.

2. Even in positions overlooked by the enemy, limbers and pack transport can be employed with success by a determined leader. In order to use transport to the best advantage under these circumstances it is necessary that the transport drivers are well trained and that the teams waste no time in unloading the equipment of the limbers or animals, otherwise heavy casualties are likely to be suffered.

8th October, 1918.

Lieutenant-Colonel,
Commanding No.5 Bn. Machine Gun Corps.

SECRET.   Copy No.......

No. 5 Battalion, Machine Gun Corps.
OPERATION ORDER No. 30.

1.   On the night 24/25th September, 1918, Company reliefs will take place in accordance with the table attached.

2.   Details of the relief will be arranged between the Company Commanders concerned.

3.   All work in connection with the defence etc. now in hand will be taken over and continued. All plans for projected work will also be taken over.

4.   Completion of relief will be notified to the Battalion Headquarters by the Code Word "ROMA".

5.   Machine Gun Companies will acknowledge.

(Sd.) R. H. Cutting

Issued at 7.15 p.m.   Lieut. Colonel,
22nd September, 1918.   Commanding No. 5 Battalion, Machine Gun Corps.

Copies to
1. 5th Division.
2. 13/Inf. Bde.
3. 15/Inf. Bde.
4. 95/Inf. bde.
5. A Company.
6. B Company.
7. C Company.
8. D Company.
9. Signalling Officer.
10. Quartermaster.
11. Intelligence Officer.
12. War Diary.
13. War Diary.
14. Office.

Table of Moves to accompany No.5 Battalion, M.G.C. Operation Order No.30.

Company.		From.	To	In relief of.	Remarks.
"A"	1 section.	Reserve.	Q.25.b and d.		Position vacated by "C" Company.
	1 section.	Reserve	Q.26.d. & Q.27.a.		Right 2 sections of "B" Company.
	2 sections		Front line		
"B" Company.		Front system.	BARASTRE.	"A" Company.	
"C"	1 section.	Q.25.b and d.	Q.21.central		Reserve section "B" Coy.
	1 section.	Q.26.d. & Q.27.a.	Q.16.b. & Q.17.a.		Left section "B" Coy.
	2 sections.	Remain in present positions.			
"D" Company.		Remain in present position.			

"C" Company H.Q. will remain in present position.

"A" Company will take over the present H.Q. of "B" Company.

S E C R E T.   Copy No............

No.5 Battalion, Machine Gun Corps.
Operation Order No.32.
Reference Sheet Map 57.d. S.E. 1/20000.
                                                            25th Sept. 1918.

1.   The Third Army is resuming the advance on a date and at a time to be notified later.
            The task of the 5th Division is to capture BEAUCAMP RIDGE and HIGHLAND RIDGE with a flank along AFRICAN TRENCH, and, if, the advance of the troops on the North, on MARCOING is successful, to advance to WELSH RIDGE and form a protective flank for the troops on the North.

2.   The attack of the 5th Division will be carried out by the 13/Inf.Bde on the right and the 15/Inf.Bde on the left. The 95/Inf.Bde will be in Divisional Reserve.

3. ACTION OF MACHINE GUNS.

    (a) "A" Company No.5 Battn.M.G.Corps will be allotted to the 13/Inf.Bde to assist in the consolidation of the captured area.
    (b) "B" Company No.5 Battn.M.G.Corps will be in Divisional Reserve and will be available for exploitation.
    (c) "C" Company No.5 Bn.M.G.Corps will be allotted to the 15/Inf.Bde to assist in the consolidation of the captured area.
    (d) "D" Company, No.5 Battalion, M.G.Corps will support the attack of the 15/Inf.Bde on BEAUCAMP with direct fire as follows:-
            One section will be in position about Q.17.c.7.8. and another section will be in position about Q.11.c.3.4. These two sections will keep the village of BEAUCAMp and the area in the vicinity under direct fire continuously from plus 152 to plus 186. Two gaps will be left in the Infantry line on this part of the front and the sections mentioned above must take every advantage of them in bringing their direct fire to bear on their targets. At plus 186 these gaps will be closed up and will thus limit the fire of these sections to direct overhead and indirect fire. From this point the advance on BEAUCAMP will be covered by direct overhead fire as long as the safety limit permits. At Zero plus 234 these sections will apply indirect fire on HIGHLAND RIDGE in accordance with the details shown in the table of tasks in sub-para. (6)
            If owing to fog or smoke direct fire is found to be impossible the two sections mentioned above will apply fire on the following line from Zero plus 152 to Zero plus 198 - Q.12.d.1.0. to Q.12.d.1.0.
    (e) During the attack and in the event of an S.O.S.call Machine Guns will apply an indirect Machine Gun Barrage in accordance with the following table. These guns will work as one group and will be under the command of Major PETRIE-HAY,M.C.No.5 Bn.M.G.C. from Zero onwards.

Coy.	No. of Guns.	Location.	Time	Targets	Rate of Fire	Remarks.
"D" Coy. No.5 Batt.	8	4 guns at Q.17.c.7.8.	plus 234 to p.242	R.7.d.15.50 to R.7.a.7.2.	60 rds. per min.	
		4 guns at Q.11.c.3.4.	plus 242 to p.250	R.7.d.5.6. to R.7.b.1.4.		
			S.O.S.	Enfilade Fifteen Ravine from R.19.a.X.1.2. to R.19.a.0.9.		Rate of fire for SOS. will be
	8	Q.16.d.0.3.	plus 152 to plus 178	Enfilade sunken road from Q.24.c.4.2. to Q.30.b.4.3.	100 rounds per minute	
			plus 178 to plus 212	Q.24.c.9.4. to Q.24.b.7.3.	60 rounds per minute.	1st 5 min RAPID.
"B" Coy. No.37 Batt.	16	4 guns at Q.16.b.7.8.	plus 152 to p.172	Q.18.d.10.65 to Q.18.b.10.90.	100 rounds per min.	2nd 5 mins. 100 rds per minute.
		8 guns at Q.16.b.6.1.	plus 172 to p.198	Q.18.b.50.15 to Q.12.c.85.60		
		4 guns at Q.16.b.8.2.	plus 198 to p.206	Q.18.b.60.35 to Q.12.d.20.70.	60 rds. per minute.	
			Plus 206 to p.214	R.13.a.3.5. to Q.12.d.60.90.		
			Plus 214 to p.222	R.13.a.7.6. to Q.12.d.95.95.		
			plus 222 to p.234	R.13.b.0.8 to R.7.a.35.10.		
			plus 234 to p.274	R.13.c.0.3. to R.13.a.8.4.		
			S.O.S.	do		

(f)   The Left Division of V Corps will apply Machine Gun Fire on the following areas from plus 152 to plus 212, and will open on these areas in case of an S.O.S. call.

    (1)   Area in vicinity of sunken roads in R.25.a.

    (2)   Area in vicinity of GREEN SWITCH in R.31.b. R.32.a., and R.26.c.

3.

4. COMMUNICATIONS. The Sections of "D" Company No.5 Bn.M.G.C. and "B" Company, No.37 Bn.M.G.C. will be connected up by wire and runners to Machine Gun Group Headquarters and to a Report Centre at TRIG POST. Machine Gun Group H.Q. will be connected up to H.Q.15/Inf.Bde by wire and runners and to Battn.H.Q. by wire, runners and visual.

A visual station will be established at Q.11.c.3.4. and "C" Company will arrange to establish a forward Report Centre near a Section H.Q. on BEAUCAMP RIDGE and get into touch with this visual station.

A runner will be kept at the double Battn. H.Q. of the 15/Inf.Bde at Q.23.a.8.3. to enable Battalion Commanders to call on the Barrage guns to engage any particular target.

The Code Call for the M.G.Group H.Q. will be M.G.B.

5. HEADQUARTERS.

H.Q. No.5 Bn.		Div.Report Centre P.24.a.3.6.
"A" Coy.	do	With 13/Inf.Bde Q.26.b.7.7.
"B" Coy.	do	NEUVILLE P.22.c.6.2.
"C" Coy.	do	With 15/Inf.Bde Q.22.a.3.2.
"D" Coy.	do	Q.15.c.9.1.
"B" Coy. No.37 Bn.M.G.C.		Q.16.b.8.2.

6. RATIONS. All companies will go into action with one complete days rations in addition to the iron ration.

7. AMMUNITION. Dumps have been formed at the following positions Q.16.d.7.9. and Q.16.d.1.5.

Battalion Reserve of S.A.A. is at NEUVILLE P.22.c.6.2.

Supply Tanks are dumping S.A.A. (bundle packed) in the forward area.

R.A.F. will drop S.A.A. from aeroplanes as follows:-

Each forward consolidating M.G.Section will take a "V" piece of white calico with it, which, if the normal means of ammunition supply fails, should be displayed in the vicinity of their position, the point of the "V" towards the enemy. The contact planes reports the position at once by wireless and the next machines endeavour to drop two S.A.A. boxes each on the spot by parachute.

8. REPORTS. The disposition of forward guns will be reported to Battn H.Q. as soon as known by Company Commanders.

Barrage guns will report S.A.A. expended and casualties to guns and personnel at Zero plus 5 hours and will report all targets engaged after this hour.

9. "B" Company will be ready to move at short notice at any time after Zero plus 3 hours to assist the 95/Inf.Bde should that Brigade receive orders to exploit the success of the operation.

The two sections of "D" Company in Q.16.c. will be ready to move forward if required to assist the 15/Inf.Bde in exploitation. O.C. "D" Company will arrange to have the routes forward reconnoitred with a view to making full use of Transport should he receive orders to move forward.

10. Watches for Barrage guns will be synchronised at Machine Gun Group H.Q. at an hour to be notified later.

11.   Zero hour for the 5th Division will be plus 152 at which hour the Artillery Barrage will come down on the initial line.

Zero will be notified later.

12.   Machine Gun Companies will please acknowledge.

(Sd) R.H. Cutting

Issued at 1 a.m.   Lieut. Colcenl,

26.9.18.   Commanding No.5 Battalion, Machine Gun Corps.

Copies to

1. 5th Division.
2. 13/Inf.Bde
3. 15/Inf.Bde
4. 95/Inf.Bde
5. C.M.C.O.
6. 37/M.G.Battn.
7. " " Coy. 37 Bn. M.G.C.
8. Right Flank M.G.Bn.
9. Left Flank M.G.Battn.
10. "A" Coy. No.5 Bn. M.G.C.
11. "B" Coy. No.5 Bn. M.G.C.
12. "C" Company. do
13. "D" Coy. do
14. Quartermaster.
15. Signalling Officer.
16. Intelligence Officer.
17. Office.
18.   do
19. War Diary.
20.   do

Army Form C.2118.
MACHINE GUN

WAR DIARY
or
INTELLIGENCE SUMMARY.
(Erase heading not required.)

Instructions regarding War Diaries and Intelligence Summaries are contained in F. S. Regs., Part II. and the Staff Manual respectively. Title pages will be prepared in manuscript.

Place	Date	Hour	Summary of Events and Information	Remarks and references to Appendices

Strength 1st. Septr:
- Officers: 46.
- O.R's: 845.

Increase during the Month. (Reinforcements)
- Officers: 7.
- O.R's: 117.

Totals: 53. / 962.

Decrease during the month.
- Killed.................: 3. / 22.
- Wounded.............: 3. / 97.
- Missing..............: -- / 4.
- To C.C.S. Sick......: -- / 45.

Decrease: 6. / 123.

Strength on 30th. Septr: 47. / 794.

Officer Arrivals & Departures.

Arrivals.

Major.A.W.L.E.FAWCETT.MC. from Base Depot. 1.9.18.
2/Lt:R.E.GORDON. from Base 6.9.18.
2/Lt:J. PAGE from Base 6.9.18.
2/Lt: L.G. CASTLE. from Base 6.9.18.
Lieut.R.S. SANDBACH. transferred to M.G.C. 28.7.1918.
2/Lt: MITCHELL. attd: from 1st:Leicester R: from 23.9.18.

Departures.

2/Lt:PICKERING Wounded 15.9.18. W'd:15
2/Lt: PAYNE. Killed 14.9.18
2/Lt:C.MASON Killed 27.9.18.
2/Lt:J.HOLLOWAY do:
2/Lt:C.I.ATTENELL. Wounded 28.9.18.
2/Lt:L.H. BRISTOWE. wounded (Gas). 29.9.18.

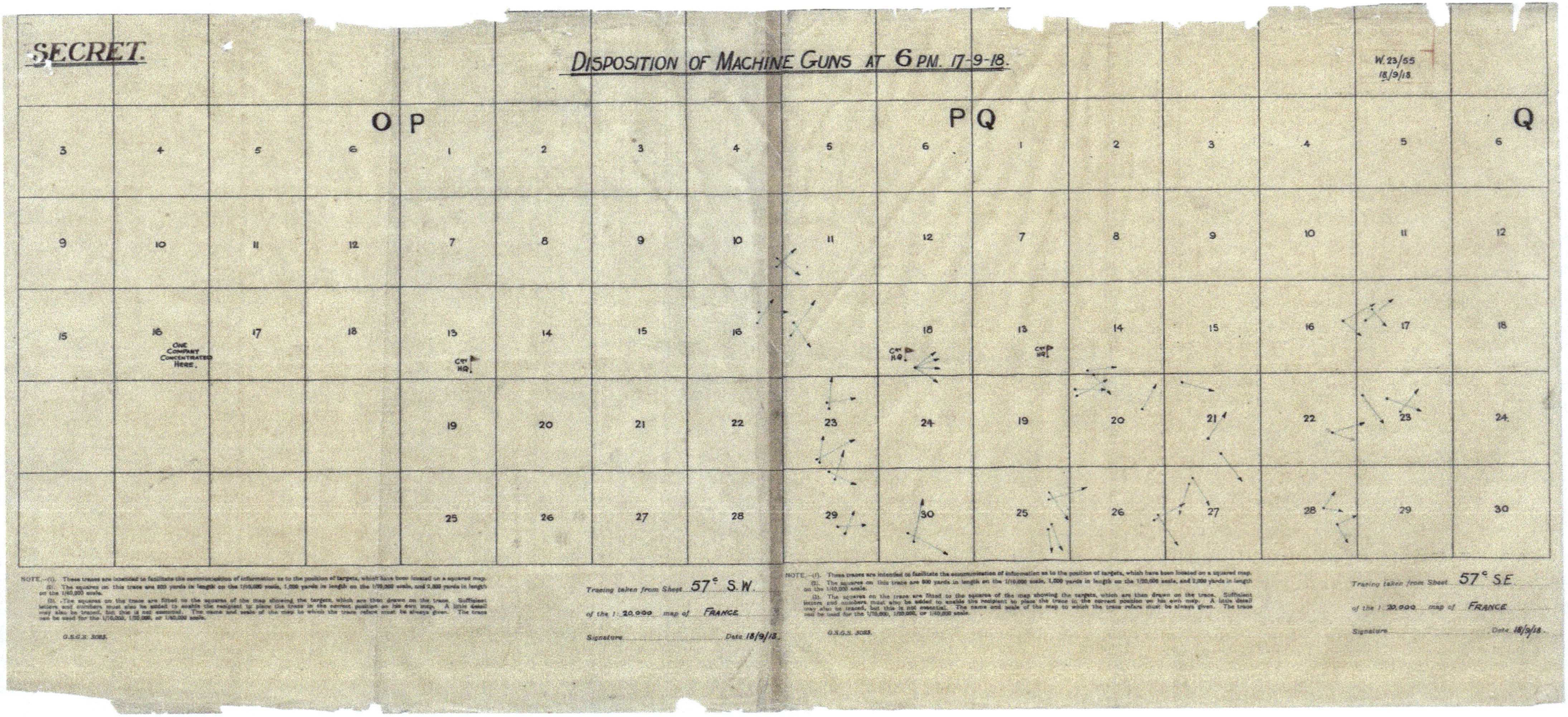

SECRET.

DISPOSITION OF MACHINE GUNS AT 6 P.M. 17-9-18.

W.23/55
18/9/18

SECRET.

→ DISPOSITION OF M.G's AT 9 A.M. 20-9-18. →

W 23/55
20/9/18

WAR DIARY.

No 5 Battalion Machine Gun Corps.

October 31st 1918.

[signature]
Major
Commanding No 5 Battⁿ M.G. Corps.

Reference Maps
57 SE. 57 SW. 1:20,000

Original

Sheet 1.

Army Form C. 2118.

WAR DIARY
—OF—
INTELLIGENCE SUMMARY.
(Erase heading not required.)

Instructions regarding War Diaries and Intelligence Summaries are contained in F. S. Regs., Part II. and the Staff Manual respectively. Title pages will be prepared in manuscript.

Place	Date	Hour	Summary of Events and Information	Remarks and references to Appendices
BERTINCOURT	1st 2/2/1918		Weather fine. Battalion concentrated at BERTINCOURT. for training carried out.	See Appendix a/1.
	2nd		-do- -do- -do-	
	3rd		-do- -do- -do-	
	4th		-do- -do- -do-	
	5th		-do- -do- -do-	
	6th		The following Officers joined Battalion from Base Depot. Major D.G. KYDD. MC. 2/Lieut R.H. CROSOER 7 2/Lieut V.P. BOND. Battalion concentrated at BERTINCOURT. Departures, Lieut RFC DARE to 15th Hants Regt.	
	7th		Battalion concentrated at BERTINCOURT.	
	8th		Battalion march to BANTOUZELLE Area. Departures Major F.N. PETRIE - HAY. MC. to IV Corps as C.M.G.O.	
BANTOUZELLE	9th		Reinforcements 2/Lt 32 ORs Joined Battalion from Base Depot. Lieut COX + Lieut CHAMBERS joined Battn from Base Depot. Lieut CULVERWELL	

Reference Map 57B N.E. 1:20000   Original   Sheet 2

Army Form C. 2118.

WAR DIARY
INTELLIGENCE SUMMARY.
(Erase heading not required.)

Place	Date	Hour	Summary of Events and Information	Remarks and references to Appendices
	10th		Battalion march to N.6.d ESNES.	See Appendix 9/2
2 June	11th		" " CAUDRY. "A" Company move forward with the 13th Infantry Brigade. Departures 2/Lieut G.E. WHITE and Lieut GLEDHILL L.D. to U.K. for four of duty at Grantham.	
-do-	12th		Companies move forward with their respective Brigades.	
-do-	13th		Disposition of Companies as follows. One Company disposed for the defence of Spur running T.12.a - T.6.a - T.6.c and D.3.c. Coy HQ at T.10.b 5.2. One Section at about T.11 central. One section at about T.4.d. 2 Sections + Coy HQ at T.22 x 50.25. One Company at BETHENCOURT. One Company at CAUDRY.	
-do-	14th		Enemy Counter-attack on BRIASTRE was repulsed. Our Artillery Barrage was very effective when S.O.S. went up. Enemy M.G. fired at intervals to NEUVILLY enfilading Road at T.36.a 30/28. Two small parties of Enemy were seen. E.26. were dispersed by our M.Gs. Reinforcements 8 O.Rs joined Battalion from Base Depot	

Army Form C. 2118.

Reference Map.
57B. N.E. 1:20000

Original   Sheet 3.

WAR DIARY
INTELLIGENCE SUMMARY.
(Erase heading not required.)

Instructions regarding War Diaries and Intelligence Summaries are contained in F. S. Regs., Part II. and the Staff Manual respectively. Title pages will be prepared in manuscript.

Place	Date	Hour	Summary of Events and Information	Remarks and references to Appendices
In Line	Oct. 1918 15th		Defence Scheme prepared. Enemy Artillery was very active on VIESLY and BRIASTRE. Gas & H.E. Shells to Front & main line. Squadron of 15 E.A. flying high, went over at 05:00 hrs. Reinforcement 1 N.C.O. + 1 O.R. joined the Battn. Weather dull.	See Appendix a/-/
-do-	16th		Enemy Artillery fairly active. VIESLY and vicinity subjected to a fairly heavy gas shell bombardment in the early morning, also to river valley and our main line of defence. Enemy M.G's fired during the night on crossroad J.6.a.10.30. Withdrawal Operation Order 36 (Company Relief) issued.	See Appendix 11 a/5
-do-	17th		Situation unchanged. Weather wet. Our M.G's carried out harassing fire, expending 8,000 rounds. Reinforcement 14 O.R's joined the Battalion from Base Depot. Warning Order No. 8 issued	See Appendix 11 a/6
-do-	18th		Weather fine. Situation unchanged. Operation Order No. 37 issued. See appendix a/-	See Appendix a/7

Reference Map 57.B.NE 1/20000   Origin 66   Army Form C. 2118.

WAR DIARY
or
INTELLIGENCE SUMMARY.
(Erase heading not required.)

Sheet 4

Place	Date Oct	Hour 1918	Summary of Events and Information	Remarks and references to Appendices
In line	19th		Situation unchanged. Weather Wet. Considerable shelling about T.O.J between 03.45 hrs & 04.15 hours. Between 05.00 hrs & 05.30 Gas shells fell in this area & also in Tien Advanced Bn. H.Q. moved up to CLERMONT CHAU. 19d 20/50.	
In line	20th		Wet. 5th Division attacked at 02.00 hrs & again at 16.00 hrs. Enemy counter-attacked at 09.30 hrs. Dispositions slight. Disposition of Companies. "B" Company in the line "D" Company at VIESLY. "A" Company at INCHY & "C" Company remained at BETHENCOURT.	See Appendix A/-9
In line	21st		"C" Company changed over with "D" Company. "D" Company moved back to CAUDRY. Operation Order 38 issued. 4 Reinforcements joined the Battalion.	See Appendix A/-8
	22nd		Advanced Battalion H.Q. moved forward to BRIASTRE.	
In line CAUDRY	23rd		5th Division attacked at 03.20 hrs & again at 01.00 hrs. 37th Brigade moved through the 5th Division Battalion consequently rejoined the Battalion. 5 Reinforcements joined the Battalion.	See Appendix A/-1

Original

Reference Map. 57.B 1:40,000 Sheet 5

Army Form C. 2118.

WAR DIARY or INTELLIGENCE SUMMARY.
(Erase heading not required.)

Instructions regarding War Diaries and Intelligence Summaries are contained in F. S. Regs., Part II. and the Staff Manual respectively. Title pages will be prepared in manuscript.

Place	Date	Hour	Summary of Events and Information	Remarks and references to Appendices
CAUDRY	24th 1918		Battalion concentrated at CAUDRY. Companies cleaning & drying, weather fine.	
	25th		Companies on Bathing Parade. The following Officers joined the Battalion from Base Depot 2/Lieut. J.M. GORNALL, 2/Lieut T.W. HARRISON, 2/Lieut W. PHILIPS + also 10 O.R's. (Extract from 5th Division Intelligence Summary d/25/10/18) "One prisoner the gunner of M.G Team stated that his gun engaged a BRITISH M.G Team which they saw coming into action, without success until the BRITISH GUN got into action & knocked out the gun & team with the exception of himself."	
	26th		Training Programme issued. Reinforcements, 20 O.R's joined the Battalion from Base Depot.	See appendix a/-10
	27th		Companies training as per Programme attached. 2 O.R's joined the Battalion from Base Depot.	
	28th		Companies training as per programme attached.	

Original

Reference Map 57^B 1:40000

Army Form C. 2118.

Sheet 6

WAR DIARY
INTELLIGENCE SUMMARY
(Erase heading not required.)

Instructions regarding War Diaries and Intelligence Summaries are contained in F. S. Regs., Part II. and the Staff Manual respectively. Title pages will be prepared in manuscript.

Place	Date	Hour	Summary of Events and Information	Remarks and references to Appendices
		1918		
CAUDRY	29		Nine Companies training as per Programme attached	See appendix 10
			The following Officer joined from Base Depot. 2/Lieut F. EVANS.	
	30		Nine Companies training as per programme attached.	
	31		Companies training as per programme attached.	
			Strength 1/4th 92 Battalion 1st 10 1918 Officers 49 OR 874
			31st 10 1918 49 872

No: 5 BATTALION MACHINE GUN CORPS. — PROGRAMME of TRAINING.

Period 4th: – 9th: October.

Date.	"A" Company.	"B" Company.	"C" Company.	"D" Company.
Friday. 4th:Oct:				
8.30. – 9.am.	P. T.	P. T.	P. T.	P. T.
9.am. – 9.30.am.	Gas Drill.	Gas Drill.	Gas Drill.	Gas Drill.
9.30. – 10.am.	Gun Drill.	Gun Drill.	Gun Drill.	Gun Drill.
10.15. – 12 noon.	Section Excercise changing from Limber to Pack Draught.	do:	do:	do:
5.30. – 6.15.pm.	Map reading for Sergts: under an Officer. Backward ren Instruction in Mechanism – I.A. and Gun Drill. Range Takers under an Officer.	do:	do:	do:
DAILY.				
Saturday 5th:Oct: (8.30. – 9.am.)	P. T.	P. T.	P. T.	P. T.
9.am. – 10.am.	T. O. E. T.	Range. Part 1 Table "C" and I. A.	T. O. E. T.	T. O. E. T.
10.15. – 12 noon.	Fire Direction.		Section Scheme introducing changing from Limber to Pack Transport.	do:
2.pm.	Inter-Company Revolver Shooting Competition.			
5.30. – 6.15.pm.	Criticism of Tactical Scheme by Coy: Comdr: to all Officers and N.C.O's who can be spared from other training.			

Date.	"A" Company.	"B" Company.	"C" Company.	"D" Company.
Monday, 7th:Oct: 8.30. am.				
9.am. - 11.am.	P. T. Section Scheme introducing changing from Limber to Pack Transport.	Company Tactical Scheme.	Route March. 8 miles.	
11.am. - 12 Noon.				
5.30. - 6.15. pm.		Criticism of Tactical Scheme by Coy: Comdr. to all Officers and N.C.O's who can be spared from other training.		
7.15. - 8.15. pm.	Night Operations.			Night Operations.
Tuesday, 8th:Oct: 3.30.am. - 9.am.	P. T.	P. T.		
9.am. - 10.am.	Range - Part 1. Table "C"	T.O.E.T. Section Tactical Scheme introducing direct over-head fire.	Company Tactical Scheme.	Route March - 8 miles.
5.30.pm. - 6.15.pm.		Criticism of Tactical Scheme by Coy: Comdr: to all Officers and N.C.O's who can be spared from other training.		
Wednesday,9th:Oct: 8.30.am. - 9.am.		P. T.		
9.am. - 11.am.	Route March 8 miles.	Section Tactical Scheme introducing changing from Limber to Pack Transport.	Range - Part 1. Table "C" and I. A.	Company Tactical Scheme.
11.am. - 12. noon.				

Date.	"A" Company.	"B" Company.	"C" Company.	"D" Company.
Wednesday.cont'd:				
5.30.pm. - 6.15.pm.				Criticism of Tactical Scheme by Coy: Comdr: to all Offrs: & N.C.O. who can be spared from other training.
7.15.pm. - 8.15.pm.	Night Operations.	Night Operations.	Night Operations.	
Thursday, 10th:Oct:				
8.30.am. - 9.am.			P. T.	P. T.
9.am. - 10.am.	Company Tactical Scheme	Route March. 8 miles.	Section Tactical Scheme introducing indirect overhead fire.	Section Tactical Scheme introducing indirect overhead fire.
11.am. - 12. Noon.				

SIGNALLERS. Signallers will receive instruction under O.C. No: 5 Section, 5th: Signal Coy: R.E.. They will be attached to Companies for Company Tactical Schemes. - Signallers will be attached to Sections for Section Tactical Schemes on application to the Signalling Officer.

GAS TRAINING. Gas Training will be introduced on all Parades, a short period being devoted to Gas Drill. (Company Commanders will pay particular attention to this subject.

SCOUTS & RUNNERS. Will be instructed in knowledge of Country by an Officer.

3rd: October.1918.

Lieut: - Colonel,

Commanding No: 5 Battalion Machine Gun Corps.

SECRET.   W.23/68.

To O.C. "A" Company.
   O.C. "B" Company.
       "C" Company.
       "D" Company.
       Quartermaster.
       Signalling Officer.
       Intelligence Officer.
       R.S.M.

1.   The Battalion will march to the BANTOUZELLE AREA. to-day.

    Route.   RUYAULCOURT - METZ - GOUZEAUCOURT - GONNELIEU.

    Dress.   Full Marching Order.

2.   Order of march of Companies will be "A","D","B","C", and "H.Q."

3.   Companies will pass the Starting Point at 5 minutes intervals.

        "A" Company.   09.00 hours.
        "D"   do   09.05   "
        "B"   do   09.10. "
        "C"   do   09.15   "
        "H.Q."   09.20   "

    Starting Point - JUNCTION of ROADS. P.2.d.0/3.

4.   Transport will move in rear of Companies.

5.   The usual intervals between Companies and Transport on the line of march will be observed.

6.   All blankets will be rolled and dumped by Companies outside the Q.M.Stores by 7 hours.

9th October, 1918.   Captain & A/Adjutant,
                                           No.5 Battn. M.G.C.

A/2

S E C R E T.   Copy No:......

No: 5 Battalion Machine Gun Corps.

Operation   Order No: 33.   9.10.18.
----

1. The Battalion will resume the march to-morrow, 10th: inst: to the
HAUCOURT - ESNES area.
Dress - full marching Order.

2. Order of March of Companies:- "C" - "B" - "D" - "A" and H.Qrs:.

3. Companies will pass the starting point at 5 minute intervals:-

   "C" Company..........................10.30.hours.
   "B" Company..........................10.35.   "
   "D" Company..........................10.40.   "
   "A" Company..........................10.45.   "
   Battn: H:Qrs:........................10.50.   "

   Starting Point - Cross Roads - M.20.d.5/0.

4. Dinners will be cooked on the line of march.

5. 1 Officer and 1 N.C.O. per Company will report to the Battn: Qr:
Mr: at 09.00. hours to act as Billeting Party.
   The Billeting Party will meet the Staff Captain of the 13/Inf: Bde:
at the S. end of VAUCELLES WOOD at 09.30.hours.

6. In view of the uncertainty of auxiliary transport being available for
carrying blankets Companies will be prepared for carrying their own
blankets folded on thier limbers.

                                                  Captain,
                                              for Lieut: - Col:,
ACKNOWLEDGE.
                                     Commanding No: 5 Battn: Machine Gun Corps.
Issued at 11.pm.

Copies to:- 1. 5th:Division.   7. Qr:Mr:.
             2. 13/Inf: Bde: 8. Signalling Officer.
             3. "A" Company.   9. Intelligence Officer.
             4. "B"   do: 10. Office.
             5. "C"   do: 12. War Diary.
             6. "D"   do: 11.   do:

a/3

SECRET.

No: 5 BATTALION MACHINE GUN CORPS.   Coyp No:......

Operation Order No: 35.   10:10: 1918.

1. The march will be continued to-morrow. Tracks will be used by Troops and Transport.

2. Companies will march as detailed below.

"A" Company. will march to CAUDRY at 09.00 hours and will then come under the order of the B.G.C., 13/Inf: Bde:. This Company will be prepared to move into the line to-morrow night.

"B" Company. will be prepared to march to CAUDRY at 09.30. hours and will tehn come under the orders of the B.G.C., 95/Inf: Bde:. This Company will be prepared to move further EAST in the afternoon.

"C" Company. will move to LIGNY at 10.00 hours and will then come under the orders of the B.G.C., 15/Inf: Bde:. This Company will be prepared to move to CAUDRY in the afternoon.

"D" Company and Battn: H:Qrs: will move to CAUDRY at 11.00 hours.

3. O.C. Companies will be responsible for getting in touch with the H.Q. of their respective Brigades, as soon as possible.

4. "B" Echelons of Companies will march with Battn: H.Q.. All Dumped Personnel will march with "B" Echelon TRansport.

5. Battalion H.Q. will close at present location at 11.00 hours and will re-open at the same hour in the vicinity of Divisional H.Q. at CAUDRY.

6. Companies will forward to Battn: H.Q. as soon as possible the location of their Company H.Qrs: and "A" Echelon Transport.

7. Machine Gun Companies will please acknowledge.

Issued at 22.45 hours.

Captain,
for Lieut:- Col:.
10th: Octr: 1918.   Commanding No: 5 Battalion Machine Gun Corps.

Copies to :- 1. 5th:Division.   10. Signalling Officer.
              2. 13/Inf: Bde:.   11. Intelligence Officer.
              3. 15/   do: 12. War Diary.
              4. 95/   do: 13.   do:
              5. "A" Company.   14. Office.
              6. "B" do:
              7. "C" do:
              8. "D" do:
              9. Qr: Mr:.

SECRET.

W.23/76.

Copy No. ....

No.5 Battalion, Machine Gun Corps
DEFENCE SCHEME.

Reference Sheet - 57.B. 1/40 000.

5th Division Defence Instructions. (Repeated for information).

(A) Divisional Boundaries.
(1). The Northern Divisional Boundary runs BETHENCOURT (inclusive) - PRAYELLE - ? .. - - VIESLY (exclusive) BRIASTRE CHURCH - BELLE VUE (exclusive).

(2) The Southern Boundary runs AUDENCOURT (incl) - BEAUMONT INCHY (excl) - NEUVILLY (excl)

(B). DISPOSITIONS.
(1) Infantry.
The Divisional Front will be held with one Infantry Brigade in the line, one in support round BETHENCOURT, and one in reserve at CAUDRY.
The Brigade in the line will maintain outposts E. of the river. They will be entrenched in depth, and the main line of resistance will be west of the river. (see Para.E.2)

(2) Artillery.
The front will be covered by three Brigades of Field/Artillery disposed in depth.

(3) Machine Guns.
One Machine Gun Company will be disposed to cover the outpost line and the main line of resistance.
Positions for a second Company covering the line of resistance will be selected and held by nucleus teams. The remainder of the Machine Gun Battalion being held in reserve at CAUDRY.

(4) Cavalry and Cyclists.
One troop of cavalry and one section of cyclists will be attached to the Brigade in the line. Remainder of the Divisional Squadron and of the Cyclist Company will be held in reserve at CAUDRY.

(C). ACTION IN CASE OF ATTACK.

The object of the outpost line is to ensure the safety of the crossings of the river SELLE against minor enterprises of the enemy. In case of an attack in force the outposts will be withdrawn to the line of resistance on the W. bank of the River. The line of resistance will be held at all costs.
The Brigade in support will be used to reinforce the line of resistance or to form a flank should the troops on the flank of the Division be forced to fall back.
The Brigade in reserve will counterattack to regain the line of resistance if lost.

The S.O.S. barrage will come down on a line roughly 300 yards in front of the outpost line (300 yards E. of the Railway.)

(D). **DEFENSIVE POLICY.**

(1). All preparations will be made for a further advance.
(2). If the enemy withdraws, Cavalry and Cyclists will be pushed forward to locate and keep touch with his rearguards.
Vigorous patrolling by day and by night must be the policy of the troops on outpost duty.

(E) **RESPONSIBILITY FOR WORK.**

(1). The Brigade in the line will be responsible for work on the outpost system.
(2) The Brigade in support with the affiliated R.E. Company will be responsible for work on the main line of resistance and should detail 4 Infantry Companies nightly for work on this line.
The line will run approximately along the reverse slope, just below crest, of the spur J.12.a. - J.6.a. and c. and D.30.a. and c.
A "Divisional Line" running approx. from J.3.central to J.16.central, will be dug when the line of resistance is finished.

(signed) G.W.GORDON HALL,
Lieut.Colonel,
13.10.18. General Staff, 5th Division.

Machine Gun Battalion Defence Scheme.

1. 1 Company is disposed to cover the outpost line and main line of resistance with positions forward of the spur in J.12.a. J.6.a. and c. and D.30.a. and c. Company H.Q. at J.5.d.60/00. "A" Echelon at J.22.a.50/25.

1 Company will cover the line of resistance from positions on the double spur running through D.29.c and d. J.5. and J.11.a. and b. These positions will be manned by nucleus teams. The remainder of the gun teams being accommodated at Company H.Q. J.22.a.50/25. A Echelon at Company H.Q.

1 Company in billets BETHENCOURT (in reserve) Company H.Q. at J.7.d.65/25.

1 Company in billets CAUDRY (in reserve) Company H.Q. at I.24.a.70/30.

O.Cs.Reserve Companies will arrange to reconnoitre routes forward and to the flanks up to and including the main line of resistance.

2. COMMUNICATIONS.

A telephone exchange has been established under Battalion Signal Officer at J.10.b.40/10. This exchange is connected to

    Company H.Q.   J.5.d.60/00.
    Company H.Q.   J.22.a.50/25.
    Company H.Q.   J.7.d.65/25.
    Battalion H.Q. L.24. central.
and Brigade in the line.

In preparation for a possible move forward Battalion Signalling Officer will get in touch with O.C. Company at J.5.d.60/00 and arrange for a visual station on the ridge forward of Company H.Q. This will not be manned till necessary.

3. AMMUNITION.

    The D.A.C. is located at I.34.d.00/30.
    The Advanced Divisional Dump at J.3.a.80/20.
    Mobile reserve remains at CAUDRY.

S.A.A. for present line will be drawn by Companies from Advanced Divisional Dump by horse transport.

In the event of a large amount of S.A.A. being required for a special operation arrangements will be made by Battalion H.Q.

4. ACKNOWLEDGE.

                              D.Kydd
                               Major

15th October, 1918.   for Lieut. Colonel,
                  Commanding No. 5 Battalion, Machine Gun Corps.

Copies to.   1. 5th Div. "G".
               2. O.C. "A" Company.
               3. O.C. "B" Company.
               4. O.C. "C" Company.
               5. O.C. "D" Company.
               6. Signalling Officer.
               7. Intelligence Officer.

SECRET.   Copy No. 12

No: 5 BATTALION, MACHINE GUN CORPS.

OPERATION ORDER No: 36.

15th October, 1918.

Reference Map - Sheet 57.b. - 1/40,000.

1. "D" Company will relieve "A" Company in the line on the night 16th/17th October.

2. On completion of relief, "A" Company will take up position vacated by "D" Company.

3. Details of the relief will be arranged between Company Commanders concerned.

4. Night firing programme and work in hand will be taken over and continued.

5. Completion of relief will be notified to Battalion H.Q. by Code Word "SCOT."

Captain & A/Adjutant,
for Lieut.-Colonel,
Commanding No: 5 Battn: M. G. C.

Issued at 21.00 hours.

Copies to:-

No: 1 - 5th Division.
    2 - 13th Infantry Brigade.
    3 - 15th   "   "
    4 - 95th   "   "
    5 - "A" Company.
    6 - "B"   "
    7 - "C"   "
    8 - "D"   "
    9 - Quartermaster.
   10 - Signalling Officer.
   11 - Intelligence Officer.
   12 - War Diary.
   13 -   -do-
   14 - Office.

Machine Gun Companies will PLEASE ACKNOWLEDGE.

SECRET. Copy No. 6

No: 5 BATTALION, MACHINE GUN CORPS.

Warning Order No: 8.

Reference Map - Sheet 57 B. N.E.

1. On a date to be notified later the Third Army will resume the offensive.

    The 5th Division will attack on right of IV Corps, 42nd Division on the left, and 17th Division on the right of IV Corps.

    The objectives of 5th Division will be:-
    1st Objective:- SOLESMES - LE CATEAU RAILWAY from E.25.b.00.70. to K.1.b.99.25.
    2nd Objective:- From E.20.c.50.55. to K.2.b.80.80.
    3rd Objective:- From E.21.a.50.40. to E.28.b.10.95.
    4th Objective: From E.22.a.50.90 to E.28.b.00.85

2. The Northern Boundary is from D.30.central to road junction at E.16.d.70.50.

    The Southern Boundary from K.1.b.99.25. through K.2.b.60.75. and E.28.b.10.95. thence to E.2a.central.

3. The attack of the 5th Division will be carried out by the 13th and 95th Infantry Brigades.

    13th Infantry Brigade will attack the 1st Objective; 95th Infantry Brigade will attack the 2nd and 3rd Objectives and exploit forward to the southern outskirts of BEAURAIN. +4th

4. ACTION OF MACHINE GUNS:-

    "A" and "D" Companies will apply a barrage in three lifts:-
    1st on Railway and Sunken Road 150 x beyond.
    2nd searching reverse slope towards and including 2nd Objective.
    3rd on valley beyond 2nd Objective (to range of 2,600 x).

    "A" Company will maintain two 8-gun batteries about J.6.d.80.40. and J.6.d.60.90.

    "D" Company will maintain two 8-gun batteries about J.6.b.25.75. and D.30.d.15.55. All these batteries to be about the 95 contour line.

    "T" bases have been arranged for and will be delivered to companies to-morrow night.

    The positions are to be sited and work commenced to-morrow. The work to be completed on night 18th/19th.

    "B" Company will be allotted to 95th Infantry Brigade to assist in the consolidation of the captured area.

    "C" Company will be in reserve at BETHENCOURT, affiliated to 15th Infantry Brigade. The orders for the move to BETHENCOURT will be issued later.

5. AMMUNITION:-

    "A" and "D" Companies will arrange to make dumps of S.A.A. in the vicinity of the Batteries.

    Lieut. R.M.BROADFOOT will be responsible for forming two S.A.A. dumps at D.30.d.15.30. and J.6.d.25.45. for the

the use of "D" and "A" Companies, respectively.

6. ACKNOWLEDGE.

Issued at 18.15 hours.
16th October, 1918.

for. Lieut.-Colonel,
Commanding No: 5 Battn: M.G.C.

Copies to:-

    No: 1 - "A" Company.
        2 - "B" "
        3 - "C" "
        4 - "D" "
        5 - War Diary.
        6 - -do-
        7 - Office.

SECRET.   Copy No. 17

No: 5 BATTALION, MACHINE GUN CORPS.

OPERATION ORDER No: 37.

Reference Map Sheet 57B. N.E., 1/20,000.

1. On a date and at an hour to be notified later the Third Army will resume the offensive.
   The 5th Division will attack on right of IV Corps, 42nd Division on the left, and 17th Division on the right of IV Corps.

2. The Objectives of 5th Division will be:-

BLUE LINE:- K.2.a.10.80. to E.19.d.15.50.
DOTTED GREEN LINE:- E.26.d.80.70. to E.27.a.20.60.
                 thence along road to E.21.a.50.30.
GREEN LINE:- E.21.d.20.00. to E.15.c.10.00.
BROWN LINE:- E.22.c.70.90. to E.15.b.70.20. (along 140 contour line).

3. DIVISIONAL BOUNDARIES:-

   The Southern Boundary is from K.2.a.10.80., K.7.a.10.55, K.1.a.50.10, E.26.d.00.00. thence to E.17.c.25.05.
   The Northern Boundary is from D.30.a.20.00., E.19.d.15.50., E.15.b.75.25. to E.10.b.30.65.

4. The attack of the 5th Division will be carried out by the 13th and 95th Infantry Brigades.
   13th Infantry Brigade will attack the BLUE LINE.
   95th Infantry Brigade will then move forward and attack the DOTTED GREEN, GREEN and BROWN LINES.

5. ACTION OF MACHINE GUNS:-

   (a) "A" and "D" Companies will apply a barrage in accordance with attached map.

   (b) "B" Company will be affiliated to the 95th Infantry Brigade and will assist both in attacking and consolidating the captured area.

   (c) "C" Company will be in Divisional Reserve at BETHENCOURT.

6. ORGANIZATION OF M.Gs. EMPLOYED ON BARRAGE WORK.

Battery.	Position.	No: of Guns.	Coy.	Commander to be appointed by.	
1.	J.6.d.30.40.	6	"A"	O.C.,"A" Coy.	) Commanded
2.	J.6.d.60.90.	8	"A"	O.C.,"A" Coy.	) by O.C.,"A" Coy.
3.	J.6.b.25.75.	8	"D"	O.C.,"D" Coy.	) Commanded
4.	D.30.d.15.55.	8	"D"	O.C.,"D" Coy.	) by O.C.,"D" Coy.
@5.	D.30.a.50.90.	2	"A"	O.C.,"A" Coy.	Commanded by O.C.,"A" Coy.

@ (Target being sunken road E.26.c.90.05. to E.26.c.40.40.).

Rates of fire will be as follows:-

ZERO to ZERO plus 4 -- 200 rounds per minute.
ZERO plus 4 to ZERO plus 12 -- 100 rounds per minute.
ZERO plus 12 to ZERO plus (-- 65 rounds per minute.
    56   ((

7. ASSEMBLY:-

Sections employed on barrage work will be in position at batteries by 23 hours "Y" day.

Four men including Gun Commander will be with the gun.

The remainder of the teams will be in reserve in the sunken road about J.5.d.30.50. The two guns from D.30.a.50.90. will report at same place on completion of their task.

8. HEADQUARTERS:-

Os.C., "A" and "D" Companies will make their H.Q. at J.11.b.60.95.

    Adv. M.G.Battalion H.Q.
      (At Adv.Div.Rept.Centre) CLERMONT CHATEAU,J.9.a.
    13th Inf.Bde.H.Q.   do   do
    95th Inf.Bde.H.Q.   do   do

9. COMMUNICATIONS:-

Company Commanders' H.Q. are connected up through M.G.Battalion Exchange at J.10.b.35.10. to Battalion H.Q. and Brigades.

Communication to Batteries will be by runner.

M.G.Battalion Visual Station will be established at J.6.a.20.00.

10. LIGHT SIGNALS:-

13th Infantry Brigade will light GREEN flares when they have gained their objective (the BLUE LINE).

11. Orders as to the synchronisation of watches will be issued later.

12. ZERO day and hour will be notified later.

13. A copy of Battery Organisation Charts will be forwarded to Battalion H.Q. by Companies on the 19th instant.

14. AMMUNITION:-

Companies will have 32 filled belts per gun at battery positions before commencement of barrage, and will arrange for teams to maintain 20 filled belts as soon as possible after conclusion of firing.

Divisional S.A.A. Dump at J.3.a.90.20.

Two dumps of 40 boxes each have also been arranged for at:-

    J.6.d.25.45.   for "A" Company.
    D.30.d.15.30.   for "D" Company.

The Mobile Reserve of S.A.A. under Lieut. R.M.BROADFOOT will move in time to be at Adv. Battalion H.Q. by 6 hours "Z" day.

15. REPORTS:-

Companies will report assembly completed by Code word 'POTUS'.

Reports as to casualties, S.A.A. expended and situation will be rendered on completion of firing.

If the flares referred to in Para: 10 are seen by the teams at the Battery Positions this will immediately be reported to Company H.Q., who will pass on the information.

16. The 42nd Battalion, M.G.C. are assisting the advance from the GREEN to the BROWN Objectives on the left flank of the 5th Division with direct overhead fire on an area bounded by -
E.15.d.70.35. - E.15.b.15.50. - E.15.b.40.60. - E.15.d.92.45. from position about E.14.d.central.

17. ACKNOWLEDGE.

[signature]
Major
Lieut.-Colonel.
Commanding No: 5 Battalion.
M.G.C.

Issued at 20 hours.

18th October, 1918.

Copies to:-
```
No: 1  -  5th Division "G".
    2  -  13th Infantry Brigade.
    3  -  15th Infantry Brigade.
    4  -  95th Infantry Brigade.
    5  -  O.C., "A" Company.
    6  -  O.C., "B" Company.
    7  -  O.C., "C" Company.
    8  -  O.C., "D" Company.
    9  -  O.C., No: 17 Battalion, M.G.C.
   10  -  O.C., No: 42 Battalion, M.G.C.
   11  -  C.M.G.O., IV Corps.
   12  -  A.M.G.O., Third Army.
   13  -  Office.
   14  -  Quartermaster.
   15  -  Intelligence Officer.
   16  -  Signalling Officer.
   17  -  War Diary.
   18  -  War Diary.
```

SECRET.　　REFERENCE SHEET. 57ᴮ N.E.　　18-10-15

No 5 Battⁿ M.G. Corps

SECRET.

A/8

No 5 BATTALION MACHINE GUN
OPERATION ORDER No 38.

Reference Map 57^B NE. 1:20000

Oct. 21st 1918

1. On a date & at an hour to be notified later, the 5th Division will continue the advance in conjunction with the Divisions on either flank. On completion of capture of Objectives, the 37th Division will pass through the 5th Division.

2. Objectives of 5th Division will be:-
   (1). E.11a.3.9. to E.11c.4.8. Hence to E.11d.4.5. to E.18a.0.6.
   (2). E.5c.8.7. E.5d.4.7. E.6c.5.1. Hence along contour line to E.12.d.7.9.

3. DIVISIONAL BOUNDARIES. The Southern Boundary is from E.17c.25.05. E.17b.5.0. to E.12.d.7.8. The Northern Boundary is from E.10.b.80.65 to E.5. central.

4. The attack of the 5th Division will be carried out by the 15th Infantry Brigade.

5. ACTION OF MACHINE GUNS. (a) "B" Company & 2 Sections of "D" Company will apply a barrage in accordance with attached table.
   (b) "C" Company will be affiliated to the 15th Infantry Bde & will assist in consolidating the captured area.
   (c) "A" Company will be in Divisional Reserve at CAUDRY.
   (d) "D" Company less 2 Sections will be in Reserve at BETHENCOURT.

6. ASSEMBLY. Sections employed on barrage work will be in positions at Batteries by 23.00 Hours on Y day. O.C. "D" Company will be responsible for his 2 Sections employed on barrage, getting into positions & preparing to fire at ZERO. These 2 Sections will then come under the orders of O.C. "B" Company at ZERO hour.

7. HEADQUARTERS. O.C. "B" Company will make H.Q.

2.

at E.21.b.5.2.
Advanced M.G. Batt. H.Q.   BRIASTRE
(at 2nd word Div. Hqrs. Cel?)   D.30.b.2.0
15th Infantry Brigade.   BRIASTRE
                                     D.30.b.2.5

8. **COMMUNICATIONS** B Company's H.Q. will be connected by wire to advanced Batt. H.Q. Communications to Batteries will be by Runner.

9. **AMMUNITION** Sections employed on barrage will have 30 filled belts per gun at firing positions before commencement of barrage & will arrange for transport to maintain 20 filled belts as soon as possible after conclusion of firing. Lieut. R.M. BROWN will form a dump of 50 boxes of S.A.A. at E.21.b.5.2. on the 22nd Inst.

10. Orders as to the reformation of Sections will be issued later.

11. ZERO hour & day will be notified later.

12. A copy of Barrage ammunition chart will be forwarded to Batt. H.Q. by Companies on 22nd inst.

13. **REPORTS** All guns will report Assembly complete by code word "INT". Report as to casualties S.A.A. expended & situation will be rendered on completion of firing.

14. Advanced Batt. H.Q. will close at CLERMONT CHAU at 8.00 hours on the 22nd & open at the same hour at D.30.b.2.0.

15. **ACKNOWLEDGE.** (M.G. Companies only)

                                         G. [signature]
                                         Capt. & Adjt.

                                         for
                                         Lieut.-Colonel
Issued at 12.00 hrs.   Commanding No. 5 Batt. M.G. Corps

No	Battery Positions	No of Guns	Coy	Targets	Times	Rate of Fire	Commander to be appointed by
1	E.22.a.35.25 – E.22.c.5.9	8	"D"	E.17.b.5.0 – E.17.a.9.8. E.17.b.9.5. – E.11.d.4.5. E.12.c.3.0. – E.11.d.8.8. E.12.c.7.2. – E.12.a.1.2.	To be issued later	1 Belt per 4 mins.	O.C. "B" Company
2	E.16.c.0.2. – E.22.a.1.9	8	"B"	E.7.a.9.8. – E.11.c.4.8. E.11.d.4.3 – E.11.a.8.2 E.11.d.8.8. – E.11.b.2.7. E.12.a.1.2 – E.5.d.6.0		—do—	
3	E.15.b.6.1. – E.15.d.8.7.	8	"D"	E.11.c.4.8. – E.10.b.8.7. E.11.a.8.2 – E.5.c.3.1. E.11.a.2.7. – E.5.c.7.6. E.5.d.6.0 – E.5.d.0.9		—do—	O.C. "D" Company

CLEARANCE: As the Battery Positions will be located in the vicinity of the leading waves of the attack, fire will not be opened until the attacking forms are at least 200 yds in front of the batteries. O.C. "B" Company will make the necessary arrangements for informing batteries when to open fire.

SECRET

No.5 Battalion, Machine Gun Corps.

Account of Operations for Period

19th October, 1918 - 23rd October, 1918.

Map Ref. Sheet. 57. B. NE. 1/20,000.

19.10.1918.   Battalion H.Q. and "C" Company in CAUDRY.
"B" Company at BETHENCOURT.
"A" and "D" Companies in line.
On night 19/20th Companies move up the line and take up position as per Operation Order No.37 attached.
Battalion H.Q. move to CLERMONT CHATEAU (J.9.a)

20.10.1918.   Zero hour for the attack 0200 hours. The BLUE and GREEN objectives were taken to time - the BROWN objective not taken. Our line ran just in advance of the GREEN objective. At 0900 hours the enemy counter-attacked from a N.E. direction and our line withdrew to the GREEN objective.
Barrage guns fired 108250 rounds in support of the attack. Total made up as follows:-

"A" Company. 48,250 rounds
"D" Company 60,000 rounds.

"B" Company moved off from billets in BETHENCOURT at 0200 hours.
Two sections pushed forward with limbers to consolidate GREEN objective. Limbers were taken up to within 700 yards of the GREEN objective, from which point the guns had to be manhandled ~~owing to~~ the limbers becoming immobile owing to the mud. The third section of this Company moved into cellars in VIESLY. The fourth section moved with Company H.Q. to J.5.d.4.3. This section was kept in reserve. At 0900 hours the Section in VIESLY was ordered forward to take up positions on GREEN objective.
The situation then was as follows :-
Our troops were holding the GREEN objective and had repulsed an enemy counter-attack. Orders were then issued for a second attack on the BROWN objective to be carried out at 1600 hours. This attack was completely successful. At 1800 hours the two Companies employed on Barrage fire withdrew to billets - "A" Company to INCHY, and "D" Company to VIESLY. The Company at VIESLY was ordered to man the ridge in E.20.c., E.26.a. and b., in the event of an emergency. Positions to be taken up were reconnoitred and sited.
After the attack the locations of the sections of "B" Company were as follows:-

1 section at E.15.d.7.7. and E.15.d.9.4.

1 section at E.22.a.2.8. and E.20.a.2.5.

1 section at E.21.a.8.2. and E.21.d.0.8.

1 section in reserve at E.30.b.2.3.

Company H.Q. at J.5.d.4.3.

21.10.1918.   95th Infantry Brigade ordered to consolidate the captured positions. The guns of "B" Company were distributed as follows:-

  1 section. (2 guns at E.22.c.7.9.
              (2 guns at E.21.b.5.3.

  1 section   (2 guns at E.16.c.1.3.
              (2 guns at E.15.d.3.1.

  1 section   (2 guns at E.21.a.8.2.
              (2 guns at E.21.d.0.8.

  1 section at D.24.d.8.2. in reserve

  Company H.Q. moved to D.24.d.8.2.

At 14.30 hours "A" Company moved back to billets at CAUDRY. "C" Company relieved "D" Company at VIESLY. "D" Company returning to BETHENCOURT.
  Orders received that 5th Division would probably continue the advance on the 23rd. "C" Company of this Battalion detailed to assist 15th Infantry Brigade in consolidation.
  "B" Company and two sections of "D" Company to be employed on barrage.
  Operation Order No.38 issued at 23 hours.

22.10.1918.   During the evening of the 22nd "B" Company and two Sections of "D" Company moved up to Battery positions as per Operation Order No.38 attached. "B" Company's Headquarters were established at E.21.b.5.2. "C" Company moved off and assembled along the sunken road in E.21.a. and b. This Company had its guns on limbers and were ordered to move forward as soon as the attacking infantry were clear of the high ground S.W. of BEAURAIN. Three sections were to go forward and one section was to be kept in reserve. "D" Company less two sections moved back to billets at CAUDRY.
  Advanced Battalion H.Q. were established with Advanced Divisional Report Centre at BRIASTRE. Battalion H.Q. were in telephone communication with "B" and "C" Companies.

23.10.1918.   Zero hour for the attack was 0320 hours.
  During the early morning of the 23rd the enemy put up two heavy barrages whilst the 15th Infantry Brigade were forming up for the attack. These barrages fell round our Battery positions but no casualties were caused.
  One Officer, "C" Company, and two signallers went forward with the leading wave of the Infantry to advise O.C. "C" Company when to move. The first attack was not a success, the two attacking Battalions of the 15th Infantry Brigade being held up in the sunken road in E.16. The third Battalion of the Brigade was then ordered forward.
  O.C. Company received information that the Battalion was pushing forward into BEAURAIN and so ordered his three sections forward to take up positions in E.12.a. These Sections moved up quickly taking transport right into the village of BEAURAIN, from where the guns were manhandled and got into position on a line approximately E.12.a.2.8. - E.12.central.

One Brigade of the 37th Division then passed through the 15th Infantry Brigade. It had been intended that the forward sections of "C" Company should support the advance of the Brigade of the 37th Division with direct overhead fire but this was only possible for a few minutes owing to a heavy smoke screen being put up by the artillery.

During the attack the barrage guns fired in all 99,000 rounds. Three guns were put out of action by enemy shell fire but the casualties were slight being in all

3 Killed 5 Wounded.

During the afternoon Headquarters and all Companies of the Battalion moved back to billets at CAUDRY.

Major,
Commanding No.5 Battalion, Machine Gun Corps.

A/10.

Date	"A" Company.	"B" Company	"C" Company.	"D" Company.
Thursday, 31st. 9.00-12.30.	Company Scheme under Company Commanders, Map location of Ground to be used will be sent in to this office.			8.50-9.15. P.T. 9.30 to Range 12.30. Firing.
Friday, 1.11.18. 8.30.	Route March - No Transport - 10 miles Route - Route to be reported to Battn.H.Q.			
15.30.	- - - - - - - - - - - Foot Inspection - - - - - - - - - -			
Saturday, 2.11.18. 8.30-9.15.	P.T.		P.T.	P.T.
9.30-10.30. 10.30-12.30.	Gun Cleaning. At discretion of Coy.Commander.		9.30 Gun Cleaning Range 12.30 Firing.	Gun Cleaning. At discretion of Coy.Commanders.

SIGNALLERS. Signallers will receive instruction under O.C.,No.5 Sec.5th Sig.Coy.R.E. They will be attached to Companies for Company Tactical Schemes.

GAS TRAINING. Gas Training will be introduced on all parades, a short period being devoted to Gas Drill (Company Commanders will pay particular attention to this subject.)

Dress. Marching Order less packs will be the dress for all parades. Lectures - Drill Order. Evening Lectures. Clean Fatigue, puttees to be worn.

27th October, 1918.

Major,
Commanding No.5 Battalion, Machine Gun Corps.

DISPOSITION OF M.G's AT 18.00 HRS: 13-10-18
Nº 5 BATTⁿ M.G CORPS.
Identification Trace for use with Artillery Maps.

SECRET.

W 23/75
13-10-18

2 GUNS FOR HARASSING

Cᵒʸ HQ.

Cᵒʸ HQ AND 1.COMPANY.

Cᵒʸ AND 2 SECTIONS 22

D. J.   D. E. J. K.

NOTE.—(1). These traces are intended to facilitate the communication of information as to the position of targets, which have been located on a squared map.
(2). The squares on this trace are 500 yards in length on the 1/10,000 scale, 1,000 yards in length on the 1/20,000 scale, and 2,000 yards in length on the 1/40,000 scale.
(3). The squares on the trace are fitted to the squares of the map showing the targets, which are then drawn on the trace. Sufficient letters and numbers must also be added to enable the recipient to place the trace in the correct position on his own map. A little detail may also be traced, but this is not essential. The name and scale of the map to which the trace refers must be always given. The trace can be used for the 1/10,000, 1/20,000, or 1/40,000 scale.

G.S.G.S. 3023.

REFERENCE.
GUNS OF LEFT FLANK BATTⁿ SHEWN THUS: <
" " RIGHT " " " : <

Tracing taken from Sheet 57ᴮ N.E.
of the 1: 20,000 map of FRANCE
Signature..................... Date 13-10-1

SECRET.

DISPOSITIONS OF M.G's AT 18.00 HRS. 14-10-18.

No. 5 Battⁿ. M.G. Corps.

REFERENCE SHEET 57^D N.E.

Guns of the Flank Batt^y Shown thus: ✗ (Vickers Teams with Guns)

Guns of Support / Coy shown thus: ✗

Guns of Forward Coy shown thus: ✗

25 N 23/2

4TH DIVISION
11TH INFY BDE

1ST BN HAMPSHIRE REGT.
MARCH, APRIL, MAY 1919 MISSING

CONFIDENTIAL.

H. Q., 5th: Division.

No. 5 BATTALION,
MACHINE GUN
CORPS.

W.5/20.

    Herewith the Original Copy of the War Diary of this Battn: for the month of Novr: 1918.

30th: Novr. 1918.

               Captain,
              for O. C.,
      No: 5 Bn: Machine Gun Corps.

ORIGINAL.

No: W.5/20.
Regd: No:
Vol: No:
Part No:

— W A R D I A R Y. —

for the Month

of

N O V E M B E R 1918.

No: 5 Battalion Machine Gun Corps.

30th: Novr: 1918.

Lieut: - Colonel,

Commanding No: 5 Battalion Machine Gun Corps.

Ref. Map Sheet 51c: 1/40000.

WAR DIARY
or
INTELLIGENCE SUMMARY.
(Erase heading not required.)

November 1918.   Sheet 1.

Place	Date	Hour	Summary of Events and Information	Remarks and references to Appendices
Battn: H.Q.				
CAUDRY.	1st.	—	Weather wet. Battalion concentrated in CAUDRY. Battn: Strength — Officers 49 — Other Ranks 867.	
— do —	2nd.	—	Weather fine. Orders received that offensive on Third Army front would be resumed on 4th Novr. Warning Order issued to Companies.	See Appendix "A".
BEAURAIN	3rd.	—	Weather wet. Battn: moved to forward area. Battn: H.Q. & D Company to BEAURAIN, marching via BERTHENCOURT — VESLY and BRIASTRE. Battn: H.Q. & D Company arrived in BEAURAIN at 02.00 hours.	
BEAURAIN	4th.	—	Weather fine. Battn: in action	Forderlalah account of operations from Novr. 4th to 12th.
NEUVILLE	5th.	—	Wet. Battn: in action	
LOUVIGNIES	6th.	—	Wet — do —	
JOLIMETZ	7th.	—	Wet — do —	
— do: —	8th.	—	Wet — do —	
— do: —	9th.	—	Wet — do —	See Appx. A/5.
PONT-SUR-SAMBRE.	10th.	—	Fine. Warning Order from Division regarding relief of 13/R.B. Relieved in the line.	
— do: —	10th.	—	Fine. 13/R.B. Bde. relieved (42/Divn.) Orders issued to move to JOLIMETZ area.	see app. A/2.
LE QUESNOY	11th.	—	Fine. Battn: H.Q. "B" & D Companies move to LE QUESNOY.	
— do —	12th.	—	Fine. A & C Companies move into LE QUESNOY	see app. A/3.
JOLIMETZ	13th.	—	Fine. Lieut. Col. R.H.Cutting, D.S.O, MC rejoins from leave. Battn: move to JOLIMETZ and are	

Army Form C. 2118.

WAR DIARY
or
INTELLIGENCE SUMMARY
(Erase heading not required.)

Sheet 2.

November 1918.

Place	Date	Hour	Summary of Events and Information	Remarks and references to Appendices
JOLINETZ	13th	contd	Concentrated in CHATEAU JOLINETZ. Major A.S. McCALL, M.C. from 2nd i/c of Bttn. to the Command of 'B' Company. Major M.W. L.E. FAWCETT, M.C. from Command of 'B' Company to 2nd i/c of 'A' Company.	See appendix A/6.
do.	14th	—	Weather wet. Lieut. Fairgrieve to U.K. on probation to R.A.F. Armistice concluded with the enemy.	
do.	16th	—	Weather wet. Thanksgiving service held at LE QUESNOY for all of the Battn.	
do.	17th	—	Weather wet. Major A.W. L.E. FAWCETT, M.C. appointed Battn. educational officer.	
do.	—	—	1st. Inspection of 'A' Company by the Commanding Officer. 'B', 'C' & 'D' Companies devoted time to cleaning of Equipment & Vehicles. Lecture given by Lieut. COLQU[...] calling B.T.O., M.G. on "Reconstruction & Demobilization."	
do.	18th	—	Weather fine. Lt. B.R. HAYDEN to GRANTHAM for tour of duty. Inspection of 'B' Company by the C.O., 'A' & 'D' Coys. Inspection by their respective O's.C. and Route March. 'C' Company — Arms, action and in Drill.	
do.	19th	—	This Lieut. FAIRGRIEVE reported. Inspection of 'C' Company by the Coy. officer. 'B' Company — Route March — "A" & D Companies, arms drill, Lectures and Gun Drills.	
do.	20th	—	The 'D' Company inspected by Commanding Officer. 'A' 'B' 'C' Coys. respective Drills.	

No. 5 BATTALION, MACHINE GUN CORPS.
Army Form C. 2118.

No. M296
Date 30.11.18.

Sheet 3.

WAR DIARY
INTELLIGENCE SUMMARY.
(Erase heading not required.)

Place	Date	Hour	Summary of Events and Information	Remarks and references to Appendices
JOLIMETZ	21st	—	Weather fine. Parade. Inspection. Squad drill without arms. Company drill without transport.	
— do. —	22nd	—	Fine. Battalion Route march, route S.10.b.1/0 – S.16.a.2/4 – CROIX ROUGE – S.1.d.4/0 – M.26.c.7/2. (Sheet 51. 1/40000 Fr. Ge.)	
— do. —	23rd	—	Weather fine. Companies placed at disposal of Company Commanders. Lt. PARRY, B Company, admce to Hospital, sick. Lt. N.E. JERVIS M.C. joined posted B Coy.	
— do. —	24th	—	Weather wet. Reinforcements from Base Depot. 10 o/ranks at Lieut N.E. JERVIS M.C. joined and posted to D Company.	
— do. —	25th	—	Fine. Orders received that British Troops are to hold COLOGNE Bridgehead. See Appendix A/7.	
— do. —	26th	—	No troops to cross today boundary from BELGIAN to GERMAN Frontier. Weather fine. Parades as per training programme appended.	Tot manner cancelled
— do. —	27th	—	Weather fine. do.	see App. A/8

WAR DIARY
of
INTELLIGENCE SUMMARY

Sheet 4

(Erase heading not required.)

No. 5 BATTALION
MACHINE GUN CORPS.
M.S/20.
30/11/19

Place	Date	Hour	Summary of Events and Information	Remarks and references to Appendices
JOLIMETZ	28th	—	(Weather wet.) Major A.S.E. FAWCETT M.C. (Battn. Education officer) transferred from 2nd Batt. M.G.C. "A" Company to Battn. HQrs. Training as per Programme.	2nd Battn. M.G.C. Education Officer O.A.S.
— do. —	29th	—	Weather wet. Training as per Programme.	
— do. —	30th	—	Weather fine. Training as per Programme. Battn. Strength. Officers 49 Other Ranks 883.	

Battle Casualties period 1st to 12th Nov.
Officers / Other Ranks

Killed	—	1
Wounded	—	7
Missing	—	—
Total	—	8

Signed A Abbey
Lieut. Colonel
Comdg No 5 Battn. M.G. Corps.

No: 5 Battalion Machine Gun Corps.

WAR DIARY.

"APPENDIX "A".

No. 5 BATTALION.
MACHINE GUN
CORPS.

30th: Novr: 1918.

ORIGINAL COPY.

6. ASSEMBLY. The 5th Div. will assemble on night
of 3/4th Oct.
(i) B Coy will march under orders of B.C.
   75th Inf. Bde.
(ii) C Coy will march under orders of B.G.C. 15th Inf. Bde.
(iii) A + D Coys + Batt HQ + B Echelon will march
   to the above under Lt. DENHAM. Route VIESLY –
   BEAUFRE – ???? – ??????. Starting point –
   Cross Roads T.18.b.9/7. Companies will pass starting
   point on 3rd Oct as under.
       A Company   19.00 hrs
       D   "   19. ?? "
       Batt H.Q.   19.10 "
       B Echelon   19.13 "

7. BILLETING. 1 Off. + 2 O.R. (mounted) from A + C
   Coys will report at Batt H.Q. at once being
   act as billeting party.

8. Packs & kits of all companies will be
   drawn on transport.

9. Blankets will be rolled in bundles of 10,
   labelled + dumped outside Coy H.Q. by approx
   on the 3rd Oct. Each Coy will provide a guard
   of 1 NCO + 1 man. The blankets will be drawn
   at the villages to which Coys are moving from.

10. B. Echelon + dumped personnel of Coys will
    report to Major A.E. ????? M.C. at the Batt
    Q.M. Stores at 18.00 hrs on the 3rd Nov.

11. The Q. SAA. ?????? as laid down in the
    Offices ?? M.14/16 will report to the R.S.M. at
    Batt Q.M. Stores at 17.00 hrs.

12. If the operations on the 4th Nov are successful
    + orders are received for the advance to be
    continued on the 5th, the objectives of the
    5th Division will be:-

SECRET.

No; 5 Battalion Machine Gun Corps

WARNING ORDER No; 10.

1.   The Battalion will be prepared to move to-morrow night.

2.   Companies will forward a nominal roll of Officers and Other ranks for Dumped Personnel by 09.00 hours, to-morrow, 3rd; inst;.

3.   The Dumped Personnel will move as a Unit in rear of the Battalion.

4.   Operation Orders will be issued later.

2nd; Novr; 1918.

Captain,

Adjutant, No; 5 Battalion M, G, Corps.

Copies to   O.C, "A", "B", "C" and "D" Companies.
Signalling Officer, Intelligence Officer, & Qr; Mr;.

SECRET.   Copy No: 13.

5th: Division Operation Order No: 273.

10/11/18.

1.   5th:Division (less Field Coys and Pioneers) will move to the HERBIGNIES - JOLIMETZ - LE QUESNOY area on the 10th: and 11th:insts:.

2   Units to move to day and their destinations are shown on the attached March Table. These Units will be prepared to move to LE QUESNOY to-morrow.

3.   Field Companies and Pioneers Battn: will remain in the present area for work.

4.   Orders for to-morrow the 11th: inst: will be issued later.

5.   ACKNOWLEDGE.   (sd). J.T.MOSTYN. Lt: Colone

General Staff 5th:Divison

Issued at 14.30. hours.

SECRET.    Copy No: 14.

5th: Division Operation Order No: 274.

1.   In continuation of 5th:Division O.O. 273 dated to day.

The Division will move to morrow the 11th: inst: in accordance with the attached Table. "A".

2.   Destination of Units and instructions regarding any further move by the 15/Inf: Bde: will be issued later.

3,   Divisional Units will ACKNOWLEDGE.

Issued at 18.00. hours.   (sd) J.T. MOSTYN.   Lieut: Col,.
----------------------------------General Staff, 5th: Division.

SECRET.   5th Division O.O.274/1.

....

In continuation of 5th Div. O.O. 274 :-

1.   Locations will be as follows :-

    Divisional H.Q. ... LE QUESNOY.
    95th Inf. Bde. ... do.
    13th Inf. Bde. ... HERBIGNIES - LE CARNOY - RUE HAUTE (N.13.c. & N.19.b.) and SARLOTAN.

    15th Inf. Bde. ... JOLIMETZ.(1 Bn.LOUVIGNIES)

    15th Bde. R.F.A.)
    27th Bde. R.F.A.) ... LOUVIGNIES and GHISSIGNIES.
    72nd Bde. R.F.A.)

    5th Bn. M.G.C. ... LE QUESNOY.

2.   The Battalion of 15th Infantry Brigade at HERBIGNIES will move under orders of B.G.C. 15th Infantry Brigade, to be clear of HERBIGNIES by 08.45 hrs.

3.   Divisional H.Q will open at LE QUESNOY at 12.00 hrs.

                                                     Lt. Colonel,

5th Division.
10/11/18.   General Staff.

SECRET.   Copy No: ......

No: 5 Battn: M. Gun Corps.

Operation Order No: 40.

1.   "D" Company and Battn: Headquarters will move to LE QUESNOY to-morrow, the 11th: inst:.
        "A" Company will move under the orders of the B.G.C., 13/Infantry Brigade.

2.   "D" Company will pass the starting Point - Road junct: U.5.c. 2/7. - at 08.40. hours and Battalion H.Q. at 08.45. hours.

3.   Route. - PONT SUR SAMBRE - U.5.c.2/7 - U.3.b. 4/5 - 0.25d.8/9. - LE GODELOT - MAISON ROUGE.

4.   One Officer and 2 Other ranks (mounted) of "D" Company will report to the Battn: H.Qrs: at 07.30 hours to act as a Billeting Party.

Issued at 20.30. hours.   (sd) A.J. SHANKS., Capt: &
                                                           Adjutant,
                                           No: 5 Battn: M. G. Corps.

10th: Novr: 1918.

Copies to - O.C. "A" Company.   Intell: Officer·
            O.C. "B" do: Office.
            Battn: H.Qrs:.   War Diary. (2).

R E T. No: 5 Battalion Machine Gun Corps.

Supply Arrangements
----

1. Rations for the 11th:inst: will be loaded on the two S.A.A. Limbers per Company (at present at Battn: H.Qrs:) under the O.M./S. and sent forward to the new Billets. Companies will connect back by means of cyclist orderlies to guide in these Limbers.

2. Rations for the 12th:inst: will be at JOLIMETZ on the 11th:inst:. Captain: Qr: Mr:DEVOTO will take over a party to the refilling point draw the rations and issue them to Companies on 1st: Line Transport.

3. The Battalion will concentrate at JOLIMETZ on the evening of the 11th: Novr:.

Issued at 12 Noon.

Captain & Adjutant.

No: 5 Battn: Machine Gun Corps.

Copies to O.C. "A" Company.   O.C. "D" Company.
         O.C. "B"   do: Battn: Qr: Mr:.
         O.C. "C"   do: Office.

S E C R E T.   No: 5 Batalion Machine Gun Corps.

                              Operation Order No: 41.

1.   "A" and "C" Companies will march from their present
Billets to Billets in LE QUESNOY forthwith.

2.   An Officer from each Company will be sent on ahead
to take over the Billets and will report to the Battn: Qr: Mr:
immediately on arrival in LE QUESNOY.

AVKNOWLEDGE.   (sd). A.J. SHANKS, CaptN :& Adjt:,

12th:Novr: 1918.   No: 5 Battalion Machine Gun Corps.
---------------   -------------------------------------

SECRET.
-o-o-o-o-o-

Copy No...12..

No: 5 BATTALION, MACHINE GUN CORPS.

Operation Order No: 41.

----

1. The Battalion will move to JOLIMETZ to-morrow, 13th instant.

2. One Officer and two O.R. per Company (mounted) will report to Battalion H.Q. at 09.00 hours to act as billeting party.

3. All Company Transport, with the exception of Cooker, Water Cart and Officers' Mess Limber, will move independently to-morrow morning:-
   "A" Company - 10.00 hours.
   "B"   "   - 10.15   "
   "C"   "   - 10.30   "
   "D"   "   - 10.45   "

4. Personnel of Companies, the vehicles mentioned in para: 3 and H.Q. Transport will move from billets at 13.30 hours, and march independently.

Issued at 20.15 hours.

Captain & Adjutant,
No: 5 Battn: M.G.C.

12th November, 1918.

Copies: 1 - O.C., "A" Company.
        2 - "   "B"   "
        3 - "   "C"   "
        4 - "   "D"   "
        5 - Quartermaster.
        6 - Signalling Officer.
        7 - Intelligence Officer.
        8 - R.S.M.
        9 - (War Diary.
       10 - (
       11 - Office.
       12 - MO

ACCOUNT OF THE OPERATIONS FROM 2nd: - 12Th: Novr: 1918.

- No: 5 Battalion Machine Gun Corps. -

2nd: Novr: 1918. The Battalion concentrated at CAUDRY. Orders received to move forward the next day to the BEAURAIN area.

3rd: Novr: Battn: H.Q. moved forward to BEAURAIN with "A" and "D" Companies. "B" and "C" Companies moved to NEUVILLE, "B" Company with the 95/ Inf: Bde: and "C" Company with the 15/Inf: Bde:.

4th. Novr. "A" Company moved to NEUVILLE. "B" Company moved to LOUVIGNIES. Orders were then received that the 95/ Inf: Bde:, at dawn, would pass through the 112th: Inf: Bde: who had gained the outskirts of the FORET de MORMAL but it was hoped that the PINK DOTTED LINE would be reached.

"C" Company moved forward at 15.30.hours to ~~LOUVIGNIES.~~

"D" Company moved to NEUVILLE.

5th: Novr:. Battn: H.Q. moved to JOLIMETZ and later to the level-crossing at T.7.b.40.80.. "A" Company moved to JOLIMETZ.

"B" Company - 95/Inf: Bde: passed through the 112th: Inf: Bde: on about a Battalion frontage - the 1st: D.C.L.I. on the left and the 1st: E.SURREY R. on the right with the 1st: DEVON R. in support. No: 3 Section followed the 1st: D.C.L.I. and No: 4 Section the E. SURREY'S. These Sections were concentrated with their Battalions about the RUE de BOIS AUBERGE about 03.30. hours.

Nos: 1 & 2 Sections were held in Reserve.

At dawn the advance commenced with very little opposition or shelling. The 112th: Inf: Bde: were passed through just West of the PINK DOTTED LINE and by night the YELLOW LINE had been reached at several points.

Great difficulty was experienced in the moving of Limbers as most of the good roads had been mined and blown up and the inferior roads were rendered almost impassable by the wet weather.

"C" Company. - 2 Sections assembled in JOLIMETZ to follow the 1st: NORFOLKS to their objectives on the road running from LE GODELOT and then to follow up the 1st: BEDFORDS when they passed through to their objectives ,(The BLACK and YELLOW Lines.)

The 2 remaining Sections were concentrated also in JOLIMETZ to assist the 1st: CHESHIRES to exploit the success of the 1st: BEDFORDS across the SAMBRE. Limbers were to be used as much as possible and guns were to assist the Infantry as much as possible by engaging the enemy where he offered resistance and by consolidating successive objectives.

Nos: 1 & 2 Sections followed the 1st:NORFOLKS by the MAISON ROUGE - LE GODELOT Roads. On this road mine craters were encountered which necessitated the guns being carried and the limbers being sent round by alternative routes. These Sections then followed the 1st: BEDFORDS by the LE GODELOT - FORESTER'S HOUSE Road where obstacles in the form of mines were again encountered but overcome. The BLACK Line was consolidated the limbers being kept close up. Strong resistance was then met with on the YELLOW Line and the guns engaged all possible targets. The YELLOW was gained about dusk and then Sections dug in and consolidated.

No: 3 & 4 Sections were moved up via MAISON ROUGE - LE GODELOT - FORESTER'S HOUSE in readiness to assist the Infantry in the exploitation of any success.

"D" Company marched to JOLIMETZ via LOUVIGNIES arriving there at 12.30.hours. At 15.30. hours they resumed the march and were eventually quartered in Hutments near LE GODELOT. Great difficulty was experienced by this Company in getting Limbers past two craters in the road.

Through one of these ran a stream and this crater was crossed by a light bridge. On this bridge the mules of one limber shied with the result that the limber fell into the stream with the mules and drivers entailing the loss of one limber and a certain amount of gun kit. Great assistance was rendered by the prompt action of Corpl: RICHARDSON of "B" Company who was present. He immediately jumped into the water which was 5ft: deep and cut the harness thereby saving the life of one of the mules.

6th: Novr: Battn: H.Q. moved in the afternoon to LA GRANDE CARRIERE.

"A" Company remained at JOLIMETZ.

"B" Company - The Line of the 95/Inf: Bde: was advanced to the BROWN Line, 1 Section of "B" Company coming into action near the Orchard midway between LA PORQUERIE and PONT SUR SAMBRE and another near HURTEBISE FARM. This latter Section had one tripod damaged by shell fire which had increased considerably but without casualties to personnel.

Very good work was done by No: 4 Section on this day in getting limbers round the cross roads South of LA PORQUERIE under heavy shell fire.

Enemy shelled LA PORQUERIE and PONT SUR SAMBRE.

"C" Company. - At 07.00. hours all 4 Sections were concentrated in LA CORNE and the defence of the YELLOW Line re-organised.

At dusk all guns were moved forward to Battery positions on the high ground in U.4.b. in readiness to put down a barrage to cover the establishment of bridgeheads across the SAMBRE. Owing to the bridges having been blown up the attack was not carried out and the guns stood by on S.O.S. Lines.

"D" Company. - At dawn positions were reconnoitred for the deployment of the Company on a line 200 yards East of the road running South from LE GODELOT to be occupied in case of an enemy counter attack. These positions were never occupied.

7th: Novr: Battn: H.Q. moved to PONT SUR SAMBRE.

"A" Company moved to LA PORQUERIE.

"B" Company. - No opposition to the crossing of the SAMBRE by the 95/Inf: Bde:. The DEVONS passed through in the morning followed by No: 1 Section, "B" Company, and by the evening the line of the RAILWAY, East of PATIGNY had been reached. This Section had to manhandle gun kit as the traffic bridge had not been completed during the morning. It was, however, finished in the afternoon and Nos: 3 & 4 Sections crossed before dark with the D.C.L.I. and the E. SURREY'S.

The DEVONS had a good many casualties mainly owing to their not being in touch with the 42nd: Division who were a long distance behind, thus enabling the enemy to enfilade the DEVONS from BOUSSIERES.

No: 1 Section had two guns knocked out and one man wounded near the Railway on the road to BOIS GEORGES.

Company H.Q. in PONT SUR SAMBRE.

"C" Company. - At 02.00. hours 2 Sections were withdrawn into Reserve at LA CORNE and at dawn the remaining 2 pushed forward to PONT SUR SAMBRE. At 13.00. hours the 2 Sections in Reserve moved forward to PONT SUR SAMBRE where the Company were concentrated.

"D" Company. - Moved to PONT SUR SAMBRE.

8th: Novr: Battn: H.Q. at PONT SUR SAMBRE.

"A" Company moved to PATIGNY. Orders received that the 13/Inf: Bde: was to relieve the 95/Inf: Bde: in the evening, the Brigade Front to be held by the 2nd: K.O.S.B.'s on the right and the 1st: R.W.KENT R. on the left.

No: 3 Section allotted to the 2nd: K.O.S.B's and took up positions in V.11.b.

No: 2 Section allotted to the 1st: R.W.KENT. R. and took up positions in V.6.B.

Nos: 1 & 4 Sections in Company Reserve in St: REMY-MAL-BATI. All Sections had their Limbers with them, good cover being found for limbers and horses.

"B" Company. — Orders issued in the night that the advance was to be continued on this day, the DEVONS being detailed to capture the GREEN and RED Lines proceeded by cyclists and cavalry. E. SURREY'S on the left and the D.C.L.I. on the right to change direction left and to make a flank attack in the direction of the BOIS de QUESNOY and HAUTMONT to assist the flank of the 42nd:Division in coming up through HAUTMONT. Cavalry and cyclists detailed to capture strategic points at cross roads leading out of HAUTMONT.

At 05.45. hours Company H.Q. moved to PATIGNY.

At 06.45. hours the advance was resumed little or no opposition being encountered until the GREEN Line was reached when hostile artillery fire became more severe and a good deal of Machine Gun fire was met with from the MAUBEUGE — AVESNES Road. FONTAINE and ST: REMY-MAL-BATI were heavily shelled and a few prisoners were captured in the latter place.

The 1st:DEVONS reached the Line FONTAINE — LA FAYE but the stream there presented a considerable obstacle and the advance was stayed.

No: 1 Section attached to the 1st:DEVONS were in action on the GREEN Line with their Limbers on the Eastern outskirts of ST: REMY-MAL-BATI.

Meanwhile the 1st: E. SURREY'S following hard on the 1st:DEVONS had gained their objective just South of the BOIS de QUESNOY and got into touch with the 42nd:Division who had advanced through the Wood.

No: 4 Section were in action with this Battalion but got few targets. They had one Limber team of mules knocked out by shell fire and the drivers wounded in ST: REMY-MAL-BATI.

The 1st: Devons had not gained their final objective. The 1st: D.C.L.I. were not all in action. No: 3 Section which was attached to them was in action just East of ST: REMY-MAL-BATI with their Limbers a few hundred yards in rear of the village.

During the day the 13/Inf: Bde: passed through the 95/Inf: Bde: and the Company was withdrawn with the Infantry to PONT SUR SAMBRE.

"C" Company. — At PONT SUR SAMBRE.

"D" Company. — At PONT SUR SAMBRE. Road to V.8.a. central reconnoitred by Section Officers.

9th: Novr: Battn: H.Q. with "B" and "C" Companies at PONT SUR SAMBRE.

"A" Company. — Orders received from the B.G.C., 13/Inf: Bde: that the Battalions in the front line to-gether with the Machine Gun Sections working with them were to push forward as far as possible. In the early morning it was found that the enemy had retired some 7 miles. The Infantry advanced to a Line running through Q.36., and W.6. and 12 but orders were received that they were to withdraw with the 2 Machine Gun Sections and establish an outpost line running through Q.33. and W.4. and 10.

During the afternoon Company H.Q. with the 2 Reserve Sections were moved to FONTAINE.

No: 3 Section with the 2nd:KOSB's. took up position in the outpost Line at W.9.b.70.80. and No: 2 Section with the 1st: R.W.KENT R. at Q.33.c.80.10.

Both these Sections had their Guns on their Limbers in readiness to move to any required point at a moments notice. Also the ground in front had been reconnoitred by Section Officers.

"D" Company. — Moved at 12.00.hours to FONTAINE.

10th: Novr: Battn: H.Q. at PONT SUR SAMBRE.

"A" Company. — Orders received at 09.00 hours that the 42nd: Division would take over the 5th: Divisional Front. This was completed by 14.30 hours and Nos: 2 and 3 Sections were withdrawn to FONTAINE. At 15.40 hours the Company moved off to ST: REMY-MAL-BATI.

"B" Company. — Moved to LA GRAND CARRIERE.

"C" Company. — Moved to JOLIMETZ.

"D" Company. — Moved to PONT SUR SAMBRE.

11th: Novr: Battn: H.Q. moved to LE QUESNOY.

"A" Company moved to SARLOTEN.

"B" Company moved to LE QUESNOY.

"C" Company at JOLIMETZ.

"D" Company moved to LE QUESNOY.

12th: Novr: The Battalion concentrated at LE QUESNOY.

15th: Novr: 1918.   Lieut: Colonel:
                                        Commanding No: 5 Battalion Machine Gun Corps.

S E C R E T.　　　　　　　　　　　　　　　　　　　　Copy No: 7.

5th: Division Operation Order No: 275.

14th: Novr: 1918.

1.　　In accordance with the Terms of the ARMISTICE the occupied portions of FRANCE, BELGIUM and LUXEMBOURG are to be evacuated by the enemy by November 26th:.

2.　　The Allied forces are to commence the advance to the RHINE on Novr: 17th:. Prior to that date the conditions laid down in 5th: Division S 70/122 dated 14th: inst: will remain good.

3.　　The advancing BRITISH Forces are being organised in two Armies - the Second and the Fourth.
　　The Fourth Army will consist of 1V., Vl., 1X and AUSTRALIAN Corps, and the 2nd: Cav: Division.

4.　　The 1X Corps on the right and the Vl Corps on the are to be the two leading Corps of the Fourth Army, 2nd: Cav: Divisions covering the whole fron tof the Army.
　　The 1V and AUSTRALIAN Corps are to be the two rear Corps and are to remain in their present areas till further orders.
　　These Corps are to move forward later, probably by train.

5.　　The 1V Corps was transferred to the Fourth Army at 12.00. hours Novr: 14th:.

ACKNOWLEDGE.

Issued at 10.00. hours.

(sd) J.P. MOSTYN, Lieut: Col.,

General Staff 5th: Divison.

SECRET.   IV Corps   No: 17/1/10/

5th: Division.

                Ref: IV Corps 17/1/10/ G.O. dated 14/11/18.
(Not sent to the 3rd: and 4th: Canadian Divisions.)

1.   British Troops are to hold the COLOGNE Bridgehead.
                The AMERICAN Army will be holding the territory on our
right and the BELGIAN Army the territory on our left.
                The BRITISH Sector of German territory will be occupied
by the Second Army.
                The Sector between the German Frontier and the Line –
AVESNES – MAUBEUGE – CHAREROI – BRUSSELS will be occupied by
the Fourth Army, which will be reconstituted to consist of IV – X
and AUSTRALIAN Corps and Cavalry Corps, less 1 Cav: Divn:.

2.   The areas which will be alloted to Corps of Fourth
Army on reconstitution are shown on the attached Map.
                The date on which it will come into force will be
notified later, and will probably be about the 4th: Decr:.

3.   The following transfers are taking place as follows:-

Formation·	From.	To.–	Remarks.
N. . Division	IV Corps.	Second Army. (11 Corps).	Date to be notified later. Will probably move by Train.
3rd: & 4th: Cadn: Divns:	Second Army. Cdn: Corps.	IV Corps.	1200. 24th: Novr:

4.   ACKNOWLEDGE.

H. Q. IV Corps.   (sd) E.H. TOLLEMACHE., Major,
24th: Novr: 1918.   for Brigadier General,
                                        General Staff, IV Corps.

                                2.

No: 5 Bn: M.G.Corps.   5th: Divison No: S. 7/131.

                        For information.

24.11.18.   (signed).   Capt;.
                                             for Lt; Col:,
                                        General Staff, 5th: Division.

No. 5 Platoon, Albert... Week Ending 30/11/...

	"A" Company	"B" Company	"C" Company	"D" Company
MONDAY				
9 to 10	T.O.E.T.	Road Safety School	Company Drill	"D" Company
10 to 11	Company Drill	T.O.E.T.	Lecture & inspection of T.O.E.T.	do
11.15 to 12.10	Lecture by NCO Re: interior econ.	Company Drill	do	do
12.10	Inspection by Section	do	do	do
12.15				
TUESDAY				
9 to 12.15	Coy Parade as detail	Coy Parade as detail	Coy Parade as detail	Company parade as detail
12.15	Inspection by Platoon officer — house by house	do	do	do
WEDNESDAY				
9 to 10	Company drill	do	T.O.E.T.	Squad drill by...

	"E" Company	"F" Company	"G" Company	"H" Company
9 to 9.15				
9.15 to 10	Setting & unpacking Instr. Wagon & O.E.I.	do.	Company Drill	T.O.E.I.
10.15		do.	Lecture by N.C.O. in the Recreation Room	Company Drill
12.15	Inspection by Section officers — Pore Drill	do.	do.	do.
THURSDAY				
9 to 10	Squad Drill by Section	S.O.E.I.	Squad Drill by Section	S.O.E.I.
10.6 to 11	S.O.E.I.	Company Dress	S.O.E.I.	Company Drill
11.15 to 12.15	Company Drill	Setting & unpacking Instr. Wagon	Company Drill	Lecture by N.C.O. in Recreation Room
12.15	Inspection by Section officers — Pore route stood	do.	do.	do.
FRIDAY				
9 to 9.15	Company complete	Route March	Company complete	Company complete
9.15	Inspection by Section officers — Slow & Quick March	do.	do.	do.

	"A" Company	"B" Company	"C" Company	"D" Company
SATURDAY 9 to 12.15	Company at disposal of Company Commander	do	do	do
	Programs to be sent in by Company to Battn H.Qrs. by 10.00 hrs on Friday			
12.15	Inspection Section officers – followed by Coys. Rolls Regt.	Inspection Section Officers (10.00 a.m) followed by Kitchens Clean?	do.	do.

Note: Section Officers will ensure that their half Coys are spick and span. This will be inspected during the first allowance to T.O.E.T. No time is to be lost by the Section officers in Inspection at 12.15. the articles laid down are to be specifically checked and are put to ensure the areas for their parades will be clean [illegible]

R.E.R.L.
Major
for O.C.
No. 6 Battn. Nigeria Regt.

ORIGINAL COPY.

No. 5 BATTALION, MACHINE GUN CORPS

Reg: No: ....
Part No: ....
Volume No: ....

No: 5 Battn: Machine Gun Corps.

WAR DIARY.

for the Month of

DECEMBER 1918.

Lieut: - Colonel,
Commanding No: 5 Battalion Machine Gun Corps.

31/12/1918.

Original

Reference Map: VALENCIENNES. 12 1:100,000

Army Form C. 2118.

WAR DIARY
INTELLIGENCE SUMMARY.
(Erase heading not required.)

Sheet 1.

Instructions regarding War Diaries and Intelligence Summaries are contained in F.S. Regs., Part II. and the Staff Manual respectively. Title pages will be prepared in manuscript.

Place	Date Dec 1918	Hour	Summary of Events and Information	Remarks and references to Appendices
	1st		Fine. Capt R.H. DADD reported the battalion from GRANTHAM, from Instructional Staff Course. Orders received from Division regarding move to new Area.	see app a/1
	2nd		Fine. Parades. A.B. + C. Companies were inspected by Coy Commanders. P.T. S.D. Lecture by Section Officer. Educational Training 11-10 to 12-10 Hrs.	
	3rd		Lieut G.P. BURDETT reported the battalion from Base Depot. Lieut R.S. SANDBACH reported the battalion from M.G. School. Battalion proceeded to LE QUESNOY for the Kings visit. His Majesty visited LE QUESNOY. Parades in the morning P.T. G+S drill the afternoon when His Majesty visited during	
JOLIMETZ	4th		Wet. His Majesty the King again visited LE QUESNOY Battalion paraded & marched there. Orders received re move forward of 17th Field Coy RE. of the division see app a/2. Prof. F.S. ADKINS gave Lectures in the Recreation Hut on the following	see app a/2

Army Form C. 2118.

Reference Map. VALENCIENNES. 1:100,000 Original Sheet 2

WAR DIARY
INTELLIGENCE SUMMARY.
(Erase heading not required.)

Place	Date	Hour	Summary of Events and Information	Remarks and references to Appendices
	DEC 1918			
	4th		Subjects (a) BELGIUM – "What it means to us" (b) Housing & Educational problems.	
	5th		Fine. Prof. F.S. ADKINS lectures on GERMANY & her War Aims.	see app a/3
	6th		For Training Parades see app a/3	
	7th		Wet. For Training Parades see app a/3	
	8th		Wet. Companies placed at the disposal of 16th Coy for church parades.	
	9th		Fine. Church Parades.	
	10th		Fine. For Training etc see app a/4.	see Appendix a/4
	11th		Wet. " " " " " "	
JOLIMETZ			Orders received that move would probably take place on the 13th. Battalion ordered to march with some under orders of the 13th Inf: Brigade Group, or "C" day afterwards with the 95th Inf Brigade Group. For Training see app a/4. Warning Order C/No 20 issued. see app. a/5.	see App. a/5.

Army Form C. 2118.

Reference Maps. VALENCIENNES, 12. NAMUR 8.
BRUSSELS, 6. 1:100,000

WAR DIARY
or
INTELLIGENCE SUMMARY

Sheet 3

(Erase heading not required.)

Place	Date Dec 1918	Hour	Summary of Events and Information	Remarks and references to Appendices
JOLIMETZ	12th		Wet. Companies bathing. Operation Order No 43 issued	see App a/5
	13th		Battalion commence the march to the BEUZET–BOVESSE Area in accordance with programme attached, will come under the orders of the 13th Inf. Brigade Group.	app a/6
	14th		– do –	
	15th		– do –	
	16th		– do –	
	17th		– do –	
	18th		Battalion resting.	
	19th		Battalion resume the march to the BEUZET–BOVESSE Area under Orders of the 95th Inf. Bde Group	see app a/6
	20th		– do –	
	21st		– do –	
	22nd		– do –	

Army Form C. 2118.

Original

WAR DIARY
~~INTELLIGENCE SUMMARY~~
(Erase heading not required.)

Reference Maps. BRUSSELS 6. NAMUR 8   1/100000   Sheet 4.

Instructions regarding War Diaries and Intelligence Summaries are contained in F. S. Regs., Part II. and the Staff Manual respectively. Title pages will be prepared in manuscript.

Place	Date	Hour	Summary of Events and Information	Remarks and references to Appendices
	Dec.r 1918			
	22nd		Battalion complete the march to the new Area. Disposition as follows. Battalion H.Q. at Chateau de Boquet, TEMPLOUX. "B" + "D" Companies in TEMPLOUX. "A" + "C" Companies in SUARLEE	
TEMPLOUX & SUARLEE	23rd		Battalion resting	
	24th		-do- The following reinforcement joined the Battalion Lieut R.E. GORDON. 2/Lieut N.C. FOUNTAIN + 3 O.Rs	
	25th		Battalion resting	
	26th		"	
	27th		Companies at the disposal of Coy Commanders	
	28th		-do-	-do-
	29th		Church Parades.	

Original
Reference Map NAMUR 8 1:100,000   Sheet 5   Army Form C. 2118.

WAR DIARY

Instructions regarding War Diaries and Intelligence Summaries are contained in F. S. Regs., Part II. and the Staff Manual respectively. Title pages will be prepared in manuscript.

(Erase heading not required.)

Place	Date Hour 1918	Summary of Events and Information	Remarks and references to Appendices
TEMPLOUX & SUARLEE	DEC 30th	Companies inspected by Company Commanders	
	31st	Classes re-commenced from 10.00 hrs to 12.30 hrs. Educational	
		— do — — do — — do —	
		— do — — do —	

ORIGINAL COPY.

Reg: No:........
Part No;........
Volume........

- No: 5 Battalion Machine Gun Corps. -

War Diary for the Month of

DECEMBER.

1918.

APPENDIX "A"
-o-o-o-o-o-o-o-o-o-o-o-o-o-o-o-o-

31st: December. 1918.

ORIGINAL COPY.

SECRET.

5th: Division.

No. 5 BATTALION, MACHINE GUN CORPS.

S. 70/136.

13/ Inf: Bde:
15/ do:
95/ do:
C. R. A.
5th: Bn: M. G. C.

NOTES ON CONFERENCE OF CORPS AND DIVISIONAL COMMANDERS HELD AT ARMY HEADQUARTERS ., 30th: NOVR: 1918.

1.   The Army will move at a date to be notified later, probably between 7th: and 13th: Decr;.

2.   The 5th:Division will march on "C" day to area BAVAI - HOUDAIN - TAISNIERES. On "D" day to area LONGUEVILLE - FEIGNIES - LOUVROUIL. On "E" day to area GRAND RENG - MAUBEUGE - "F" day Halt. On "G" day to area CROIX - PESSANT - BINCHES. On "H" day to area TRIVIERES - MANAGE. On "I" day Halt. On "J" day to area SENEFFE - NIVELLES - BOUSVAL. "L" day to area.

3.   Reconnaisance of the above areas will be carried out at once by the 5th:Divisional Staff.

Army Troops are already in occupation of some of the places in these areas. They will remain there. Any places now occupied by troops of the N. Z. Division will be available for the 5th: Division.

4.   **Divisional Artillery** will march complete, i.e. it will not form part of Brigade Group.

5.   Army Headquarters will be at NAMUR.

30th: Novr; 1918.

(sd) S. GORE-BROWNE.,
Lieut; Col.,
General Staff, 5th: Division.

SECRET.

> No. 5 BATTALION, MACHINE GUN CORPS.
> Copy No. .....

5th: Division Operation Order No: 276.

4th: Decr: 1918.

1. One Field Company per Division, IV Corps, will move to the new area in accordance with the attached March Table, to prepare the new area for occupation.

2. The Field Companies of the 5th: and 37th: Divisions will continue their march together from the BAVAI area as far as FONTAINE L'EVEQUE under the Command of Major. CLOUTMAN, 59th: Field Company, R. E..

3. Administrative instructions will be issued by 5th: Divn; "AQ".

4. 5th: Division and C. R. E. to acknowledge.

Issued at 14.00. hours.

(sd) G. W. GORDON. HALL.,
Lieutenant Colonel,
General Staff 5th: Division.

Copies to :-

1. IV Corps "G"	2. IV Corps "Q".
3. 37th: Division.	4. 13/ Inf: Bde:
5. 15/ Inf: Bde:	6. 95/ Inf: Bde:
7. C. R. A.	8. C. R. E.
9. A. D. M. S.	10. 5th: Bn: M. G. C.
11. 14th: R. War: R.	12. 5th: Division "Q".
13. 5th: Divn: Train.	14. S. S. O..
15. D. A. D. O. S.	16. D. A. P. M.
17. D. A. D. V. S.	18. 5th: Signal Company.
19. War Diary.	20. War Diary.
21. Office Copy.	

No:5 Battalion Machine Gun Corps.

PROGRAMME OF TRAINING — For Thursday & Friday, 5th: & 6th:

	"A" Company.	"B" Company.	"C" Company.	"D" Company.
THURSDAY.				
9. to 9.30.	Company Commanders Inspection.		Company at the disposal of the Company Commander.	Coy: Commdr's Inspection
9.30. to 10.	Squad Drill.	Gun Drill.		Physical Training.
10. to 10.30.	Physical Training			Lecture by the M.O.
10.30. to 11.	Lecture by Section Officers on Fire Direction.	Physical Training.		
11.10. to 12.10.	EDUCATIONAL TRAINING.			
1215.	Section Officers Inspection of Mess Tins and Field Dressings.			
FRIDAY.				
9. to 9.30.	Inspection by Company Commanders		Company at the disposal of the Company Commander.	
9.30 to 10.	Physical Training.	Company Drill.		Squad Drill.
10. to 10.30.	Lecture by the M.O.			Physical Training.
10.30. to 11.		Physical Training.		Lecture by Section Officers on Fire Direction.
11.30 to 12.10.	EDUCATIONAL TRAINING.			
12.15.	Section Officers Inspection of Water Bottles.			

Captain.,
Adjutant, No: 5 Battn: Machine Gun Corps.

O.C. "A" Company.
O.C. "B"   do:
O.C. "C"   do:
O.C. "D"   do:
Signalling Officer.

No. 5 BATTALION.
MACHINE GUN
CORPS.

1:100,000
Ref: Sheet VALENCIENNES.

Reference the Programme of Training for the period 9th: to the 11th: Decr:. The detail of the Route March as laid down for Wednesday is amended as follows;-

Companies will parade independently and will pass the starting point at the following hours:-

"B" Company.........................09.20. hours.
"C" Company.........................09.22.   "
"D" Company.........................09.24.   "
No:5 Section, 5th: Sig: Coy:......09.26.   "

Starting Point. The CROSS ROADS at the Battalion Recreation Hut.

ROUTE:-   Junction of roads ¼ mile North of the "E" in JOLIMETZ, across the RAILWAY to Pt: 214, the Southern outskirts of VILLEREAU, (Junction of roads North of the "T" in POTELLE), thence to the junction of roads at "B" in BASSEEVILLE and along the main LE QUESNOY Road.

10th: Decr;.1918.

Capt; & Adjt:.,

No: 5 Battn: Machine Gun Corps:

Amended Programme of Training from 9th to 11th Decr.1918.

	"A" Company.	"B" Company.	"C" Company.	"D" Company.
MONDAY.9.12.18				
9.00 to 9.30	Coy.Comdr.Inspection.	Company Cdr.Inspection.	Company at the disposal of the Coy.Commander.	Coy.Comdr.Inspection.
9.30 to 10.00	Gun Drill	Physical Training.		Squad Drill.
10.00 to 10.30		Company Drill.		Physical Training
10.30 to 11.00	Physical Training	Company Drill.		Lecture by Section officers
11.10 to 12.10	Educational Training. All ranks not engaged in Educational Training will be at the disposal of Company Commanders for parade purposes during this hour.			
12.15	Section Officers Inspection — — of Iron Rations.			
TUESDAY.10.12.18				
9.00 to 9.30	Company Comdrs. Inspection and Coy.	Coy.Cmdr.Inspection.	Company at the disposal of Company Commander.	Coy.Comdr.Inspection
9.30 to 10.00		Squad Drill.		Physical Training
10.00 to 10.30	Route March.(Coy. less Transport) March to commence at 09.15	Physical Training		T.U.E.T.
10.30 to 11.00		Lecture by Sect.Officers		
11.10 to 12.10	Educational Training. All ranks not engaged in Educational Training will be at the disposal of Company Commanders for parade purposes during this hour.			
12.15	Section Officers Inspection — — — of Holdalls and Towels.			
WEDNESDAY.11.12.18				
9.00 to 9.15	Company - Commander's - - - - Inspection.			
9.15 to 11.15	Route March West on the CHATEAU Square. Companies less Transport. Parade in close Column,facing			
11.20 to 12.20	Company at the disposal of the Company Comdr.	Educational Training. All ranks not engaged in Educational Training will be at the disposal of Company Commanders for parade purposes during this hour.		

December 9th,1918.

Captain,
Adjutant,No.5 Battalion,Machine Gun Corps.

SECRET.

No: 5 BATTALION, MACHINE GUN CORPS, WARNING ORDER No. 20.

5th Division march to GEMBLOUX Area on 13th December, 1918.

I. The 5th M.G.Battalion will march under the orders of the 13th Infantry Brigade on 13th, 14th and 15th instant, and march under the orders of the 95th Infantry Brigade for the remainder of the march.

II. A halt of one day will be made on the 5th day in the BINCHE Area. The Battalion will arrive in the new area on 22nd instant.

III. DRESS:-

Leather jerkins will be carried rolled on top of the pack. The remainder of the equipment will be carried in accordance with Battalion Standing Orders on the subject.

IV. TRANSPORT:-

Baggage wagons will march with the Battalion.

V. BILLETING PARTIES:-

Special instructions will be issued on this subject.

VI. MARCH DISCIPLINE:-

The Orders laid down in Fourth Army G.S.128 will be adhered to during this march.
There will be no interval within each Company's Transport.
There will be an interval of 10 yards between a Company and its Transport.
"When on the march to the new area, the following method will be adopted in order to ensure the whole column moving on, as nearly as possible, at the same moment at the end of each clock hour halt.
(1) When the clock hour halt takes place, equipment will be slipped off. Limbers and wagons will not be so closed up as to render it impossible for all to start pulling out at the same moment.
(2) One minute before the clock hour, the Unit Commanders will sound one long whistle, on which Company Commanders order men to dress and fall in, in fours, at side of road. Transport men mount.
(3) At clock hour, Unit Commanders sound two whistles, whereupon Company Commanders immediately give order "Quick March"."

SMOKING:-

All ranks will be discouraged from smoking during the march.

VII. UNFIT PERSONNEL:-

No provision is being made for the dumping or transport of Category "B" personnel, or any personnel recommended as unfit for marching.

Lieut.-Colonel,
11th December, 1918.   Commanding No: 5 Battalion, M.G.C.

Copies to:-   "A", "B", "C" & "D" Companies, Qr. Mr., M.O., Signalling Officer, Education Officer, R.S.M., War Diary (2), Office.

No: 5 BATTALION, MACHINE GUN CORPS.

SECRET.

Ref. Maps:- VALENCIENNES.
NAMUR.
BRUSSELS.
1/100/000.

OPERATION ORDER No: 43.

I. The 5th Division will move to the GEMBLOUX Area on the 13th instant - "C" Day.

II. The 5th M.G.Battalion will march to the BEUZET and BOVESSE Area in accordance with the attached table.

III. The 8th Group Lovat's Scouts will be attached to the Battalion for the move.

IV. The order of march of Companies for "C" Day will be "A", "B", "C" and "D" Companies, and on "D" Day "B" Company will lead followed by "C" Company, and so on in rotation. H.Q. will always march in rear. The 8th Group Lovat's Scouts will follow H.Q.

V. The Company on duty will detail a mounted officer to ride in rear of the Battalion to collect stragglers, and, if necessary, march them in rear of the Battalion. He will be assisted by the Provost Corporal. From "F" Day, inclusive, the Company on duty will also detail a mounted officer to assist in Traffic Control. This Officer will report at Brigade H.Q. at an hour which will be notified in Battalion Orders.

VI. The orders laid down in Fourth Army G.S. 128 will be adhered to during the march.

VII. Special instructions re Billeting have been issued separately.

VIII. Watches will be synchronised each morning before the Battalion moves.

ACKNOWLEDGE.

12th Decr: 1918.

Capt. & Adjt.,
No: 5 Battn: M.G.C.

Copies to:- 5th Div. "G"., 13th, 15th & 95th Inf.Bdes.,
"A", "B", "C" and "D" Coys., Qr.Mr., M.O.,
E.O., S.O., 8th Group Lovat's Scouts,
War Diary (2), Office (3).

No: 5 BATTALION, MACHINE GUN CORPS.

PROGRAMME of MARCH.

Day.	From.	To.	Bde. Group S.P.	Time.	Route.	Remarks.
C.	JOLIMETZ.	LE LOUVION.			AMFOIPRET – BAVAI.	March under orders of 13th Inf. Bde. Group.
D.	LE LOUVION.	SOUS LE BOIS.	Cross Roads. VAL.3.k.16.56.	09.10.	LE GROS CHENE, FEIGNIES.	--do--
E.	SOUS LE BOIS.	JEUMONT.	Cross Roads. VAL.3.L.70.40.	10.30.	PONT ALLANT, BOUSSOIS.	--do--
F.	JEUMONT.	VILLEREILLE.	Cross Roads. NAM.3.B.24.63.	09.09.	MERBES LE CHATEAU.	March under orders of 95th Inf. Bde. Group.
G.	H	A	L	T.		
H.	VILLEREILLE.	BAUME.	Cross Roads. NAM.2.C.1.6.	09.00.	BINCHE Cross road. NAM. 1.C.12.12. PONT ST. VAAST – HAINE ST. PAUL.	--do--
I.	BAUME.	ARQUENNES.	Cross Rds. BRUS.6.C.90.13.	10.20.	SENEFFE.	--do--
J.	ARQUENNES.	HOUTAIN LEVAL.	Cross. Rds. BRUS.5.E.24.19.	10.39.	JERUSALEM.	--do--
K.	HOUTAIN LEVAL.	CORTIL NOIRMONT.	Cross Rds. BRUS.5.F.70.17.	09.17.	MELLERY – GENTINNES.	--do--
L.	CORTIL NOIRMONT.	BEUZET & BOVESSE Area.	Bridge on NAMUR.Rd. BRUS.6.I.60.58.	09.31.	NAMUR Rd. to Cross Rds. BRUS.6.J.19.23. – ST.DENIS.	--do--

THE BATTALION STARTING POINT & TIME WILL BE ISSUED
IN BATTALION ORDERS OF THE PREVIOUS NIGHT.

12th Decr: 1918.

Captain & Adjutant
No: 5 Battn: M.G.C.

No. 5 BATTALION,
MACHINE GUN
CORPS.
No.............
Date...........

O R I G I N A L.

Regd; No: W/5/20./14.
Volume No:...........
Part No:.............

W A R D I A R Y.

for the month of

J A N U A R Y 1919.

No: 5 Battalion Machine Gun Corps.

-o-o-o-o-o-o-o-o-o-o-o-o-o-o-o-o-o-o-o-o-o-

Major
for Lieut: Colonl,

Commanding No: 5 Battn. Machine Gun Corps.
-o-o-o-o-o-o-o-o-o-o-o-o-o-o-o-o-o-o-o-o-o-o-o-o-o-o-

1st: Feby. 1919.
-o-o-o-o-o-o-o-o-o-

Reference Map NAMUR 8. 1:100000   Original

Army Form C. 2118.

Sheet 1

WAR DIARY
INTELLIGENCE SUMMARY.
(Erase heading not required.)

Instructions regarding War Diaries and Intelligence Summaries are contained in F. S. Regs., Part II. and the Staff Manual respectively. Title pages will be prepared in manuscript.

Place	Date 1919	Hour Jany	Summary of Events and Information	Remarks and references to Appendices
TEMPLOUX & SUARLEE		1st	No Parades. Disposition as follows "A" + "C" Coys at SUARLEE "B" & HQ at TEMPLOUX	
		2	Company Commanders inspection, followed by Company Drill + Educational classes. 4 ORs proceeded to the UK as Watford Details - 10 ORs to the UK for demobilization	
		3rd	Company Commanders inspection, followed by Company Drill + Educational classes.	
		4th	-do- -do- -do-	
		5th	Church Parades	
		6.	Company Commanders inspection, followed by Company Drill + Educational classes.	
		7th	-do- -do- -do-	
		8th	Reinforcements. 24 ORs joined the Battalion from Base Depot Company Commanders inspection, followed by Company Drill + Educational classes	
		9th	-do- -do- -do- 4 Officers + 2 ORs proceeded to the UK for demobilization	

Reference Map. NAMUR 8 1:100000

Original
WAR DIARY
or
INTELLIGENCE SUMMARY.
(Erase heading not required.)

Army Form C. 2118.

Sheet 2

Instructions regarding War Diaries and Intelligence Summaries are contained in F. S. Regs., Part II. and the Staff Manual respectively. Title pages will be prepared in manuscript.

Place	Date 1919	Hour JANY	Summary of Events and Information	Remarks and references to Appendices
TEMPLOUX		10th	Training programme issued. See appendix a/1.	See a/1.
		11th	" as per programme. 4 Officers + 16 O.R's proceeded to the U.K for demobilization	
		12th	Church Parades. 14 O.R's proceeded to the U.K for demobilization	
		13th	Training as per programme	
		14th	— do — — do — — do — — do — 1 O.R to U.K for demobilization	
		15th	— do — — do — — do — — do —	
&		16th	— do — — do — — do — — do —	
SUARLEE		17th	Joined the Battalion from Base Depot 2 Officers + 104 O.R's The following Reinforcements	
		18th	Training as per programme. — do —	
		19th	Church Parades. 1 Officer + 136 O.R's proceeded to the U.K for demobilization	
		20th	Company Commanders inspection followed by Company Drill + Educational classes.	
		21st	— do — — do — — do —	

Original

Reference Map NAMUR 8. 1:100,000

Army Form C. 2118.

Sheet 3

WAR DIARY
INTELLIGENCE SUMMARY.

(Erase heading not required.)

Instructions regarding War Diaries and Intelligence Summaries are contained in F. S. Regs., Part II. and the Staff Manual respectively. Title pages will be prepared in manuscript.

Place	Date 1919	Hour	Summary of Events and Information	Remarks and references to Appendices
	JAN			
	22nd		Company Commanders inspection followed by Company drill & Educational classes	
	23		-do- -do- -do- -do-	
	24		-do- -do- -do- -do-	
	25		-do- -do- -do- -do-	
TEMPLOUX	26		3 ORs joined the Battalion from Base Depot. Church Parade. 89 ORs proceeded to the U.K. for Demobilisation	
&	27		Company Commanders inspection followed by Company drill & Educational classes c/o 5 Section of No 5 Company R.E. Signals rejoined Division H.Q.	
SUARLEE	28		Company Commanders inspection followed by Company drill & Educational classes	
	29		-do- -do- -do- -do- 2 ORs joined from Base Depot	
	30		-do- -do- -do-	
	31		-do- -do- -do-	

NEW YEARS HONOURS DESPATCH. Extract from London Gazette 4/1/1919
Lieut H. Evans (Mentioned in Despatches 11/1/19)
279440 Sgt Urquhart A. R. (Awarded D.C.M. 1/1/19)
16192 Sgt Martin A. R. " M.S.M. 1/1/19
65710 Sgt Cherry J. T. " M.S.M. 1/1/19

W.5/20./14.

ORIGINAL.

W A R D I A R Y
for the month of
JANUARY - 1919.

No: 5 Battalion Machine Gun Corps.

A P P E N D I X   "A"

1st: Fabry. 1919.

No. 5 BATTALION,
MACHINE GUN
CORPS.

No.....................
Date...................

Plan of 5th Div. Wing.
Infantry Barracks, Charleroi.

FIRST FLOOR

14TH R. Warwicks.   262
5TH M.G Bn 253. 254. 257. 258
15TH Inf: Bde. 249. 250. 251. 252.
5TH Sig: C.R.E. 243. 244. 245. 246.
Div: H.Q. 254. 255. 256. 257.

No. 5 BATTALION,
MACHINE GUN
CORPS.

PROGRAMME of TRAINING for the Week Ending 18th: Jany. 1919.

Company.	Monday.	Tuesday.	Wednesday.	Thursday.	Friday.	Saturday.
Battn: Headquarters.	Squad Drill & Rifle excercises.	P. T.	Route March.	Drill.	P. T.	Kit and Billet Inspection.
"A" Company.	Route March.	Section Drill.	Squad Drill.	Route March.	Section Drill.	Inspection Parade.
"B" Company.	Route March.	P. T.	Squad Drill.	Gun Drill.	P. T.	Route March.
"C" Company.	Gun Drill.	Route March.	P. T.	Squad Drill Arms Drill.	Arms Drill Squad Drill.	Company Drill.
"D" Company.	Squad Drill & handling of arms.	Route March.	Company Drill.	P. T.	Baths.	Route March.

Education will be carried out as per the attached Programme. The following Lectures will take place:—

Place.	Time.	Subject.	Lecturer.
SUARLEE.	18.30. hours.	"STARS" How they are made.	Revd: LEE - WARNER.
TEMPLOUX.	18.30. hours.	Readings from Shakespeare.	Revd: KENWORTHY.
do:	14.30. hours.	France and the French.	Prof: HATZFIELD.

Men not employed on Education will be at the disposal of Company Commanders.

12th: Jany. 1919.

A. J. Shanks
Captain, for O. C.,
No. 5 Battn. Machine Gun Corps.

CONFIDENTIAL.

Reg; No. ....
Vol. No. ....
Part No. Vol II

W A R   D I A R Y.

No; 5 BATTALION MACHINE GUN CORPS.

for the Month of February, 1919.

E. Hyde
Lieut. Colonel,
Commanding No: 5 Battn. Machine Gun Corps.

28/2/1919.

Original

Army Form C. 2118.

WAR DIARY
INTELLIGENCE SUMMARY
(Erase heading not required.)

Reference Map NAMUR 8. 1:100000

Instructions regarding War Diaries and Intelligence Summaries are contained in F. S. Regs., Part II. and the Staff Manual respectively. Title Pages will be prepared in manuscript.

Sheet 1

Place	Date 1919	Hour	Summary of Events and Information	Remarks and references to Appendices
	FEBY			
		1st	Company Drill followed by Educational Classes	
		2	Church Parades	
		3	Company Drill followed by Educational Classes	
		4	-do- -do- -do-	
		5	-do- -do- -do- 1 Officer	
			and 71 O.R's proceeded to the U.K. for demobilization	
		6	Company Drill followed by Educational Classes	
			-do- -do- -do- 1 Officer	
		7	and 6 O.R's proceeded to the U.K. for demobilization	
TEMPLOUX		8	Company Drill followed by Educational Classes 2 O.R's	
AND			proceeded to the U.K. for demobilization	
SUARLEE		9th	Church Parades. Lieut-Col R.H. CUTTING D.S.O. M.C evacuated	
			to the U.K. sick	
		10th	Company Drill followed by Educational Classes Major O.G. KYDD M.C	
			appointed Lieut-Col on taking over the command of the Battalion.	
			Orders received from Divisional H.Q. for the 8" Group Lou's "Scots"	
			to proceed to NAMUR for entrainment to MERLIEMONT	
		11th	Company Drill followed by Educational Classes 5 O.R's	
			proceeded to the U.K. for demobilization	

2449 Wt. W14957/M90 750,000 1/16 J.B.C. & A. Forms/C.2118/12.

Original

Army Form C. 2118.

Reference Map. NAMUR 8. 1:100,000

WAR DIARY
-or-
INTELLIGENCE SUMMARY

(Erase heading not required.)

Sheet 2

Instructions regarding War Diaries and Intelligence Summaries are contained in F. S. Regs., Part II. and the Staff Manual respectively. Title Pages will be prepared in manuscript.

Place	Date 1919	Hour	Summary of Events and Information	Remarks and references to Appendices
	Feb 12		Company Drill followed by Educational Classes 12 O.R's proceeded to the UK for demobilization	
	13		Company Drill followed by Educational Classes 3 O.R's proceeded to the UK for demobilization. Orders received from Divisional H.Q. to be prepared to dispatch 3 Officers & 100 O.R's to the 3rd Batt. M.G.C. in the Army of Occupation	
TEMPLOUX	14		Company Drill followed by Educational Classes 1 O.R to UK for demobilization	
AND	15		-do- -do- -do- 1 O.R to UK for demobilization	
			demobilization. Reinforcement 1 O.R joined from Base Depot	
	16		Church Parades	
SVARLEE	17		Company Drill followed by Educational Classes	
	18		-do- -do- -do- Orders received	
			to cancel draft for the 3rd Batt. M.G.C.	
	19		Company Drill followed by Educational Classes 6 O.R's	
	20		-do- -do- -do- proceeded to the UK for demobilization	

Reference Map NAMUR 8 1:10000

Original
WAR DIARY
or
INTELLIGENCE SUMMARY
(Erase heading not required.)

Army Form C. 2118.

Sheet 3

Place	Date 1919 FEB.Y	Hour	Summary of Events and Information	Remarks and references to Appendices
	21		Company Drill followed by Educational Classes	
	22		-do- -do- -do-	
			Animals of Class "Z" were dispatched to 4th V.E.S. CHARLEROI for sale to the Belgians. 2 Riders 1st L.D. Horses + 25 L.D. Mules. Total 41 Animals	
	23rd		Church Parades. The following Officers were appointed Acting Ranks from the dates shewn. Capt D.G. McI. ABBOTS to be A/Major from 12/1/19. Capt G.P. BURDETT apptd A/Major from 23/2/19. Lieut R.M. BROADFOOT apptd A/Capt from 23/2/19. Lieut P.A. BREEN apptd A/Capt from 23/2/19. Lieut A.F. FROST to be Lieut from 1/2/19	
TEMPLOUX AND SUARLÉE	24		Company Drill followed by Educational Classes	
	25		-do- -do- -do- 1 Officer to DAK for demobilization	
	26		-do- -do- -do- 2 O.O.Rs " " "
	27		-do- -do- -do- " " "
	28		-do- -do- -do- " " "

Original

Regd. No. W.28
Part No. 3
Vol. No. 2

W A R   D I A R Y.

of

No. 5 Battalion Machine Gun Corps for Month of March 1919.

Came under orders of IV Corps, 16 March.

31. 3. 1919.

Captain & Adjutant,

No. 5 Battn. Machine Gun Corps.

Army Form C. 2118.

Original
WAR DIARY
OF
INTELLIGENCE SUMMARY.
(Erase heading not required.)

Reference Map NAMUR 8. 1:100000   Sheet 1.

Instructions regarding War Diaries and Intelligence Summaries are contained in F. S. Regs., Part II. and the Staff Manual respectively. Title pages will be prepared in manuscript.

Place	Date 1919	Hour MAR	Summary of Events and Information	Remarks and references to Appendices
		1st	Company Commanders inspection, followed by Company Drill	
		2nd	Church Parades.	
		3rd	Company Commanders inspection, followed by Company Drill. The Battalion provided the following parties to attend the funeral of a BELGIAN SOLDIER who died whilst on leave at TEMPLOUX. 12 OR's to act as the Bearer party + 1 Sergeant + 12 OR's for the Firing party. 2/Lieut E.R. ELPHICK was in charge of the Parade.	
TEMPLOUX AND SUARLEE		4th	Orders received to commence the Storage of Equipment of this Unit at the Infantry Barracks, CHARLEOI. Plan showing location of rooms allotted attached. see append. A/1.	See append. A/1
		5th	Company Commanders inspection, followed by Company Drill - do - - do - - do - - do -	See append. A/2
		6th	- do - - do - - do - - do -	
			Further orders issued in reference to the storage of kit at CHARLEROI.	See append. A/3
			Orders received from Divisional H.Q. giving communication during the forthcoming move	

Original
Army Form C. 2118.

Reference Map. NAMUR. 8. 1:100.000   Sheet 2.

WAR DIARY
of
INTELLIGENCE SUMMARY.
(Erase heading not required.)

Place	Date 1919	Hour MAR.	Summary of Events and Information	Remarks and references to Appendices
TEMPLOUX AND SUARLEE		7th	Lieut-Col. W.V.L. PRESCOTT- WESTCAR. D.S.O. joined from G.H.Q. Lewis Gun School, & assumed command of the Battalion. Company Commanders inspection, followed by Company Drill.	
		8th	-do- -do- -do- -do- Capt & Q.M. W. L. DEVOTO proceeded to the 104th Batt'n M.G.C. for duty	
		9th	42 Animals of the "Z" Class were dispatched to 5/V.E.S. for sale to the Belgians	
		10th	Commanding Officers conference was held at the H.Q. CHATEAU at 09.00 hrs.	
		11th	10 O.R's proceeded to the U.K. for demobilization	
		12th	45 Animals of the Z Class were dispatched to 5/V.E.S. for sale to the Belgians. Orders received from 5th Division H.Q. that this Unit would form part of the "RHINE" Army	
		13th	Orders received from Division H.Q. for this Unit to move to SOMBREFFE Area.	

Original

Army Form C. 2118.

Reference Maps. NAMUR & BRUSSELS G. 1:100000

Instructions regarding War Diaries and Intelligence Summaries are contained in F. S. Regs., Part II. and the Staff Manual respectively. Title pages will be prepared in manuscript.

WAR DIARY
or
INTELLIGENCE SUMMARY.
(Erase heading not required.)

Sheet 3

Place	Date 1919	Hour MAR	Summary of Events and Information	Remarks and references to Appendices
		13th		see appen a/5.
TEMPLOUX AND SUARLEE		14th	Operation Order No 44 issued in reference to the move to SOMBREFFE. The 5th Divisional "H.Q. will cease to exist as such at midnight 15th/16th March 1919. This Unit will come under the orders of the H.Q. IV Corps at that hour	See append a/4.
		15th	Company Commanders inspection followed by Company Drill	
		16th	Sunday. No Parades	
		17th	The Battalion move to SOMBREFFE. Companies move at independently Special Order of the day by Major Gen. J. PONSONBY. C.B. C.M.G. D.S.O. bidding farewell to the Division	See append a/6.
		18th	Commanding Officers conference was held at Batt: Orderly Room	
		19th	15 Animals of the "Z" Class were despatched to 5/ V.E.S. for sale to the Belgians	
SOMBREFFE		20th	Two Companies "A" & "B" withdraw Stores & Equipment from Infantry Barracks CHARLEROI.	
		21st	IV Corps H.Q. will close at WAVRE from midnight 21/22 March 1919 + re-open at the same hour at DUREN.	

Army Form C. 2118.

Original
WAR DIARY
or
INTELLIGENCE SUMMARY.
(Erase heading not required.)

Reference Map BRUSSELS C 1/10000

Instructions regarding War Diaries and Intelligence
Summaries are contained in F. S. Regs., Part II.
and the Staff Manual respectively. Title pages
will be prepared in manuscript.

Sheet 4

Place	Date 1919	Hour MAR.	Summary of Events and Information	Remarks and references to Appendices
SOMBREFFE	22nd		All Leave and Demobilization suspended, including despatch of "CADRES". Order by the War Cabinet owing to the threatened Strikes in ENGLAND. Two Companies C & D withdraw all Stores & Equipment from Infantry Barracks CHARLEROI.	
	23rd		Sunday Battns. bathing at Liverpool Baths GEMBLOUX	
	24th		Company Commanders inspection followed by Company drill	
	25		-do- -do- -do- -do-	
	26		-do- -do- -do- -do-	
	27		-do- -do- -do- -do-	
	28		-do- -do- -do- -do-	
	29		-do- -do- -do- -do-	
	30		Sunday etc parades	
	31st		Company Commanders inspection, followed by Company Drill. Warning Order Nº 10 issued in reference to the move to Germany	see appx A/17

Original

A P P E N D I X "A"

W A R D I A R Y

of

No. 5 Bn. Machine Gun Corps.

March 1919.

O. C. "A" Company.
O. C. "B" do:
O. C. "C" do:
O. C. "D" do:
Battn. Sr. NCO.

No. 5 BATTALION,
MACHINE GUN
CORPS.
No................
Date................

1.   The storage of the Cadre Equipment of this Battalion will commence on Wednesday, the 5th: March as per the table below.

2.   Accommodation for the storage has been allotted at the Infantry Barracks, CHARLEROI for the Division. Rooms numbered 253, 254, 257 and 258 have been allotted to this Battalion.

3.   The rooms are not all of the same dimensions but each room is capable of holding the complete Cadre Equipment of one Company.

4.   Limbers will parked in the space provided outside the entrance to the Barracks.

5.   Each Company will take down all Gun Limbers complete with Section Gun Kit and the Headquarters Limbers loaded with Signalling Stores and spare lead harness. Cookers, Watercarts and S. A. A. Limbers will remain for the present with Companies. The Equipment will be carefully unloaded and stored in the room allotted each Company and the Limbers parked as in para 4.
        The unloading party and the horses will remain at CHARLEROI for one night and will return early the next day. Billets can be obtained at the Barracks. Officers Commanding Coys. will make the necessary arrangements re rationing the Party.

6.   It is hoped to be able to obtain padlocks for each room - if this can be arranged it will only be necessary to leave a small Guard for the whole Battalion.

7.   "A" Company will detail the first Guard which will consist of 1 Corporal and 3 Men. The Guard will be held responsible for all stores left under their charge. The Guard will take rations for two days together with blankets. They will then come under the Command of Major, R. ECCLES. M. C., O. C. of the Divisional Wing of the Barracks.

8.   On arrival at the Barracks the Officer in charge of the Company must first report at the Office of Major ECCLES.

9.   Days allotted for Companies are as follow:-

Company.	Date.	Hour of Departure.	Room Allotted.
"A".	5th:	06.00. Hours.	No: 253.
"B"	6th:	06.00. "	No: 254.
"C"	7th:	06.00. "	No: 257.
"D"	8th:	06.00. "	No: 258.

                                                        Capt. & Adjt.,
                                                        for. O. C.,
4th: March, 1919.
                    No: 5 Bn. Machine GunCorps.

O. C. "A" Company.
O. C. "B"   do:
O. C. "C"   do:
O. C. "D"   do:
Battn. Quartermaster.
Lieut. E. P. RANKINE.

D. 1/156.

With reference to the dumping of Gun Kit, Belt Boxes and spare Saddlery in CHARLEROI. "B" Company will continue as ordered in this Office No: B.1/156 of the 4th: Inst.;

"C" and "D" Companies will each be allotted one Motor Lorry reporting to - morrow morning at SUARLEE and TEMPLOUX CHURCHES respectively at 08.00. hours. These Lorries are to be loaded up by 09.00. hours and are to be accompanied by 4 Men each of "C" and "D" Companies to assist the unloading parties at CHARLEROI.

The Lorries should arrive at CHARLEROI at 12. 00. hours.

Lieut. E. P. RANKINE should arrange to return with his unloading party by one of the empty returning lorries leaving the "A" Company Guard in charge. This Guard together with the brakesmen of "B" Company will be sufficient to unload "B" Coy's Stores.

"C" Company will send off their G. S. Waggons empty to - morrow, the 5th:inst: the men and horses to return on the 7th:inst:.

"D" Company will send off their G. S. Waggons empty on the 7th:inst: and the horses and Men will return on the 8th: inst:.

Any removable fittings on these Waggons are to be handed in to Company Dumps under the charge of the N. C. O. of " " Company.

5th: March. 1919.

Lieut. Colonel.,
Commanding No: 5 Bn. Machine Gun Corps.

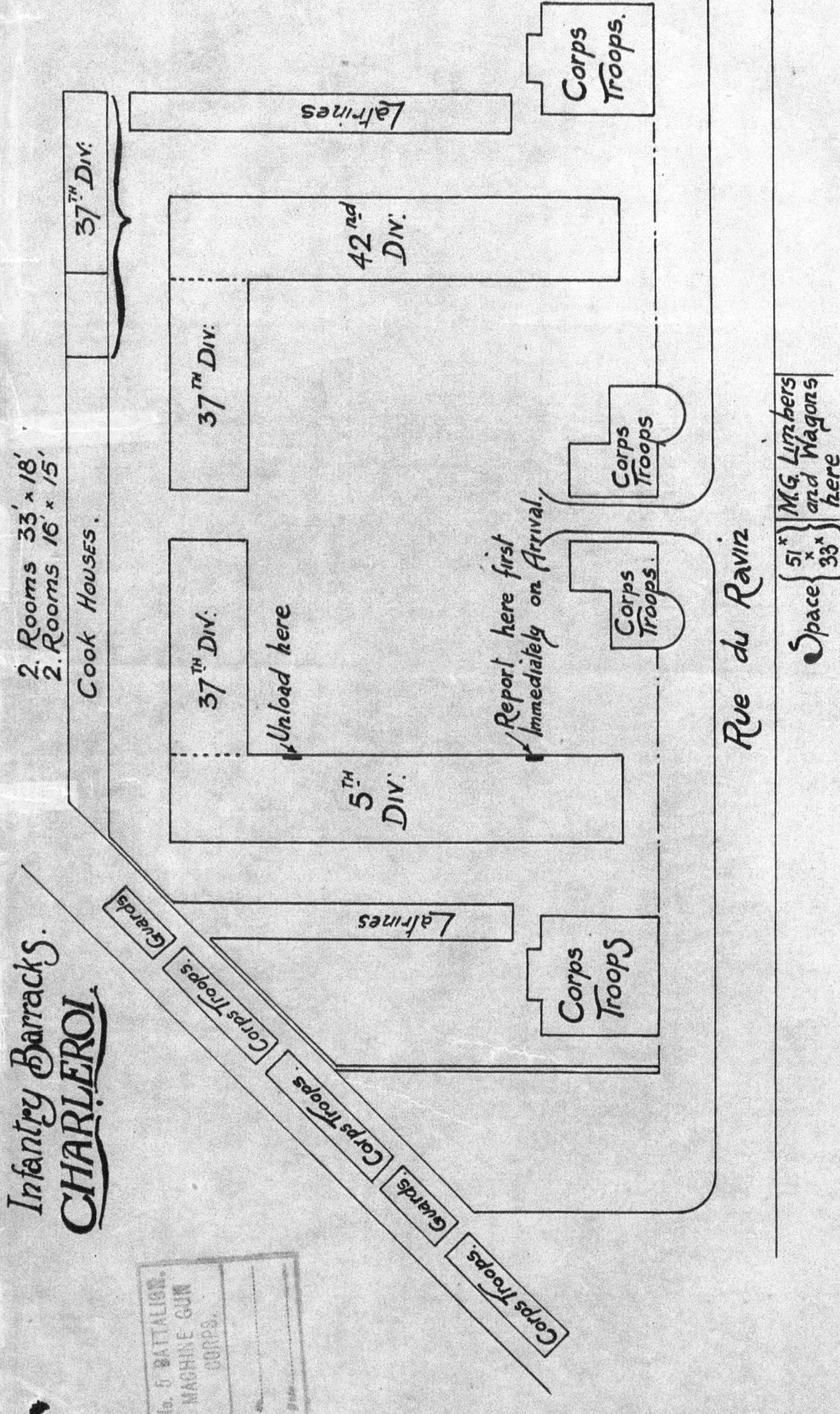

No: 5 Battn. M. G. Corps.
....

5th: Division.
S. 55/17/1.
....

      During the forthcoming move communication will be by telephone, where possible, and D. R. . Each Infantry Brigade and Divisional Artillery Headquarters will have one Motor Cyclist from O. C. Signals.

      D. R's will leave Divisional H. Q. for Brigades etc. at 09.00. hours and 16.00. hours daily commencing on the 9th:inst:. Special D. R's runs must be reduced to a minimum.

      As no Signal Personnel is available for laying signal and Telephone Lines, Headquarters must be established near existing communications.

No. 5 BATTALION.
MACHINE GUN
CORPS.

6th: March. 1919.
-o-o-o-o-o-o-o-o-

(sd).   Capt.
for
Lieut. Colonel.,
General Staff, 5th: Division.
-o-o-o-o-o-o-o-o-o-o-o-o-o-o-o-o-o-o-o-

No. 5 BATTALION
MACHINE GUN
CORPS.

No.............
Date...........

a/4

5th:Divn. A.A. /3900/ 436.

The 5th:Divisional Headquarters will cease to exist as such at midnight 15th:/16th: March 1919, when Brigadier General. R.D.F.OLDMAN, C.M.G., D.S.O., Commanding 15th: Infantry Brigade will take over the Command of all troops of the 5th: Division less the 5th: Divisional Artillery, including the 72 nd. Army Field Artillery Brigade and the 5th: Battn. M. Gun Corps.

5th:Divisional Artillery will come under the orders of the G. O. C., R. A., IV Corps. and

5th:Bn. Machine Gun Corps will come under the orders of the Headquarters IV Corps at that time.

Moves ordered in 5th:Divn. G. O. No; 282 dated 13. 2. 1919. will be carried out.

Units detached as above will continue to be rationed by the 5th:Division.

C. R. A., and O. C. 5th: M. Gun Battn. will report to this Office by 12.00. hours on the 15th:inst:, without fail, particulars of Units as follows;-

    (a). Numbers of retainable Other Ranks.
    (b). Numbers of releasable Other Ranks.
    (c). Numbers of animals by Classes and Categories.
    (d). Location of Units.

13. 3. 1919.
-o-o-o-o-o-

(Sd) D. S. INMAN, Major.,

D. A. A. G. 5th: Division.
-o-o-o-o-o-o-o-o-o-o-o-o-o-o-o-o-o-

(2).

Battn. Or. Mr.
-o-o-o-o-o-o-o-

Forwarded for your information.

14. 3. 1919.
-o-o-o-o-o-

Capt. & Adjt.,
No. 5 Bn. M. G. Corps.
-o-o-o-o-o-o-o-o-o-o-o

With reference to O. O. No. 44, para 5. - Blankets will be rolled in bundles of ten, clearly labelled and dumped outside Company Qr. Mr. Stores by 10.00. hours, to morrow. Labels will show the Company and the Number of the Section. Tables and other articles of Educational furniture will also be dumped outside Company Qr. Mr. Stores at the same hour.

A Guard of 2 men will be detailed per Company over these dumps and after loading will travel on the lorry. One Lorry will call and collect the Blankets and another lorry will collect Educational Furniture. The Quartermaster will detail one N.C.O. to be in charge of the Blanket Lorry and O.C. "D" Company will detail one N.C.O. to be in charge of the furnitue Lorry. This N.C.O. to report to Qr.Mr. Stores at 10.00. hours (with equipment).

On arrival at SOMBREFFE all Blankets and furniture will be formed into two dumps at the new Qr. Mr. Stores and will be re-issued to Companies under the supervision of the Quartermaster.

This order does not apply to "A" Company who will make their own transport arrangements.

Capt. & Adjt.,
No. 5 Bn. M. Gun Corps.

16.3.1919.

Distribution as for O. O. No. 5 44.

S E C R E T.

No. 5 Battn. Machine Gun Corps Operation Order No. 44.
-o-o-o-o-o-o-o-o-o-o-o-o-o-o-o-o-o-o-o-o-o-o-o-o-o-o-o-o-o-o-

1. The Battalion will move to SOMBREFFE on the 17th:inst.

2. Companies will march independently and will pass the starting point at the following hours.;-

    H.Qrs................ 13.00. hours.
    "D" Coy.............. 13.15. "
    "B" Coy.............. 13.30. "
    "C" Coy.............. 13.45. "
    "A" Coy.............. 14.00. "

Starting Point. Main Gates of the Bn. H.Qrs, CHATEAU.
The usual halt will be observed at 10 minutes to the clock hour.

3. BILLETING. Capt. P.A. BREEN, "A" Coy will take over the duties of Town Major, SOMBREFFE as from the 14th:inst. O's C. Coys. will detail one Officer to report to Capt. BREEN at 13.00. hours on the 17th:inst. to take over Company Billets.

4. Os.C. "B" & "C" Coys. will detail one Officer to remain behind to investigate and settle any claims that may arise for the villages of TEMPLOUX and SUARLEE respectively. The inhabitants should be warned of the move and warned that all claims must be submitted within 24 hours of the departure of the troops to the Officers remaining behind. The inhabitants will find the Officers concerned at their respective Messes.

5. Coys. will move on their existing Transport. Arrangements are being made to secure Lorry accomodation for Blankets – further instructions will be issued later.

6. In order to arrange for each Company to have sufficient animals to draw their vehicles the following temporary transfers will take place;-

    "A" Coy. to draw 5 Mules from "B" Coy.
    "D" Coy. to draw 2 Mules from "B" Coy.
    Bn. H.Q. to draw 3 Mules from "B" Coy.

Os. C. Coys will arrange to draw these animals from O.C. "B" Company on Sunday, 16th:inst: and will return them on the completion of the move. Animals will be handed over with rugs, nosebags, headcollars and chains. – harness will not be handed over.

7. The RHISNES Guard will remain in its present location until relieved under arrangements to be made by the Fourth Army.

ACKNOWLEDGE.

Issued at 16.00. hours.
                                              Capt. & Adjt.,

13th:March 1919.   No. 5 Battn. Machine Gun Corps.

Copies to;-   Os.C. "A", "B", "C" and "D" Companies., Qr. Mr., Capt. BROADFOOT., War Diary., Office.

SPECIAL ORDER OF THE DAY.

B Y

Major-General J. PONSONBY, C.B., C.M.G., D.S.O.

    In bidding farewell to the Division, I should like to express to all ranks my sincere thanks for the loyal support extended to me during the time I have been in command.
    The 5th Division, before I took over command, had already made their name as being one of the very best Divisions in the Expeditionary Force, and I feel very proud that this reputation has been maintained during the time I have had the honour to command it.
    This is entirely due to the magnificent "Esprit de Corps" that has invariably existed in the Division, and also to the unexampled courage and bravery shown by Officers and men during all the severe fighting which has ended in a victory over the enemy.
    I wish you all the best of luck in the future and whatever the path of duty directs you, I know that you will always maintain the great tradition of the 5th Division.
    I can only add that I take leave of the Division with the happiest past memories and with the greatest regret at leaving you.

                            (signed)   JOHN PONSONBY.

                                             Major-General.

March 17vh., 1919.

No 5 Battn. Machine Gun Corps Warning Order No. 10.
....

    The Battalion will be prepared to move by train route to GERMANY on the 3rd: and 4th: insts. as follows;-

    "A" and "B" Company..... By train from CHARLEROI on the 3rd:inst:.
    "C" and "D" Company..... By train from CHARLEROI on the 4th:inst:.
    Battn. H. Qrs............ By train from CHARLEROI on the 3rd:inst.

31. 3. 1919.
....

                              RMillerBroadfoot Cpt
                              for Capt. & Adjt.,
                No. 5 Bn. M. Gun Corps.
....

Copies to:- All Companies, Batt'n. Or. Rr. Capt. BROADFOOT, War Diary., Office.

No. 5 BATTALION,
MACHINE GUN
CORPS.

No.........................

Date.......................

Regdd No. W/20

Part No. 4

Vol. No. 2

ORIGINAL.

WAR DIARY.

OF

No. 5 Battalion, Machine Gun Coprs for the month of April, 1919

J.R. Hood.

Lieut. & Adjutant,
No. 5 Battalion, Machine Gun Corps.

30.4.1919

WAR DIARY or INTELLIGENCE SUMMARY

Army Form C. 2118.

Place	Date	Hour	Summary of Events and Information	Remarks and references to Appendices
SOMBREFFE	1		Orders received from H.Q. Corps "Q" for this unit to move to Germany. Orders received from different units of 6"D Divn to hug guns to establishment No. 5 Sec. his 5 signal Coy came for duty. Buses rec'd for entrainment of Battalion at Ottignies.	Appendices A/1
(CHARLEROI) (Ref. Map NAMUR S 1/100.000)	2			A/2 A/3 A/4
CHARLEROI	3		Buses received guns, entrainment & detraining of Battalion.	
			"A" & "B" Coy & Bttn. Headquarters entrain for the Rhine.	
	4		"C" & "D" Coy entrain & "A" & "B" Bttn HQrs detrain at TROISDORF, and billet "A" at ESCHMAR "B" at ESCHMAR, Bttn HQrs at SIEGLAR	
	5		"C" & "D" Coy detrain TROISDORF. Battalion now in billets as follows Bttn. H.Q. "A" Coy SIEGLAR "B" Coy ESCHMAR "C" Coy KREIGSDORF "D" OBERLAR.	
	6		Parades devoted to cleaning up.	
SIEGLAR	7		111 LDH exclusive of Buchs ride de la) for mules & reinforcements join from 101st MG Bttn (Buchs ride de la) Germany.	
	8		93 OR's from 11 Bn M.G.C. & 2 from 55 Bn. join as reinforcements.	
	9		26 Officers, 52 ORs & H Changes from Bn as reinforcements.	

WAR DIARY or INTELLIGENCE SUMMARY

Army Form C. 2118.

Rellman January 1/100,000

Place	Date	Hour	Summary of Events and Information	Remarks and references to Appendices
(?)	10		Major D.S. Hynd (MC) proceeds to UK for demobilization	
	11		Draft to Bonham Parades	
	12		4 Officers & 115 OR proceed to UK for demobilization	
	13		5 Officers & 31 OR proceed to UK for demobilization	
SIEGLAR	14		118 OR re-inforcements from 2nd M.C. Btn.	
KRIEGSDORF	15		5 Officers re-inforcements from Grantham	
OBERLAR	16		1 Off. & 1 OR from 101st Coln M.G.C & OR from 18 Btn. 52 OR from 7th Coln MGC	
ESCHMAR	18		Good Friday. Observed as a Sunday throughout the Army area	
	19		Company Parades	
	20		Divine Service (C of E)	
	21		6 Officers re-inforcements from Grantham	
	22		Company Parades	
	23		1 Officer (Capt. & Adjt.) A.J. Banks to UK for demobilization. 1 Off & 7 OR to course NEWMARKET	
	24		Company Parades	
	25			
	26			

Army Form C. 2118.

WAR DIARY
or
INTELLIGENCE SUMMARY.
(Erase heading not required.)

Ref. M & B Company 2 1/400.000

Instructions regarding War Diaries and Intelligence Summaries are contained in F. S. Regs., Part II. and the Staff Manual respectively. Title pages will be prepared in manuscript.

Place	Date	Hour	Summary of Events and Information	Remarks and references to Appendices
	27.		1 Officer & 16 O.R. to UK for demobilization	
			2 O.R. to Education Course Bonn (Expo)	
	28.		Company trained	
	29.		Company parades	
	30.		Company parades	

APPENDIX "A".

WAR DIARY.

OF

No. 5 Battn, Machine Gun Corps.

April. 1919

To   5th: Division CADRE.
      5th: M. Gun Battalion.

Q. C./127.   31st.

5, 37 and 42nd. M. G. Bns. will move by rail to the 2nd. Army as follows aaa 5th: M.G.Bn. ½ on the 3rd: and ½ on the 4th:, 37th: Battn. ½ on the 5th: and ½ on the 6th:, 42nd. Battn. 1/3 on the 7th:, 1/3 on the 8th: and 1/3 on the 9th: aaa Entraining strength has been taken as follows 5th: Battn. 33 Offrs. 402. O. R's., 235 Animals, 126 axles., 37th: Battn 20 Offrs. 260 O. R's., 235 Animals 126 axles., 42nd. Battn 23 Offrs. 300 O.R's., 235 Animals., 126 axles. Wire immediately any difference in axles entraining strength. Entrainment will take place at CHARLEROI axle Station and times later aaa Detraining Station 5th: and 37th: Battns. COLOGNE., 42nd. Battn BEVEL aaa Destination 5th. and 37th: Battns. COLOGNE., 42nd. Battn. BONN. aaa When mobility is removed send releasable personn on the strength of Battns to CONCENT. Divisions concerned to arrange this aaa 2 Days rations and fuel and blankets to be taken on trains aaa HALTE REPAS at HUY and VERVIERS WEST aaa Divisions concerned to wire departures giving rations strengths and the da to which rationed to 2nd. Army aaa repeated to 4/Area "Q" and this Officeaaa addressed 5, 37, and 42nd. M.G. Battns., 5, 37, and 42nd. Division Cadres. aaa

Time of handing in 18.40. hours

From 4/Corps "Q" Dembn.

RM.

Battn. Qr. Mr.

          Forwarded for your information and necessary
action as regards Rations and Fuel.

No. 5 BATTALION,
MACHINE GUN
CORPS.
No. 1. 4. 1919.
Date

                                              Capt. & Adjt.,
                              No. 5 Bn. M. Gun Corps.

5th: Division AM. /3900/533.

1. 5th:Battn. M.G. Corps will move to the Army of the RHINE by rail as follows;-

   Half Battn. on 3rd:inst.
   Half Battn. on 4th:inst.

2. The Battalion will entrain at CHARLEROI (Station to be notified later) and detrain at COLOGNE.

3. Times of entrainment will be notified later.
   Halte Repas will be observed on the journey at HUY and VERVIERS WEST Stations.

4. A Loading Party and Entraining Officer for each train will be detained by O. C. Battalion.

5. Water Carts and Water Bottles will be full on entrainment.

6. Two days rations and fuel, in addition to the day of entrainment, will be carried on the train.

   O. C. 5th: Divisional Train will arrange direct with O. C. Battalion for the additional days rations and fuel to be delivered at the Station on the 3rd: and 4th: inst.

7. Each man will entrain carrying full equipment including ammunition, steel helmet, box respirator and 3 Blankets.

8. Supply Waggons will be entrained full.

9. Breast ropes for Horses will be provided by the Unit.

10. A C K N O W L E D G E.

1st: April. 1919.

(sd). C. DOUGLAS. Lieut.
for. Major.
D. A. A. G., 5th: Division.

Copies to ;- 5th: Bn. M. G. Corps., 13/Inf. Bde., 5th:Div; Train., D. A. D. O. S., W. O. i/c. Posts., Commdt., 5th: Divn. Recptn. Camp., 5th: Signal Co.

a/3

5th: Battn. M. G. Corps.

From   IV Corps Dembn. "Q"

No. Q.C./140.   1st: April.

        Reference Q. C.127, 31st: aaa Detraining Station
5th: M. G. Battn.   TROISDORF.   aaa
37th:M. G. Battn.   MULHEIM.   aaa
42nd.M.G. Batn.   EHRENDLD.   aaa

        addressed 5, 37, and 42. M. Gun Battns.
        repeated 5, 37, and 42. Divisional Cadres.

No. 5 Battn. Machine Gun Corps Operation Order No. 81.
_____

1.   The Battalion will entrain at CHARLEROI on the 3rd & 4th: insts. as follows:-

           Bn. H.Qrs. "A" and "B" Coys on the 3rd: inst; at CHARLEROI SUD Station at 15.00. hours - train will depart at 18.00. hours

           The times of parade will be:-

                "A" Company............11.00. hours.
                "B" Company............11.30.   "
                Bn. H. Qrs............11.45.   "

           "C" and "D" Companies on the 4th: inst: at CHARLEROI SUD Station at 15.00. hours, - train will depart at 18.00. hours

           The times of parade will be:-

                "C" Company............11.00. hours.
                "D" Company............11.30.   "

2.   Detraining Station will be TROISDORF.

3.   The entraining Officer will wire the departure of each train direct to Second Army "Q" repeating to L/Area "Q", IV Corps Dembn. and 5th: Divn. Cadre, giving ration strength on train and the date to which rationed.

Issued at 12.00. hours.
....9/1..... Lieut. for
SOMBREFFE.   Adjt., No. 5 Bn. M. G. Corps.
....

Copies to :-   O. C. "A" Company.   Major, D.G. HYDD., MC.
                O. C. "B" Company.   R. S. Major.
No. 5 BATTALION. O. C. "C" Company.   Office.
MACHINE GUN   O. C. "D" Company.   Bn. Or. Rm.
CORPS.   Capt. R.M. BROADFOOT.   War Diary, (2).

No. 5 BATTALION.
MACHINE GUN
CORPS.

No.........
Date.........

Original.

Regd. No. W/20
Part No. 5
Vol No. 2

WAR OF DIARY

No. 5 Battalion, Machine Gun Corps for the month of May, 1919.

[signature]
Captain and Adjutant,
No. 5 Battalion, Machine Gun Corps.

31.5.1919

Army Form C. 2118.

Believue War Diary May 2 1/100,000   Sheet 1

WAR DIARY
INTELLIGENCE SUMMARY
(Erase heading not required.)

Instructions regarding War Diaries and Intelligence Summaries are contained in F. S. Regs., Part II. and the Staff Manual respectively. Title pages will be prepared in manuscript.

Place	Date 1920 MAY	Hour	Summary of Events and Information	Remarks and references to Appendices
SIEGLAR		1.	Coy Commanders inspection followed by Parades.	
			Rides to M.T.	
		2.	Coy Parade. 1 Offr for evening class	
KREIGSDORF		3.	Coy Parades. Coy Commanders conference at Siegler	
		4.	Divine Service. Parade Service (C of E) at 11.00 hrs. 6 O.R. from 10th M.G.Btn	
			R.C. vaccinations voluntary 18.00 hrs	
ESCHMAR		5.	Coy Parades	
		6.	Batn handed as strong as possible for Parade for Kiew. Men any 60 men from Windorf to COBLENTZ being to stay at eleven.	
			feet only under PUCEFFNACH. Parades not to exceed one enemy	
		7.	Coy Parades	
		8.		
OBERLAR		9.	Kit inspection. 1 Off. + 1 O.R. proceed to Doncaster.	
		10.	Divine Service. Parade Service (C of E) at 11.00 hrs	
		11.		
		12.	Baths for battalion.	
		13.	Coy Commanders inspection followed by Parades. 1 Offr joined from 18. M.G.Btn	

WAR DIARY
or
INTELLIGENCE SUMMARY.
(Erase heading not required.)

Army Form C. 2118.

Place	Date	Hour	Summary of Events and Information	Remarks and references to Appendices
GODESBERG	14		3 O/Rs to Divn. Educational Course. Capt. O.R. Ovens left to A.Coy. proceeded off for 3 weeks privilege leave to England nett. return army.	Appendix 9/1
	15		1,000 Horses by march route to GODESBERG. Oths Horses to follow on by rail.	
	16		Remaining 2 Coys moved by march route to GODESBERG. Bn. now in billets in GODESBERG.	
	17		O.C. Coy Commander. Lectures previous by General	
	18		Divn. Sports. Battn. Educational Course (Stage 6) 10 O/Rs & 1 Off. to to attend same. Army Service Corps tests re-written form.	
			Have received from N. Eng. for rehabilitation to be raised to a cadre of 2 Offs. & 130 O/Rs. the following additional [illegible] personnel were also received were also received	
	19		were drafted at 1 Off, 1 Col, 23 O/Rs, 1 Farrier, 1 Saddler [illegible] 10 1 Col, 10 [illegible]	APPENDIX 9/2
			Personal officers 2 drafts 50 & 50 arrived to 5th & 7th Coys 6 C O.R's 8 to join 'B' Coy 3 to join 'C' Coy Transport of approved - Rifles to Lancashire Divn. Remainder to be used.	

Army Form C. 2118.

WAR DIARY
or
INTELLIGENCE SUMMARY.
(Erase heading not required.)

Sheet 3

Place	Date	Hour	Summary of Events and Information	Remarks and references to Appendices
GODESBERG		20	[illegible handwriting]	

WAR DIARY
or
INTELLIGENCE SUMMARY.

(Erase heading not required.)

Army Form C. 2118.

Place	Date	Hour	Summary of Events and Information	Remarks and references to Appendices
GODESBERG			Raid on Godesberg. Electric Stores & concentration of taxis or buses	

APPENDIX "A".

WAR DIARY

OF

No. 5 Battalion, Machine Gun Corps.

Month of May, 1919.

NO 5 BATTN, MACHINE GUN CORPS.   OPERATION ORDER NO 91.

---

1.   The Battalion will move to billets at GODESBERG on the 15th and 16th instants.

2.   Companies will march independently, and will pass the starting point at the following hours:-

'B' Company............... 09.30 hours)
)
'A' Company............... 09.45   "   )   15.5.19.
)
Headquarters.............. 10.00   "   )

'C' Company............... 09.30   "   )
)   16.5.19.
'D' Company............... 09.45   "   )

Starting Point:- 'B' Company Officers' Mess, ESCHMAR.

The usual halt will be observed at 10 minutes to the clock hour.

3.   Dress:-   Full marching order with exception of blankets and leather jerkins.

4.   Transport:-   One motor lorry will report to each Company at 09.30 hours to take surplus stores, blankets, jerkins and officers' baggage and will complete double journey, if necessary. A loading party of 4 men per Company will be detailed and will accompany the lorry.
   A guard of 1 N.C.O and 3 men per Company will be left in charge of stores and equipment unable to be carried on first load and will form loading party for the second journey.

5.   Billets:-   Officers Commanding Companies will carefully inspect all billets before the Companies move.
   All billets and their surroundings must be left perfectly clean. Latrines will not be removed.

SEIGLAR (RHINE).   Captain and Adjutant,
14.5.19.   No 5 Bn, M.G.Corps.

5th Bn, Machine Gun Corps.   Xth Corps No Q/507/Q.

        With reference to No O.B./2 dated 16th May. attached.

1.   The 5th M.G. Battalion, 90th and 104th Field Ambulances have been selected for disbandment.

2.   The M.T. vehicles of 90th Brigade, R.G.A will remain where they are now parked pending further instructions.

3.   A return showing the amount of ammunition handed in to Seigburg Dump will be rendered to Xth Corps 'Q'.

                                        (Signed)   A.H. Mead.
                                                      Capt
                                        for Lieut. Colonel.
19th May, 1919.   A.Q.M.G., Xth Corps.

Xth Corps.   S E C R E T .   O.B/2.   A/2

                                                  Xth Corps No G.43/2/15.

1.   It has been decided that the following units will be disbanded, detailed instructions as to the disposal of personnel being issued by the D.A.G.

Brigade H.Q.   23.   39.   56.   60.   68.   90.
                26 (Army.)   31 (Army.)   73 (Army).

Batteries.   6-in How:- 106.   114.   144.   168.   183.
              206. 211. 220. 242. 244. 263. 266.
              277. 281. 299. 305. 319. 342.

              8-in How:-   25.   70.   256.

              9.2-in How:- 133.   136.   175.

              12-in Gun:-   92.

              12-in How:-   65.   86.   243.   381.   444.
              493.   514.

              6-in Gun:-   58.   189.   393.   450.
              498. or 544.

              9.2-in Gun:-   461.   523.

MACHINE GUN BATTALIONS. - 5 Battalions - one per Corps. -
        to be selected by Corps and designations wired to
        G.H.Q. as soon as possible.

FIELD AMBULANCES. - 10 Field Ambulances - 1 per Division -
        as ordered in my O.B/2 of 14.5.19.

2.   The following procedure will be adopted for the disposal of horses, and for the care and custody of equipments of units to be disbanded.

SIEGE ARTILLERY.

    (a) The 32nd Army Bde R.G.A., will be reconstituted and will consist of:-
                H.Q.
                481 Siege Batty.
                488 Siege Batty.
                498 or 544 Siege Batty (9th Corps to decide and report).

        The following Batteries will be transferred from 32nd Army Bde R.G.A. to 73rd Army Bde, R.G.A.

                461 Siege Batty.
                444 Siege Batty.
                86 Siege Batty.
and, from 73rd Army Bde R.G.A. to 32nd Army Bde, R.G.A.
                498 or 544 Siege Batty.

    (b) Brigade H.Q. will be reduced to:-
                Lieut-Colonel., Adjutant, 1 Sergt Major, and 2 O.Rs.

        Batteries to:-
                1 Officer (Major or Capt), 1 Q.M.S., 1 N.C.O. and 19 O.Rs.
                (limber gunners included).

        M.T. Columns attached will be reduced to:-
                1 N.C.O. in charge of each column
                1 driver R.A.S.C. for every three M.T. vehicles., and
                1 driver R.A.S.C. for every two caterpillars.

    (c) Detailed instructions for the disposal of all ordnance stores

                                                            P.T.O.

on charge of Brigades and Batteries will be issued later. Meantime the nucleus personnel will be responsible for the care and custody of all their Stores.

(d) M.T. Vehicles will be parked under Corps arrangements and will be cared for by the personnel referred to in (b) above. Instructions for the ultimate disposal of these vehicles will be issued later.

(e) Ammunition of Batteries being disbanded will be returned forthwith to ammunition depots as follows:-

```
2nd Corps Q.V.      LANGENFELDT.
4th Corps Q.V.      VOCHEN.
6th Corps Q.W.      SEIGBURG.
9th Corps Q.V.      VOCHEN.
10th Corps Q.W.     SEIGBURG.
```

(f) Horses on charge of Brigade H.Q. R.G.A. will be disposed of under instructions to be issued later.

MACHINE GUN BATTALIONS AND FIELD AMBULANCES.

(g) Machine Gun Battalions and Field Ambulances will be reduced to a necessary minimum in personnel with equipment, except as regards motor ambulances and motor cycles which will be handed over to the Divisional M.T.Coy concerned. Instructions as to the ultimate disposal being issued later.

```
Strength:    M.G.Battalion  - 2 x 120 O.Rs.
             Fld Amb. -        5 x  50 O.Rs.
```

(h) Arrangements are being made for 6 trains of horses to be evacuated during the week ending 31.5.19 by which date all animals should be disposed of. All animals will be evacuated through the Army animal collecting camp under instructions which will be issued later, but meantime nucleus personnel are responsible for the care of horses.

(i) Ordnance Stores will be disposed of under instructions to be issued later. Meantime nucleus personnel will be responsible for the care and custody of all their stores.

(j) S.A.A. of the Machine Gun Battalions will be returned to the ammunition depots mentioned in 2 (e).

3. Units will forward reports through the usual channels to reach G.H.Q. not later than the 22nd, showing deficiencies on their G.1098.

Nil reports to be rendered.

General Headquarters.
16.5.19.

(Signed) G.A. BOYD. Brig-Gen
for Major-General,
C. G. S.

TENTH CORPS.   Rhine Army No A 602/1(O)
----

1.   With reference to GHQ letter O.B/2 dated 16.5.19, the
following instructions are issued regarding disposal of personnel
becoming surplus in consequence of the re-organisation therein referred
to.

2.   ROYAL ARTILLERY - OFFICERS -
            O.C. Batteries and Seconds in Command of Batteries will be
disposal of in accordance with orders which will be issued by this
office.
        Corps will select and notify to this office the names of
officers retained for the Nuclei of Brigades and Batteries as described
in para 2 (b) of the communication under reference.
        All other officers will be sent to England and will report to
the Secretary, War Office, in writing, quoting the number of this
letter as authority for doing so.
        No applications for transfer for personal reasons to other
units of the Rhine Army can be entertained.
        Nominal Rolls showing the names of officers ordered to
England and dates of departure will be submitted to this office.

3.   ROYAL ARTILLERY - OTHER RANKS.
        (a) Other Ranks (retainable) personnel becoming surplus will
be cross-posted by Corps to make up existing deficiencies in the establishment of R.G.A. units of the Corps.
        (b) Before disposing of any signallers or men with experience
of telegraph or telephone work in civil life arrangements will be made
by Corps for such men to be interviewed by their chief Signal Officer
with a view to their Transfer to Corps or Divisional Signals Units if
found suitable.
        Transfers (which will be compulsory under A.C.I. 2084)
will be carried out in accordance with the instructions contained in
this office A.600 (O) dated 16.5.19.
        (c) There is a most urgent need for men of good physique
and character not less than "good" in the Military Police (Mounted and
Foot).
        Only volunteers (gunners) can be accepted. It is thought
that a considerable number of suitable men can be found in these R.G.A.
units, and it is hoped that all officers concerned will do their utmost
to ensure that the largest possible number of men of the right stamp
may be forthcoming for this service.
        Men whose attachment is approved will be appointed
A/L/Cpls. Men who re-enlist receive the usual bounty.
        The daily rates of pay (including Bonus under Army
Order XLII of 29.1.19) for Privates are:-
            M.M.P.   4/2d plus War Pay.
            M.F.P.   3/9d plus War Pay.
        After attachment to Military Police, providing they
fulfil the requirements of the Metropolitan Borough Constabularies
men may be recommended for service in such forces.
        Men volunteering for duty in the Military Police will
be despatched for attachment to G.H.Q. under arrangements to be made
direct between Corps and P.M. G.H.Q.
        (d) N.C.Os and men are also wanted for transfer to R.A.O.C.
and it is essential (after the above requirements have been met) that
every effort should be made to secure the services of suitable personnel
for transfer to this Corps.
        Such transfers will be compulsory under A.C.I. 2084
and men will retain their present rates of pay if more advantageous.
        Each Corps (except 4th Corps) will, if available,
select 60 men for attachment as clerks and 100 men for attachment as
store-keepers. Fourth Corps will, if available, provide 120 of the
former and 200 of the latter categories.
        Men will be sent in batches for attachment to Ordnance
Units under arrangements to be made between Corps and D.O.S, G.H.Q.
direct. If suitable they will be transferred after 21 days probation.
        Personnel in excess of the requirements in (a), (b),
(c) and (d) above will be cross-posted by Corps to R.G.A. Units on
whose strength they will be held supernumerary.

                                                              P.T.O

(e) The selections and cross-posting described above will be completed by 5th June, 19.

4. **R.A.S.C. (M.T) - OFFICERS DOING DUTY WITH SIEGE ARTILLERY UNITS -**
Officers will be disposed of under instructions to be issued by this officer.

5. **R.A.S.C. (M.T) - OTHER RANKS DOING DUTY WITH SIEGE ARTY UNITS -**
Releasable O.R. personnel will be demobilised.
Retainable O.R. personnel will be posted by Corps to fill vacancies in the establishment of their M.T. Units.
Personnel required for duty with Army Troops Units will be withdrawn from Corps under arrangements to be made by Corps with D of S and T direct.

6. **MACHINE GUN CORPS - OFFICERS -**
Releasable officers of the disbanded Battalions will be forthwith demobilised.
Corps will post regular or volunteer officers from the disbanded Battalions to complete their remaining M.G. Units to the following establishment (i.e. War Establishment, plus 25% of Captains and Subalterns).

```
Lieut-Colonel...1
Major..........5
Captains ...... 6   (may include the Adjt).
Subalterns ....45
Q.M. ..........1
              ──
              58
              ──
```

Care must be taken to post the surplus officers so that, as far as is possible, Battalions may have an equal share of officers holding the various substantive ranks.
All compulsorily retained officers in excess of the establishment given above will be demobilised.
The cross-posting and demobilisation of officers as above will be completed by 5th June when nominal rolls of officers of all Battns in order of seniority will be forwarded to this office. The substantive and acting or temporary rank of each officer should be stated and each name should be marked in accordance with the following:-
Reg - Regular.   V - Volunteer under A.O.55
S.R - Special Reserve.   C.R - Compulsorarily retained under AO 55.
T.F - Territorial.   T.C - Temporary Commission.

7. **MACHINE GUN CORPS - OTHER RANKS.**
Surplus other ranks personnel will be cross-posted by Corps to complete the remaining M.G. Units of the Corps and demobilisation of releasable personnel will proceed on a basis of length of service.
The X-posting and demobilisation of men so released will be completed by 10.6.19, on which date a return showing by ranks the surplus or deficiency in each Battn will be forwarded to D.A.G., G.H.Q.,
The number of other ranks compulsorarily retained (after the above operations, will be forwarded to D.A.G., G.H.Q.

8. **R.A.M.C - OFFICERS.** - Officers becoming surplus will be disposed of under orders to be issued by this office.

9. **RAMC - O.Rs.** - Surplus other ranks personnel will be cross-posted to the remaining Fld Ambs of the Divn and demobilisation of releasable personnel will at once proceed on a basis of length of service.

(Signed) A.G. Sillem. Major-General.
D.A.G.

G.H.Q.
B.A of R.
18.5.19.